The Possibility of Naturalism

Since _The Possibility of Naturalism_ has been one _philosophy_ of science and social _cornerstones_ of the critical realist position, which is now widely seen as offering perhaps the only viable alternative to positivism and post-modernism. This revised edition includes a new foreword.

Roy Bhaskar is the founder of the critical realist movement. He has taught both philosophy and social science as the universities of Oxford, Edinburgh and Sussex, as well as holding research fellowships at Linacre College, Oxford and City University, London. He is currently the Chair of the Centre for Critical Realism, London. His other publications include _A Realist Theory of Science, Scientific Realism and Human Emancipation, Reclaiming Reality, Dialectic: The Pulse of Freedom_ and _Plato Etc._

The Possibility of Naturalism

A Philosophical Critique of the Contemporary Human Sciences

Third edition

ROY BHASKAR

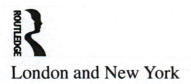

London and New York

First published 1979 by Harvester Press Ltd
Second edition published 1989 by Harvester Wheatsheaf
a division of Simon & Schuster International Group

Third edition published 1998
by Routledge
2 Park Square, Milton Park, Abingdon, Oxon, OX14 4RN

Simultaneously published in the USA and Canada
by Routledge
270 Madison Ave, New York NY 10016

Transferred to Digital Printing 2005

British Library Cataloguing in Publication Data
A catalogue record for this book is available from the
British Library

Library of Congress Cataloging in Publication Data
A catalog record for this book has been requested

ISBN 0–415–19873–9 (hbk)
ISBN 0–415–19874–7 (pbk)

Contents

Foreword to the Third Edition

The Possibility of Naturalism has been out of print for a couple of years now and the second edition (1989) is being reprinted here, in substantially unchanged form, by Routledge in the new *Critical Realism: Interventions* series to coincide with the publication of *Critical Realism: Essential Readings* and the Second Annual Conference of the Centre for Critical Realism at the University of Essex in September 1998.

Since 1989 I have developed first level critical realism – roughly transcendental realism, as expounded in *A Realist Theory of Science* and subsequently augmented in works of the 1980s, and critical naturalism, as presented in *The Possibility of Naturalism* and likewise further elaborated in works of the 1980s – into the system of dialectical critical realism. The development of critical naturalism into dialectical critical naturalism is registered most sharply in *Dialectic: The Pulse of Freedom* (Verso, London 1993), Chapter 2.9, and *Plato Etc.* (Verso, London 1994), Chapter 5. I have thought it impractical and wrong – since dialectical critical naturalism is essentially a preservative development and sublation of critical naturalism and dialectical critical naturalism is itself justified by the whole structure of dialectical critical realism as essayed in those books – to attempt a summary of these developments here. In any event I have little or no quarrel with *The Possibility of Naturalism*, at least in its second edition form, and first moment critical naturalism, as presented here, is the necessary basis for dialectical critical naturalism and its further developments. Moreover I will shortly be publishing a number of books – most notably *Transcendence and Totality* and *The Philosophy of Money* – which further expand on and rework its themes.

I would like to take this opportunity to thank my fellow Trustees of the Centre for Critical Realism (CCR), namely Margaret Archer, Andrew Collier, Tony Lawson, Alan Norrie and Sean Vertigan, and all those, including Mike Jellicoe, Roberta Keenan and Maria Perna, who have helped in its establishment and that of the International Association for Critical Realism (IACR). I am enormously indebted to Alan Jarvis of Routledge for organising and supervising the launch of the *Critical Realism: Interventions* series and for the publication with exemplary efficiency and rapidity of *Critical Realism: Essential Readings* and this edition of *The Possibility of Naturalism*. Thanks are also due to Steve Jarman, Belinda Dearbergh and everyone else at Routledge concerned with the production of these two initial books in what looks like becoming an extremely valuable series.

Roy Bhaskar, *May 1998*

Preface to the Second Edition

When the first edition of this book was published in September 1979 it was billed as Volume I of a two-volume study on 'Philosophy and the Human Sciences'. It was my intention then to proceed fairly rapidly to complete Volume II, provisionally entitled *Philosophical Ideologies*, which would comprise a social scientific critique of leading schools of philosophy – as *The Possibility of Naturalism* had engaged a philosophical critique of the contemporary human sciences, or at least of their metatheoretical and methodological underpinnings, provided most notably by positivism and hermeneutics. In the interim I have not abandoned the project of *Philosophical Ideologies* – and I have attempted an explanatory critique of positivism as an ideology in Chapter 3 of *Scientific Realism and Human Emancipation*.* But it does now seem to me to require the resolution of major conceptual and theoretical problems in the reconstruction, analysis and criticism of philosophical ideas, on which I, along with others, am working.

The Possibility of Naturalism is therefore being republished in this new edition on its own. This is the way in which, as I made clear in the first edition, I wanted it to be read, used, critically appropriated and judged. This edition has been completely reset and contains a substantial number of corrections, as well as a postscript in which I take the opportunity to respond to some criticisms of the book or its project and to comment briefly on some developments of it. In making corrections to the text of the original I have not changed or recast the theory argued in it in any essential way. In preparing this edition I have been enormously helped by William Outhwaite and Gregory Elliott. My thanks are also due to the new team at Harvester, and Farrell Burnett in particular, for the prompt and efficient way in which they have produced this edition of this book.

Roy Bhaskar
January 1989

---

* Verso (London 1986).

Preface to the First Edition

This book and its sequel *Philosophical Ideologies* are concerned with the connection between the social, and more generally the human, sciences and philosophy. Together they comprise an attempt to elucidate the possibilities of a philosophical critique of contemporary social science and a social scientific critique of contemporary philosophy. The first is written on the terrain of the philosophy of social science, the second on that of the sociology of knowledge. Sociology is necessary if we are to avoid 'that kind of criticism which knows how to judge and condemn the present, but not how to comprehend it'.* But philosophy is essential if we are to situate the possibility of any social scientific criteria of understanding at all. I am thus committed to what might be called 'strong programmes' in both the sociology of knowledge and philosophy. That is to say, I believe all ideas, including purely philosophical ones, to be susceptible of scientific explanation. But I also believe philosophy to be irreducible and essential, *inter alia*, to science. Although the themes of the two volumes are interconnected, this book, as a positive elaboration of theories of society and mind, stands on its own. In Volume II the results established here are utilized in the development of collateral theories of philosophy and ideology.

In Chapter 1 I show how recent developments in the philosophy of science lay the ground for a resolution of the old problem of naturalism: the problem of whether social objects can be studied in essentially the same way as natural ones, that is, 'scientifically'. Both the dominant naturalist tradition, positivism, and its anti-naturalist hermeneutical foil rest on an ontology rendered obsolete by these developments. The time is therefore overdue for a 'sublation' of their historic confrontation.

In Chapters 2 and 3 I attempt a transcendental deduction of the properties that societies and people respectively must possess if they are to be (or demarcate the sites of) possible objects of scientific knowledge. In both cases it is seen that it is not their similarities with, but precisely their differences from, natural objects that makes a scientific knowledge possible. The upshot of the analysis is a new *critical naturalism*, entailing a transformational model of social activity and a causal theory of mind. The transformational model necessitates a relational conception of the

* K. Marx, *Capital I* (London 1965), p. 505.

subject-matter of sociology and a series of ontological, epistemological and relational limits on (or conditions for) a naturalistic science of society. It also permits, through the reconstruction of the idea of an explanatory critique, a resolution of the traditional fact/value dichotomy. Similarly, the theory of mind elaborated in Chapter 3 enables a resolution of the reason/cause and mind/body problems. Thus, it is argued that reasons can and must be causes (of a specific type), and that only a 'synchronic emergent powers materialism' is consistent with the metaphysical and scientific data.

In Chapter 4 the argument of the book is completed with a critique of the leading traditions in the philosophy of social science. Transcendental refutations of both the positivist and hermeneutical schools are obtained. On the new naturalist conception that emerges social science is critical, self-reflexive and totalizing. Its objects remain transfactually efficacious. But they are now both concept-dependent in their mode of operation and irreducibly historical. And among such objects are, of course, philosophies.

Roy Bhaskar
September 1978

Acknowledgements

Linda Alexander, Barry Barnes, George Davie, Roy Edgley, Daniel Garrad, Richard Gunn, Rom Harré, Martin Hollis, John Llewelyn, Steven Lukes, John Mepham, William Outhwaite, Maeve Power, Norman Stockman, Hilary Wainwright, Richard Walsh and David Will; and Basil Blackwell for permission to use – in Chapter 2 – material that originally appeared in the *Journal for the Theory of Social Behaviour*.

Chapter 1

Transcendental Realism and the Problem of Naturalism

The Problem of Naturalism

In this book I want to situate, resolve and explain an old question that dominates philosophical discussions on the social sciences and invariably crops up, in one guise or other, in methodological controversies within them: *to what extent can society be studied in the same way as nature?*

Without exaggerating, I think one could call this question the primal problem of the philosophy of the social sciences. For the history of that subject has been polarized around a dispute between two traditions, affording rival answers to this conundrum. A naturalist tradition has claimed that the sciences are (actually or ideally) unified in their concordance with *positivist* principles, based in the last instance on the Humean notion of law. In opposition to positivism, an anti-naturalist tradition has posited a cleavage in method between the natural and social sciences, grounded in a differentiation of their subject-matters. For this tradition the subject-matter of the social sciences consists essentially of meaningful objects, and their aim is the elucidation of the meaning of these objects. While its immediate inspiration derived from the theological *hermeneutics* (or interpretative work) of Schleier-macher,[1] the philosophical lineage of this tradition is traceable back through Weber and Dilthey to the transcendental idealism of Kant. But both traditions have older antecedents and wider allegiances. Positivism, in assuming the mantle of the Enlightenment, associates itself with a tradition whose Galilean roots lie in the new Platonism of the late Renaissance;[2] while hermeneutics, finding early precursors in Herder and Vico[3] and possessing a partially Aristotelian concept of explanation,[4] has always flourished in the humus of romantic thought and humanist culture.[5] Significantly, within the Marxist camp an exactly parallel dispute has occurred, with the so-called 'dialectical materialists' on one side, and Lukács, the Frankfurt School and Sartre on the other.

Now, with the partial exception of the 'dialectical materialists' (whose specificity will be considered later), the great error that unites these disputants is their acceptance of an essentially positivist account of natural science, or at least (and more generally) of an empiricist ontology. Consider, for example, Winch's *The Idea of a Social Science*, probably the most influential tract written within the self-styled 'analytical' school. Winch, it will be remembered, wants to demonstrate an essential identity between philosophy and social science, on the one hand, and a fundamental contrast between social and natural science, on the other. When one examines his arguments for such a contrast one finds that they reduce, in essence, to just two. The first is an argument to the effect that constant conjunctions are neither sufficient nor (contrary to, for example, Weber) even necessary for social scientific explanation, which is achieved instead by the discovery of intelligible connections in its subject-matter.[6] This may be granted. But the required contrast is only generated if one assumes that the discovery of intelligible connections in *its* subject-matter is not equally the goal of natural scientific explanation (or that the identification of constant conjunctions could be necessary and sufficient for this). Winch's second argument is that social things have no existence, other than a purely physical existence, that is, as social things, apart from the concepts that agents possess of them.[7] Besides leaving the ontological status of concepts unclear, once more the desired contrast only gets off the ground if one tacitly assumes that, with the privileged exception of thought itself, only material objects can properly be said to be 'real', that is, that in natural science *esse est percipi*. Winch's anti-naturalism thus depends entirely on empiricist theories of existence and causality. Now if, as I shall argue shortly, science employs a causal criterion for ascribing reality, and causal laws are tendencies, his contrast collapses. Of course it does not follow from this that there will be no differences between the natural and the social sciences (or, for that matter, that Winch's idea of a social science is entirely incorrect). But, by effectively ceding natural science to positivism, Winch precludes himself from locating them. The anti-naturalist faction within Marxism typically makes the same mistake.

Now I think that recent developments in the philosophy of science (and in particular those that I have elsewhere systematized under the title of 'transcendental realism'[8]) permit what the current crisis in the human sciences necessitates: a reconsideration of the problem of naturalism. *Naturalism* may be defined as the thesis that there is (or can be) an essential unity of method between the natural and the social sciences. It must be immediately distinguished from two species of it: *reductionism*, which asserts that there is an actual identity of subject-matter as well; and *scientism*, which denies that there are any significant differences in the methods appropriate to studying social and natural objects, whether or not they are actually (as in reductionism) identified. In contrast to both these forms of naturalism, I am going to argue for a qualified anti-positivist naturalism, based on an essentially realist view of science. Such a naturalism holds that it is possible to give an account of science under which the proper and more or less specific methods of both the natural and social sciences can fall. But it does not deny that there are significant differences in these methods, grounded in real differences in their subject-matters and in the relationships in which their sciences stand to them. In particular it will be shown that *ontological, epistemological* and *relational* considerations all place limits on the possibility of naturalism (or rather, qualify the form it must take); and that these considerations all carry methodological import. However, it will transpire that it is not in spite of, but rather just *in virtue of*, these differences that social science is possible; that here, as elsewhere, it is the nature of the object that determines the form of its possible science. So that to investigate the limits of naturalism is *ipso facto* to investigate the conditions which make social science, whether or not it is actualized in practice, possible.

It would seem clear that my first task is to establish the elements of an adequate account of natural science, in relation to which the possibility of social scientific knowledge can be reappraised. But such an undertaking seems immediately vulnerable to the objection that it is guilty of assuming what it is trying to prove. For how can conclusions taken from reflection on the natural sciences be transposed to the context of social science unless the truth of naturalism (that is, the essential comparability of the two domains) has already been presupposed? Now this objection rests on a misinterpretation of the modal status of my conclusions, which concern merely the *possibility* of a social science. Philosophy, indeed, can neither anticipate the results nor guarantee the success of a naturalistic science of society; what it can do is to specify the (ontological) conditions that make, and the (epistemological) conditions that must be satisfied, for such a project to be possible. its realization is, however, the substantive task, and contingent outcome, of the practice of science itself.

But this objection pales into insignificance in the face of two logically anterior ones. What reason is there to suppose that a unitary account of scientific method, or rather of its essence, can be given, so that the question of whether or not it could embrace social science (that is, the problem of naturalism) can even be meaningfully posed? For surely, it might be said, science is just whatever scientists do, and their doings may be as varied as any randomly selected group of persons. Now this objection may be countered with a dilemma. For either there are *real* differences between the activities of scientists and bigamists, bimetallists and people whose surname begins with a 'P', in virtue of which the predicate 'scientific' is applicable to the former but not the latter; or else there are no grounds for *consistently* using the term 'scientist' to designate one rather than another group of people. On the second horn nominalism itself is impaled. But to fall back on the first is to concede the case for a real definition of science. Once achieved, such a definition will then allow us to discriminate between more and less scientific work within the 'scientific community'; that is, to judge the activity by the concept, so giving us some critical purchase on science.

But why, given that the case for a real definition is conceded, should we presume that *philosophy* can provide it? Surely this task is best left to the scientists themselves, or perhaps to *their* scientists (that is, sociologists of science)? What business does a philosopher as such have pronouncing on science at all? Indeed, how can a philosopher, operating so it would seem by the exercise of pure reason alone, say anything *at all* about the world, without scientific *naïveté* or at least susceptibility to substantive scientific refutation? How, that is to say, is a philosophy of science possible?

How is a Philosophy of Science Possible?

What is the relation between science and philosophy? Do they compete with one another or speak of different worlds? Neither position is acceptable. To ignore the historical links between them would be folly. Indeed, no distinction between them can be drawn in the case of pre-Socratic thought, and no sharp one even in the seventeenth century. (It is salutary to remember that 'metaphysics' is merely the name that Aristotle's literary executors, so to speak, gave to the work they classified after his physics,[9] and that Hume fancied himself engaged in experimental science.[10]) It is only in Kant that one finds a clear, if ultimately untenable, non-reductionist distinction between philosophy and science. After Kant the *status quo ante* was, for the most part, restored: with a romantic and idealist strain, of varying quality, tending to cosmological speculation, very much in the old style; while an empiricist and positivist current proved increasingly unable to sustain an intelligible concept of either science or itself. In this impasse an offshoot of the latter, with conventionalist and pragmatist leanings, openly welcomed the breakdown of the philosophy/science distinction. On this view, they are to be distinguished, if at all, only by the generality of their questions (that is, their removal from the data of sense) – a distinction which may be a matter of degree (Quine) or kind (Lakatos).

Now there is a quota of truth in this picture, historically speaking. Philosophy has tended to develop in symbiosis with science. It can codify, and even motivate it; while science has given philosophy its essential analogies,[11] as well as data for its results. However, no philos-

opher can argue with any confidence from the history of his subject to
approval of the conception with which it seems to accord. Moreover,
taken consistently, the Quine/Lakatos conception is ultimately subversive of *any* claims for philosophy. For once crude empiricist criteria
of scientificity are abandoned there is no reason why philosophy, as so
conceived, should not just be assimilated into science. For its results
must be as potentially transient as, and cannot differ significantly in
epistemological status from, substantive scientific theories. At most they
can only be characterized by a relative immunity to revision – an
immunity which, it would seem, must ultimately be justified, if it can be
justified at all, on a posteriori grounds.

If philosophy is to be possible (and I want to contend that it is in
practice indispensable) then it must follow the Kantian road. But in
doing so it must both avoid any commitment to the content of specific
theories and recognize the conditional nature of all its results. Moreover
it must reject two presuppositions which were central to Kant's own
philosophical project, viz. that in any inquiry of the form 'what must be
the case for ϕ to be possible?' the conclusion, X, would be a fact about
us[12] and that ϕ must invariably stand for some universal operation of
mind. That is to say, it must reject the idealist and individualist cast into
which Kant pressed his own inquiries.

In fact, if the general form of a philosophical investigation is into the
necessary conditions for social activities as conceptualized in experience, then it must be recognized that both the activity and its
conceptualization may be historically transient; that the activity may
depend upon the powers that people possess as material things rather
than just as thinkers or perceivers; and that its analysis may establish
transcendental realist, rather than idealist, and so epistemically rela-
tivist, rather than absolutist (or irrationalist), conclusions. On this
conception, then, both the premises and conclusions of philosophical
arguments remain contingent facts, the former (but not the latter) being
necessarily social, and hence historically transient. It is only in this
relative or conditional sense that philosophy can establish synthetic
a priori truths (truths about the world investigated by science).
Philosophy, then, operates by the use of pure reason. But not by the use
of pure reason alone. For it always exercises that reason on the basis of
prior conceptualizations of historical practice, of some more or less
determinate social form.

Thus conceived, philosophy can tell us that it is a condition of the
possibility of scientific activities ϕ and ψ that the world is stratified and
differentiated, X and Y. But it cannot tell us *what* structures the world
contains or *how* they differ. These are entirely matters for substantive
scientific investigation. Scientific activities are contingent, historically
transient affairs. And it is contingent that the world is as described in

'X', 'Y', and 'Z'. But given ϕ_i, X *must* be the case. A demonstration, or 'deduction', of this necessity (which may be termed 'transcendental') will normally consist of two parts: a straightforward 'positive' part, in which it is shown how X makes ϕ intelligible; and a complementary 'negative' part (in general only analytically separable from the positive part), in which it is shown how absurd, incoherent, counter-intuitive or counterfactual results flow from the failure to sustain the concept of X,[13] typically expressed in the form of one or more theories that explicitly or implicitly deny the activity as conceptualized in 'ϕ_i'. Now misunderstandings about the intentions of transcendental arguments often stem from the failure to appreciate the critical contexts in which they are developed – against existing philosophical theories. Thus it is certainly the case that there is no way of demonstrating the uniqueness of X in advance of every conceivable philosophical theory about ϕ_i.[14] But the transcendental consideration is not deployed in a philosophical vacuum: it is designed to situate or replace an existing theory; and may of course come, in time, to suffer a similar fate. Moreover both the (warranted) acceptability and the (actual) acceptance of some piece of philosophical reasoning will depend upon the minor premises (ϕ_i, ψ_j, etc.) concerned. Further, both the activity and its conceptualization may depend upon different sets of historical circumstances; and both may be, perhaps essentially, contested.[15]

On this conception, then, philosophy is distinguished by the kinds of considerations and arguments it employs. It does not consider a world apart from that of the various sciences. Rather it considers just that world, but from the standpoint of what can be established about it by a priori argument, where it takes as its premises generally recognized activities as conceptualized in experience. But neither does it compete with science. For its task is to show what must be the case for the ensemble of scientific activities to be possible. In doing so, it analyses notions that denote only on the condition that they are used syncategorematically, that is under some particular description, in science. It is thus especially important not to reify or hypostatize a conclusion in philosophy as referring to, or dependent upon, objects distinct from those investigated by the various sciences. Now to posit an object as noumenal (or unknowable) is already to hypostatize it. Hence one difference between transcendental realism and idealism is that, for transcendental realism, what is presupposed in any given scientific activity is at once a possible object of scientific explanation; so that what is apodeictically demonstrable is also scientifically comprehensible; that is, what is synthetic a priori is also (contingently) knowable a posteriori. Philosophy consists in an irreducible level of discourse; it does not constitute an autonomous order of being (whether such an order is conceived as real or glossed as merely ideal). Moreover, as such, it is itself in principle susceptible to substantive scientific (sociological) explanation. Only the spell of actualism misleads us into thinking that to explain a phenomenon, such as philosophy, is to dissolve it. The characteristic error of 'critical theory', to suppose that to demystify a phenomenon is to destroy it, is grounded in the same mistake.

Suppose, though, that philosophical and scientific accounts were to clash. What would this show? Merely that one had come up against the limits of a particular scientific form, just as the limits of the possibility of measurement may be given by quantum theory. But that measurement has limits does not mean that nothing can be said a priori about what the world must be like for measurement to be possible within those limits. What it does mean is that there is no way in which philosophy can legislate in advance for the transportation of particular scientific procedures; so that the minor premises of philosophy's arguments may have to be developed afresh in the case of each specific science. Indeed, were philosophy able to anticipate the form of or stipulate criteria *ex ante* for successful scientific practices, the historic aspirations of absolute idealism and post-Cartesian, precritical, rationalism (including empiricism) would stand vindicated. For science would now appear as the simple realization of philosophy or as the automatic product of a practice (or method) authenticated by it.

Some implications of the conception of philosophy advocated here should be registered straightaway. Firstly, according to it, there is no connection between (a) what lies beyond sense-experience and (b) some special sphere of philosophy. For at least once a non-reductionist account of science is accepted then some 'transcendent' entities, such as magnetic fields, may quite properly be regarded as objects of scientific investigation. But their 'transcendence' is a contingent fact about the world, and philosophy speaks with no special authority about it. The familiar conflation of (a) and (b) in a unitary concept of metaphysics[16] must be assiduously avoided. It has proved a prop for a positivism that has systematically scouted the cognitive potential of both philosophy and science. Secondly, by making the possibility of philosophical discourse contingent upon the actuality of particular social practices it provides, in ways to be elaborated in the sequel to this study, a way of reconciling transcendental and sociological analyses of social activities such as science[17] – and philosophy. Finally, this conception situates the possibility of apodeictic inquiries into non-scientific, and even non-cognitive, human activities (such as economic exchange), where these are conceptualized in the experience of the agents concerned. For the possibility is bound to arise of posing transcendental questions of the form 'what must be the case for ϕ to be possible?' for social practices other than science. The answer to such a question will consist in a statement of necessary conditions for the particular activity. However, in opposition to a neo-Kantian stream of thought, transcendental realism holds that such conditions are both real and subject to historical transformation, so that the resultant hermeneutics becomes contingently critical.

Philosophy, then, like science, produces knowledge. But it is knowledge of the necessary conditions for the production of knowledge – second-order knowledge, if you like. If philosophy is, as I believe it can be, a conceptual science, then like any science it ought to be able to tell us something we did not already know: it ought to be able to surprise us. For, as Marx astutely observed, 'all science would be superfluous if the outward appearances and essences of things directly coincided'.[18] Conceptual discovery is, I believe and hope to show, possible.

In response to its echo in sceptical doubt, modern philosophy has typically set itself the task of showing how our knowledge is justified, or more specifically how science is rational. As Lukács characterized it: 'acknowledging as given and necessary the results and achievements of the special sciences, philosophy's task is to exhibit and justify the grounds for regarding the concepts they construct as valid'.[19] Now such an exercise presupposes both a certain view of knowledge (so that it is intrinsically circular); and implicitly of the world (that is, of the way the world must be for knowledge of the presumed sort to be possible). Given the nature of its implicit ontology this curious epistemological project must, as is evinced by the history of post-Humean philosophy of science,[20] end in formal failure. I am therefore going to propose a reversal in our conception of the programme of philosophy. On it, one no longer implicitly makes certain (extraordinary) assumptions about the world overtly to demonstrate, but perhaps covertly to deny, the rationality of science. Rather, one assumes at the outset the intelligibility of science (or rather of a few generally recognized scientific activities) and asks explicitly what the world must be like for those activities to be possible. This programme not only yields new insight into the structure of scientific knowledge (the form that it must take if it is to be knowledge of a world investigated by such activities), but enables us to see that the tacit presupposition (of a closed world, completely described) on which the traditional problem of its rationality was hung is inconsistent with its very possibility.

What activities can furnish the premises for such a philosophical investigation? Traditionally, epistemology has been dominated by the dispute between the contending claims of experience and reason. Since Kant we know that both must play a part in science. However, neither are sufficiently differentiated to yield the premises needed to produce an account capable *inter alia* of generating a real definition of science. So let us attempt their substitution by the more specific concepts of *experimental activity* and *scientific development*, in the context of which the real epistemic significance of experience and reason respectively will be found to lie.

Experiment and Application: The Intransitive Dimension

I want first, then, to undertake an analysis of experimental activity, together with a logically related feature of science. Now in considering experimental activity we immediately encounter a paradox. Although everyone agrees that it plays a role in science, no one (or virtually no one) has analysed it. And the few who have given it some attention, such as Anscombe and von Wright, have failed to grasp its point.

In an experiment scientists produce a pattern of events. In itself there is nothing special about this. For, as causal agents, we are co-responsible for events all the time. And scientists could, in fact, produce a vast array of events, most of no conceivable significance. What is so special about the patterns they deliberately produce under meticulously controlled conditions in the laboratory is that it enables them to identify the mode of operation of natural structures, mechanisms or processes which they do not produce. What distinguishes the phenomena the scientist *actually* produces from the totality of the phenomena she *could* produce is that, when her experiment is successful, it is an index of what she does *not* produce. A *real* distinction between the objects of experimental investigation, such as causal laws, and patterns of events is thus a condition of the intelligibility of experimental activity. And it can now be seen that the Humean account depends upon a misidentification of causal laws with their empirical grounds. Notice that as human activity is in general necessary for constant conjunctions, if one identifies causal laws with them then one is logically committed to the absurdity that human beings, in their experimental activity, cause and even change the laws of nature! The objects of experimental activity are not events and their conjunctions, but structures, generative mechanisms and the like (forming the real basis of causal laws), which are normally out of phase with the patterns of events which actually occur.[21]

But of course we not only experimentally establish, we practically *apply* our knowledge – in systems, which may be characterized as *open*, where no constant conjunctions of events obtain. If this activity is to be rendered intelligible causal laws must be analysed as the tendencies of things, which may be possessed unexercised and exercised unrealized, just as they may of course be realized unperceived (or undetected) by people. Thus in citing a law one is referring to the transfactual activity of mechanisms, that is, to their activity as such, not making a claim about the actual outcome (which will in general be co-determined by the activity of other mechanisms). Here again failure to make an ontological distinction between causal laws and patterns of events results in absurdity. For if causal laws are constant conjunctions of events then one must ask: what governs phenomena in systems where such conjunctions do not obtain. The actualist is now faced with an impossible dilemma: for s/he must either say that nothing does, so that nature becomes radically indeterministic; or that, as yet, science has discovered no laws![22]

Once made, however, the ontological distinction between causal laws and patterns of events allows us to sustain the universality of the former in the face of the non-invariance of the latter. Moreover, the actualist analysis of laws now loses all plausibility. For the non-invariance of conjunctions is a condition of an empirical science and the non-empirical nature of laws a condition of an applied one.

Did we not know this all along? Of course it is at one with our intuitions. Thus we do not suppose that, for example, Ohm's law holds only in the laboratory. And as every schoolchild knows, no experiment goes properly the first time.[23] We can *use* the laws of science for the explanation of events and the making of things in open systems, where deductively justified predictions, and hence decisive test situations, are impossible. And yet in the reflective consciousness of philosophy, as distinct from the spontaneous practice of science, it has seldom been doubted that the Humean analysis specifies at least necessary conditions for the attribution of laws.

Of course transcendental idealists and others have long contended that a constant conjunction of events is not a sufficient condition for a causal law. They have seen that scientists never fail to distinguish a necessary from an accidental sequence (even if they are not always sure into which class a given sequence falls). But the problem has always been to ground this intuition in such a way as to sustain a concept of *natural* necessity, that is, a necessity in nature quite independent of human beings and their activity.

On the transcendental realist system a sequence A, B is necessary if and only if there is a natural mechanism M such that when stimulated by A, B tends to be produced. And it is a condition of the possibility of science (and in particular of the experimental establishment and practical application of our knowledge) that such objects exist and act, as what may be termed the *intransitive* objects of scientific inquiry, independently of their identification.

Now it follows from the fact that causal laws must be analysed as tendencies (which are only necessarily manifest in empirical invariances under closed conditions) that, contrary to the specific claims of Popper and Hempel and the tacit presupposition of Winch, deducibility from empirical invariances, depending upon the availability of constant conjunctions of events, can be neither necessary nor sufficient for a natural scientific explanation. There is an ontological gap between causal laws and their empirical grounds, which both parties to the naturalist debate have hitherto ignored. This not only renders standard positivist methodological injunctions patently inapplicable, but vitiates the most familiar hermeneutical contrasts. Thus, just as a rule can be broken without being changed, so a natural mechanism may continue to endure, and the law it grounds be both applicable and true (that is, not falsified), though its effect (i.e. the consequent) be unrealized.[24]

If the objects of our knowledge exist and act independently of the knowledge of which they are the objects, it is equally the case that such knowledge as we actually possess always consists in historically specific social forms. Thus to think our way clearly in the philosophy of science we need to constitute a *transitive* dimension or philosophical sociology to complement the intransitive dimension or philosophical ontology already established. A moment's reflection will show that, unless one does so, any attempt to establish the irreducibility of knowable being to thought must end in failure.

Discovery and Development: The Transitive Dimension

Once we constitute an intransitive dimension we can see how changing knowledge of unchanging objects is possible. But here again we encounter a paradox. For those philosophers, such as Popper and Kuhn, who, in opposition to the classical inductivist view, have drawn attention to the phenomena of scientific discontinuity and change, have found it difficult to reconcile this with the idea that science involves a cumulative growth in our knowledge of nature.

The analysis of experimental activity shows that the objects of scientific investigation are typically structured and intransitive, that is, irreducible to patterns of events and active independently of their identification by human beings. But how, given that they are, can science come to possess knowledge of them? How, that is to say, is scientific discovery possible? It is clearly a condition of the intelligibility of scientific discovery that, in the intransitive dimension, what is discovered exists independently of its discovery; and that, in the transitive dimension, it is not known prior to its discovery. Now if one is to avoid the absurdity of the assumption of the production of such knowledge *ex nihilo*, it must depend upon the employment of antecedently existing cognitive materials (which I have called the 'transitive' objects of knowledge). So science must be seen as a social process, whose aim is the production of the knowledge of the mechanisms of the production of phenomena in nature – the intransitive objects of inquiry.

Typically, then, the construction of an explanation for, that is, the production of the knowledge of the mechanism of the production of, some identified phenomenon will involve the building of a model, utilizing such cognitive materials and operating under the control of something like a logic of analogy and metaphor,[25] of a mechanism, which *if* it were to exist and act in the postulated way would account for the phenomenon in question (a movement of thought which may be styled 'retroduction'[26]). The reality of the postulated explanation must then, of course, be subjected to empirical scrutiny. (For, in general, more than one explanation will be consistent with the phenomenon concerned.) Once this is done, the explanation must then in principle itself be explained. And so one has in science a three-phase schema of development in which, in a continuing dialectic, science identifies a phenomenon (or range of phenomena), constructs explanations for it and empirically tests its explanations, leading to the identification of the generative mechanism at work, which now becomes the phenomenon to be explained, and so on. In this continuing process, as deeper levels or strata of reality are successively unfolded, science must construct and test its explanations with the cognitive resources and physical tools at its disposal, which in this process are themselves progressively trans-formed, modified and refined.

Now, in this dialectic, it is important to note that science employs two criteria for the ascription of reality to a posited object: a perceptual criterion and a causal one. The causal criterion turns on the capacity of the entity whose existence is in doubt to bring about changes in material things. Notice that a magnetic or gravitational field satisfies this criterion, but not a criterion of perceivability. On this criterion, to be is not to be perceived, but rather (in the last instance) just to be able to do.[27] The standard hermeneutical fork, generated by the conceptual/perceptible dichotomy of classical empiricist ontology, which we have already seen invoked by Winch, ignores precisely those possibilities opened up by a causal criterion for ascribing reality. Thus both parties to the naturalist dispute have assumed that the social must be either merely empirically real or in effect transcendentally ideal, so producing either a conceptually impoverished and deconceptualizing empiricism, or a hermeneutics drained of causal import and impervious to empirical controls.

Knowledge of deeper levels may correct as well as explain, knowledge of more superficial ones. In fact one finds in science a characteristic pattern of description, explanation and redescription of the phenomena identified at any one level of reality. But only a concept of *ontological depth* (depending upon the concept of real strata apart from our knowledge of strata) enables us to reconcile the twin aspects of scientific development, viz. growth and change. Such a reconciliation is essential if the one-sidedness of the accounts of both continuists, such as Nagel, and discontinuists, such as Popper, is to be avoided; and, in opposition to, for example, Feyerabend and Kuhn, the rationality of scientific transformations sustained.[28] Moreover, only the concept of ontological depth can reveal the actual historical stratification of the sciences as anything other than an accident.[29] For this can now be seen as grounded in the multi-tiered stratification of reality, and the consequent logic – of discovery – *that* stratification imposes on science.[30]

A critique of empiricism is achieved by noting how knowledge at the Lockean level, viz. of real essences, is possible, so resolving the paradoxes and problems (most notoriously, of induction) that stem from the dogmatic assumption of empirical realism. But a complementary critique of rationalism is achieved by noting that such knowledge is produced a posteriori – in the transitive, irreducibly empirical, process of science.[31]

On this transcendental realist view of science, then, its essence lies in the *movement* at any one level from knowledge of manifest phenomena to knowledge of the structures that generate them. The question of naturalism can thus now be posed as follows: to what extent is it possible to suppose that a comparable move can be made in the domain of the human sciences?

The Social Sciences and Philosophy

Our analysis of science immediately pinpoints an internal difficulty in this project. For the objects of scientific inquiry are neither empirically given nor even actually determinate chunks of the world. Rather, they are real structures, whose actual presence and appropriate concept have to be produced by the experimental and theoretical work of science. Thus, it would seem that we must first know what kinds of things societies (and people) are before we can consider whether it is possible to study them scientifically. Indeed without some prior specification of an object of inquiry, any discourse on method is bound to be more or less arbitrary. The question to which this essay aspires to make a contribution may therefore be set as follows: *what properties do societies and people possess that might make them possible objects of knowledge for us?*

But to pose the question in this way immediately invites the objection that such a specification can only be achieved by the work of science itself, so that philosophy is once again, as it were, 'running idle'. For it would seem that if naturalism has been achieved, there is nothing for the philosopher to add; and, if it has not, there is nothing s/he can say. What this objection presupposes is that there is nothing that can be said a priori about societies (and persons).

Now it would clearly beg the question to pick on some or other forms of social scientific activity to act as premises for a transcendental inquiry. For such activities are themselves the subject of substantive theoretical controversy, and presuppose different and conflicting conceptions of society. But it does not follow from this that one cannot isolate more or less universally recognized features of substantive social life itself, which do not beg the issue at the outset in favour of one type of social science rather than another. Indeed reflection on natural science, which is a social activity, conducted by people, is sufficient to show the scope for philosophical argument here. For, if it is to be possible, people must be material objects capable of acting intentionally on a world of other material objects and communicating the results of their activity to other intentional agents and for subsequent moments of time. Moreover, if it is to be possible, knowledge must be a reproduced process irreducible to a purely individual acquisition. Indeed, one might be tempted to take results such as these as premises for a formal 'deduction' from science. However, such a programme could not license the inference from scientific activity to social activity in general. But it is in any event unnecessary to restrict ourselves to what can be said a priori about science. For the properties that scientific activity depends upon are not instantiated in scientific practice alone. Indeed they turn on features that are a necessary condition for any social life at all. So, in developing my argument in Chapter 2, I shall draw on aspects taken from the wider ambit of general society, thereby allaying any suspicion that I might be trying to squeeze a general moral out of the special case of science. Of course as any account of society must be consistent with science, the latter may serve as a useful check on, and illustration of, the general account.

In considering the italicized question above, it is important to note that I must establish that any such properties, and *a fortiori* their bearers, are real. That is to say, I must show not only that in explanations in the domain of the human sciences social (and psychological) predicates are irreducible (which is consistent with a transcendental idealist interpretation of their status), but that a realistic interpretation of social scientific (and psychological) theory is in principle acceptable; that is, that some possible objects designated by social scientific (and psychological) theory are real. For unless this is done our analysis of science entails that the possibility of a non-reductionist naturalism must straightaway collapse.

Analysis of experimental activity and scientific development shows that knowledge must be viewed as a produced means of production, with intransitive objects existing and acting independently of it. Now the orthodox tradition in the philosophy of science, including both its em- piricist and neo-Kantian wings, has uncritically accepted the doctrine, implicit in the empirical realist dissolution of ontology, of the actuality of causal laws, and it has interpreted these, following Hume, as empirical regularities. In this way causal laws are reduced to sequences of events, and events to experiences. Anything further, any 'surplus element' in their analysis, is then supposed to be contributed by mind. Now analysis of experimental (and applied) activity shows that causal laws cannot be explicated as sequences of events and consideration of the possibility of scientific change (or even of any scientific redescrip- tion, implied *inter alia* by the necessity for a scientific training) shows that events cannot be explicated in terms of experience. Research and teaching are the two most obvious, yet philosophically under-analysed, *tasks* of scientists, just as the laboratory and the classroom are the two most obvious *sites* of science.

By secreting an ontology based on the category of experience, three domains of reality (the domains of the real, the actual and the empirical) are collapsed into one.[32] This prevents the crucial question of the conditions under which experience is, in fact, significant in science from being posed. And it prevents the way in which these three domains of reality are aligned in scientific practice – viz., by the transformation of nature (in experiment) and thought (in redescription) – from being described. What the orthodox tradition omits from its account of science is the nature of scientific activity as *work*; or when, as in transcendental idealism, it does recognize it, it considers it only as intellectual and not also as practical labour.[33] Accordingly, it cannot see knowledge, or at least the achievement of a closure, as a transient social product. Underlying the undifferentiated ontology of empirical realism is thus an individualistic sociology, in which people are seen as passively sensing (or else, as conventionally deciding upon) given facts and recording their constant conjunctions.

I said earlier that a philosophy of science was not only possible, but in practice indispensable for science. I have yet to substantiate this claim. Now it follows from my argument that scientists, when they are practising science, are implicitly acting on transcendental realism. But it does not follow, any more than it did with M. Jourdain and his prose, that they *realize* they are. Nor does it follow that transcendental realism is the *only* or even, at any moment of time, the dominant philosophy they are acting on. One is therefore, qua philosopher of science, at perfect liberty to criticize the practice of any science for its lack of scientificity. The importance of this should be clear. For example, instrumentalist and fictionalist interpretations of scientific theories may be used quite generally (in chemistry and physics as much as in economics and psychology) to impede attempts to build realist scientific theories. But the intervention of philosophical reflection in the practice of a science or putative science needs no stressing when one focuses on the social sciences. Their *Angst*-ridden state already renders them particularly prone to philosophical suggestion. And it is clearly in the social sciences, with their evident *malaise* and their invocation of flaccid philosophies in support of widely discrepant practices, that philosophy might be expected to do something more than paint its grey on black.

Now a closer link is bound to exist between philosophy and the social sciences than between it and the natural sciences for another and necessary reason. For it is *internal* to the subject-matter of the social, but not the natural, sciences. That is to say, it is itself a possible object of social scientific explanation; and in the sequel to this study some of the ways in which philosophies may be explained will be delineated. We shall see, for instance, how the positivist concept of a fact as what is more or less immediately apprehended in sense-perception generates characteristic ideologies *for* and *of* science; how the former rationalizes the practice of what Kuhn has called 'normal science',[34] and how the latter produces mystiques of common sense and/or expertise. Or again, how the Humean theory of causality, presupposing a view of the world as closed and completely described, encourages a conception of the social world as unstructured (hence as 'obvious'), as undifferentiated and unchanging; so underpinning certain substantive theories of social life (which are themselves regurgitated in social science). It is a mistake to think that philosophy functions in the social sciences only via methodological injunctions (or prohibitions). It acts in a number of other ways, most obviously via what I shall call 'resonance'. In resonance philosophies come to reflect, and so reinforce, the interests, preoccupations and assumptions of substantive social science (as in the structural homologies already noted between empiricism and behaviourism, and conventionalism and voluntarism). These in turn may themselves reflect, or be otherwise generated by, interests at work in the rest of society.

Now transcendental realism can under-labour for the social sciences in at least three ways. Firstly, it can help to debunk the claims to scientificity made by practices which merely ape the image of science projected by positivism or one of its mutant forms. In this way it can cut into the web of mutually supportive resonance effects sustaining the various homoeomorphs secreted by the social order. Secondly, it can set the terms for a more rational appraisal of the real problems the social sciences face by enabling a fairer contrast to be drawn between their conditions and possibilities and those of the sciences of nature. And, finally, by exploring an affinity which philosophy shares with social science in that both seek, as at least part of their project, to identify and describe the conceptions of agents engaged in social practices, it can, in ways to be explored in the next chapter, illuminate a kindred mode of discovery. If these claims are warranted then philosophy could turn the tables on Hegel's jibe (and Bradley's that it merely produces bad reasons for what we believe on instinct) and yet play a part in the continuing *Kampfplatz* between social ideologies and social science.[35] And one could then agree with Winch that there *is* an essential connection, while insisting (against him) that it is not one of identity, between the tasks of philosophy and the social sciences.

Towards a New Critical Naturalism

As already indicated, over the last hundred years or so two broad positions in the philosophy of social science have dominated the scene: the one naturalist, the other anti-naturalist. But the dominant naturalist tradition has been based on a very different conception of science (and philosophy) from that advocated in this chapter. It has seen science as consisting essentially in the registration of (or refutation of claims about) empirical invariances between discrete events, states of affairs and the like. The hermeneutical tradition has accepted this account of natural science (or at least its implicit ontology), subjecting it at best to relatively minor qualifications. But it contends that social science is (or should be) concerned with the elucidation of meaning and the tracing of conceptual connections – activities clearly lacking counterparts in the study of the inanimate world of nature. Besides this positive claim, defenders of *Verstehen* can point, with justice, to the complete absence of explanations in social science conforming to positivist prescriptions, and in particular to the absence of universal empirical regularities of a significant kind. In response to this, positivists tend to argue that the social world is much more complex than the natural world ('inter-actionism', already prefigured by Mill[36]) or that the regularities that govern it can only be identified at a more basic level ('reductionism', prefigured by Comte), and that, in any event, concepts (or meanings), to the extent that they are explanatorily relevant at all, can only be identified, or hypotheses about them tested, empirically (i.e., behaviourally). Neither party doubts for a moment that empirical invariances are necessary for laws, or that the conceptual and the empirical jointly exhaust the real.

The basis of the hermeneutical tradition lies in the Kantian and Hegelian dichotomies of phenomenon/noumenon and nature/spirit. Its heyday was reached in the Manichean world of late nineteenth-century

German thought which drew sharp distinctions between causal explanation (*Erklären*) and interpretative understanding (*Verstehen*), the
nomothetic and the ideographic, the repeatable and the unique; and an
absolute contrast between the science of the physical non-human world
of nature and the science of the world of mind, of culture and of history.
This was at least in part a reaction to the positivism of Comte and Mill
(and their German epigones), and before them to the kind of chiliastic
claims made by the Enlightenment for the new science of mechanics.
And it was against this Manichean dualism – or its real or imaginary
effects – that the latest wave of positivism, in the form of the systems of
Popper and Hempel and their followers, was very largely aimed. The
epistemological ground for this reassertion of positivism in the philosophy of the social sciences was laid by the logical atomism and
positivism of the 1920s and 1930s, itself traceable through the work of
the early Wittgenstein, Russell and Moore, to a reaction against the
same idealism that informed the intellectual milieu of Dilthey, Simmel,
Weber and Rickert. It was understandable, then, that in the wake of the
anti-positivist turn taken by the later Wittgenstein and the Oxford of the
1950s one should see the emergence of a reformed and analytically
sophisticated hermeneutics, represented most notably perhaps by the
works of Anscombe, Dray, Charles Taylor and Winch (a partial
reaction to which is evident in the writings of Davidson and, for
example, Mandelbaum,[37] on reductionist and interactionist lines respectively). In Germany this development was paralleled by the critical
and dialectical hermeneutics of Gadamer, Apel and Habermas, which
immediately became the target of polemical attack by Popper and his
school.[38]

Much of the history of the philosophy of the social sciences can thus
be seen as a kind of historical see-saw, an oscillation to-and-fro between
variants of these basic positions. Now the conception of science
developed here sees science, like the positivist tradition, as unified in its
essential method; and, like the hermeneutical tradition, as essentially
differentiated in (or specific to) its objects. But my account of scientific
method is diametrically opposed to that of positivism; and partly
(though not only) in virtue of this, my account of the specific differences
of the social sciences also departs in fundamental respects from that of
the hermeneutical tradition.

To posit an essential unity of scientific method is to posit an account
which conceives the sciences as unified in the form that scientific
knowledge takes, the reasoning by which it is produced and the concepts
in terms of which its production can be most adequately theorized or
reconstructed. (These aspects correspond roughly to the traditional
fields of epistemology, logic and metaphysics respectively.) Now the
transcendental analysis of science sketched above reveals that its

essence consists in the movement, at any one level of inquiry, from manifest phenomena to the structures that generate them. It shows that experimental and practical activity entails an analysis of causal laws as expressing the tendencies of things, not conjunctions of events ('epistemology'); that scientific discovery and development entails that scientific inferences must be analogical and retroductive, not simply inductive and/or deductive ('logic'); and that the process of knowledge-production necessitates a conceptual system based on the notion of powers ('metaphysics').[39] From this perspective, then, things are viewed as individuals possessing powers (and as agents as well as patients). And actions are the realization of their potentialities. Historical things are structured and differentiated (more or less unique) ensembles of tendencies, liabilities and powers; and historical events are their transformations.

Taken together, these three shifts in standpoint imply a radically different ontology and account of science. The prima-facie plausibility of positivism may then be seen to rest largely upon the illicit generalization, and incorrect analysis, of a special case: that of an epistemically significant closure. Realism can accommodate (and what is more explain) that case too. But it is a case without application to the social sciences, and, if treated as a norm, cannot be acted upon without generating in practice the most damaging overt and covert effects.

Now the fact that, upon any serious reflection, positivist prescriptions can be seen to be so patently inapplicable to the social sciences no doubt accounts for the greater intuitive plausibility of hermeneutical positions there. Thus most writers within this tradition have not found it difficult to show that some positivist assumption or rule is inapplicable to some or other area of social life. But they characteristically draw the wrong conclusions from this. In some cases, where it is just a matter of their extracting an anti-naturalist moral from a fundamentally correct point, the error is easily undone: by showing how the point can be accommodated within the more expansive, less restrictive account of science provided by transcendental realism. But in other cases the point itself is mistaken. And, where it is, I think that this is often traceable not just to an inadequate conception of their contrast (natural science), but to their taking over of some still more fundamental positivist assumption into their conception of social science. Indeed, upon analysis, anti-naturalist theories of social science may often be seen to consist entirely in, or at least depend essentially on, the inversion or displacement, transformation and/or condensation of characteristically positivist themes. In this sense the effects of positivism, or rather of the philosophical problem-field that underpins it, on the philosophy of social science have been hegemonic. This problem-field is defined by an ontology of experience, *empirical realism*, and a sociology of man, *sociological individualism*, and it incorporates transcendental idealist and collectivist variants. It is this couple (empiricism/ individualism) that I think must be held largely responsible, or rather that acts as the metatheoretical trustee for the practices responsible, for the social scientific *malaise*.

To illustrate the tacit dominance of positivist thought, consider the fact of human agency, upon which anti-positivists have quite properly wished to insist. However their acceptance of the actualist presupposition that laws fully describe, and so completely control, the everyday world of perceived things, together with their well-grounded fear that if this notion were to be applicable to social life there would be no room left for human agency, has often encouraged them into a total voluntarism. This is nothing but the simple inverse of positivism's blanket determinism. Sartre's (or Goffman's) freely chosen selves and Durkheim's (or Parsons') internalized values reflect in the last instance the same mistaken notion of law. In fact, in given circumstances and considered in relation to their own peculiar mode of operation, social structures may be just as 'coercive' as natural laws. And, conversely, just as rules can be broken, so natural tendencies may fail to be realized. Again, by and large, writers within the hermeneutical tradition have adopted the positivist view that the objects of knowledge are events (or their counterpart in the domain of the human sciences, actions). Transposed to the hermeneutical perspective, this misconception has encouraged a definition of the social by reference to the category of *behaviour*, albeit of a particular, for example intentional or rule-governed, sort. Now the notion 'social science' is at present enormously confused. It is very much a hotchpotch, and requires analysis. But its distinct subject-matters cannot be separated out by using the category of behaviour. Rather one will have to look to the distinct *structures* that mesh together in the field of social life. Substituting an ontology of structures for one of events, and recognizing that social individuals are in general both complex and changing, provides a way of avoiding at the outset the false oppositions, such as between theory and history or the universal and the unique, on which the hermeneutical dualisms turn.

According to the non-positivist naturalism developed here, the *predicates* that appear in the explanation of social phenomena will be different from those that appear in natural scientific explanations and the *procedures* used to establish them will in certain vital respects be different too (being contingent upon, and determined by, the properties of the objects under study); but the *principles* that govern their production will remain substantially the same. It is the argument of this book that although, because social objects are irreducible to (and really emergent from) natural objects, and so possess qualitatively different features from them, they cannot be studied in the same way as them,[40] they can still be studied 'scientifically'. Indeed, it is only because social objects possess such a 'non-natural surplus' (as it were), differentiating them from purely natural ones, that it makes sense to suppose that they can be studied scientifically, as *social* objects, at all. There can be identity of essence here, only *because* there is difference in substantival form.

The positivist tradition is correct to stress that there are causal laws, generalities, at work in social life. It is also correct to insist (when it does) that these laws *may* be opaque to the agents' spontaneous understanding. Where it errs is in the reduction of these laws to empirical regularities, and in the account that it is thereby committed to giving of the process of their identification. For in the absence of spontaneously occurring, and given the impossibility of artificially creating, closed systems, the human sciences must confront the problem of the direct scientific study of phenomena that only ever manifest themselves in open systems – for which orthodox philosophy of science, with its tacit presupposition of a closure, is literally useless.[41] In particular it follows from this condition that criteria for the rational appraisal and development of theories in the social sciences, which are denied (in principle) decisive test situations, *cannot be predictive* and so must be *exclusively explanatory*.

The hermeneutical tradition is correct to point out that the social sciences deal with a pre-interpreted reality, a reality already brought under concepts by social actors, that is, a reality *already brought under the same kind of material in terms of which it is to be grasped* (which is the only possible medium of its intelligibility). So that, to put it crudely, the human sciences stand, at least in part, to their subject-matter in a subject-subject (or concept-concept) relationship, rather than simply a subject-object (or concept-thing) one. It is also correct to insist upon the methodological significance of this difference. Where it errs is in a reduction of social science to the modalities of this relationship, and its consequent failure to situate, through the possibility of reference to aspects of reality at once social and inadequately conceptualized, the possibility of rationally defensible conceptual criticism and change, most fully in the development of the concept of ideology.

Now it is in their common commitment to the ontology of empirical realism, and the individualist sociology that it presupposes, that the root source of these divergent errors will be found, in Chapter 4, to lie. In rejecting this ontology and sociology, transcendental realism also situates the possibility of a new *critical naturalism* (which will be elaborated in Chapters 2 and 3). Such a naturalism, it will be shown, can do justice to the proto-scientific intuitions of both positivism and its hermeneutical foil. However in contrast to positivism, it can sustain the *transfactuality* of social structures, while insisting on their *conceptuality* (or concept-dependence). And in contrast to hermeneutics, it can sustain the *intransitivity* of both beliefs and meanings, while insisting on their susceptibility to scientific explanation and hence *critique*, in a spiral (rather than circle) which reflexively implicates social science as a moment in the process that it explains.

It is important to stress that the upshot of the analyses of Chapters 2 and 3 will not be a substantive sociology and psychology, but formal or a priori conditions for them. However if my argument in the previous section is correct, such philosophical investigations may yet prove to be *practically* indispensable conditions for the emancipation and successful development of the 'human sciences'.

NOTES

1. See W. Outhwaite, *Understanding Social Life*, ch. 2 (London 1975).
2. See, for example, E. A. Burtt, *The Metaphysical Foundations of Natural Science* (London 1964), esp. chs. 2 and 3, or A. Koyré, *Metaphysics and Measurement* (London 1968), esp. chs. 1 and 2.
3. 'The world of civil society has certainly been made by men, and . . . its principles are therefore to be found within the modifications of our human minds. Whoever reflects on this cannot but marvel that the philosophers should have bent all their energies to the study of the world of nature, which, since God made it, He alone knows; and that they should have neglected the study of the world of nations, or the civil world, which, since men made it, men could come to know', G. Vico, *Scienza Nuova*, trans. as *The New Science of Giambattista Vico* (Ithaca 1969), sec. 331. See, for example, L. Pompa, *Vico* (Cambridge 1975), ch. 15.
4. See G. H. von Wright, *Explanation and Understanding* (London 1971), ch. 1.
5. See H.-G. Gadamer, *Truth and Method* (London 1975), pp. 5–39.
6. P. Winch, *The Idea of a Social Science* (London 1958), esp. pp. 114–5.
7. *Ibid.*, esp. pp. 108, 124–5.
8. *A Realist Theory of Science*, 1st edn (Leeds 1975), 2nd edn (Hassocks and New Jersey 1978).
9. See, for example, R. Collingwood, *An Essay in Metaphysics* (Oxford 1940), pp. 3ff.
10. *The Treatise* is subtitled 'An attempt to introduce the experimental method of reasoning into moral subjects'.
11. See, for example, G. Buchdahl, *Metaphysics and the Philosophy of Science* (Oxford 1969), p. 3 and *passim*.
12. See R. Harrison, *On What There Must Be* (Oxford 1974), p. 27.
13. See, for example, W. H. Walsh, *Kant's Criticism of Metaphysics* (Edinburgh 1975), pp. 102–6.
14. S. Körner, *Categorial Frameworks* (Oxford 1970), p. 72.
15. See W. B. Gallie, 'Essentially Contested Concepts', P.A.S. 56 (1955–6).
16. See, for example, P. Duhem, *The Aim and Structure of Physical Theory* (New York 1962), esp. ch. 1.

17. See, for example, P. Colvin, 'Ontological and Epistemological Commitments and Social Relations in the Sciences', *Sociology of the Sciences Yearbook 1977: The Social Production of Knowledge*, E. Mendelsohn, P. Weingart, R. Whitley (eds.) (Dordrecht 1977).
18. K. Marx, *Capital*, 3 (London 1966), p. 817.
19. G. Lukács, *History and Class Consciousness* (London 1971), p. 110.
20. See, for example, R. Harré, *The Principles of Scientific Thinking* (London 1970), ch. 1 and *passim*.
21. See my *A Realist Theory of Science*, ch. 1.
22. *Ibid.*, ch. 2.
23. See J. R. Ravetz, *Scientific Knowledge and its Social Problems* (Oxford 1971), p. 76.
24. See *A Realist Theory of Science*, ch. 2, sec. 4.
25. See, for example, R. Harré, *op. cit.*, ch. 2; and M. B. Hesse, *The Structure of Scientific Inference* (London 1974), esp. chs. 9 and 11.
26. See N. R. Hanson, *Patterns of Discovery* (Cambridge 1965), pp. 85ff.
27. See *A Realist Theory of Science*, p. 182.
28. See my 'Feyerabend and Bachelard: Two Philosophies of Science', *New Left Review* 94 (1975), esp. pp. 31–47.
29. See, for example, H. Putnam, 'Explanation and Reference', *Philosophical Papers Vol. II: Mind, Language and Reality* (Cambridge 1975), p. 210.
30. See my 'Forms of Realism', *Philosophica* 15 (1975), esp. pp. 108–14.
31. See *A Realist Theory of Science*, ch. 3, secs. 5 and 6.
32. *Ibid.*, ch. 1, sec. 6.
33. Marx's comments on Hegel to the effect that 'the only labour Hegel knows and recognizes is *abstract mental labour*. So that which above all constitutes the essence of philosophy . . . Hegel *knows* by *doing* philosophy' (K. Marx, *Early Writings* (Harmondsworth 1975), p. 386) provide an ironically apt epitaph on the entire (superficially very un-Hegelian) orthodox tradition in the philosophy of science.
34. T. S. Kuhn, *The Structure of Scientific Revolutions*, 2nd edn (Chicago 1970), esp. ch. 2.
35. See L. Althusser, 'Lenin and Philosophy', *Lenin and Philosophy* (London 1971), p. 57.
36. 'The agencies which determine human character are so numerous and diversified . . . that in the aggregate they are never in two cases exactly similar . . . [Nevertheless] any facts are fitted, in themselves, to be a subject of science, which follow one another according to constant laws; although these laws may not have been discovered, nor ever be discoverable by our existing resources', J. S. Mill, *A System of Logic* (London 1961), bk. 6, ch. 3.
37. 'The laws through which we explain a particular event need not be laws which state a uniform sequence concerning complex events of the type which we wish to explain. Rather, they may be laws which state uniform connections between two types of factor which are contained within those complex events', M. Mandelbaum, 'Historical Explanation: The Problem of Covering Laws', *History and Theory* 1 (1961), reprinted in P. Gardiner (ed.), *The Philosophy of History* (Oxford 1974), p. 57.
38. See T. Adorno (ed.), *The Positivist Dispute in German Sociology* (London 1976).
39. See *A Realist Theory of Science*, esp. ch. 3, sec. 3. See also R. Harré and E. H. Madden, *Causal Powers* (Oxford 1975), *passim*.

40. Thus it is obvious that one can no more set out experimentally to identify (or non-vacuously simulate) the causes of the French Revolution than one can sensibly contemplate interviewing a gene. But is it surprising, in view of the fact that nation states are not at all *like* molecules, that knowledge of them should have to be obtained in radically different ways?

41. See *A Realist Theory of Science*, esp. appendix to ch. 2.

Chapter 2

Societies

Introduction

What properties do societies possess that might make them possible objects of knowledge for us? My strategy in developing an answer to this question will be effectively based on a pincer movement. But in deploying the pincer I shall concentrate first on the ontological question of the properties that societies possess, before shifting to the epistemological question of how these properties make them possible objects of knowledge for us. This is not an arbitrary order of development. It reflects the condition that, for transcendental realism, it is the nature of objects that determines their cognitive possibilities for us; that, in nature, it is humanity that is contingent and knowledge, so to speak, accidental. Thus it is because sticks and stones are solid that they can be picked up and thrown, not because they can be picked up and thrown that they are solid (though that they can be handled in this sort of way may be a contingently necessary condition for our *knowledge* of their solidity).[1]

In the next section I argue that societies are irreducible to people and in the third section I sketch a model of their connection. In that and the following section I argue that social forms are a necessary condition for any intentional act, that their *pre-existence* establishes their *autonomy* as possible objects of scientific investigation and that their *causal power* establishes their *reality*. The pre-existence of social forms will be seen to entail a *transformational* model of social activity, from which a number of ontological limits on any possible naturalism can be immediately derived. In the fifth section I show how it is, just in virtue of these emergent features of societies, that social science is possible; and I relate two other types of limit on naturalism (viz. epistemological and relational ones) back to the fundamental properties of the transformational model itself. In the last section I use the results established in the previous section to generate a critique of the traditional fact/value dichotomy; and in an appendix to the chapter I illustrate the notion of social science as critique in the reconstruction of an essentially Marxian concept of ideology. Now it is important to note that because the causal power of social forms is mediated through human agency, my argument can only be formally completed when the causal status of human agency is itself vindicated. This is accomplished in Chapter 3 in the course of a parallel demonstration of the possibility of naturalism in the domain of the psychological sciences.

The transformational model of social activity developed here will be seen to entail a *relational* conception of the subject-matter of social science. On this conception 'society does not consist of individuals [or, we might add, groups], but expresses the sum of the relations within which individuals [and groups] stand'.[2] And the essential movement of scientific theory will be seen to consist in the movement from the manifest phenomena of social life, as conceptualized in the experience of the social agents concerned, to the essential relations that necessitate them. Of such relations the agents involved may or may not be aware. Now it is through the capacity of social science to illuminate such relations that it may come to be 'emancipatory'. But the emancipatory potential of social science is contingent upon, and entirely a consequence of, its contextual explanatory power.

Consider for a moment a magnet F and the effect it has on iron filings placed within its field. Consider next the thought T of that magnet and its effect. That thought is clearly the product of science, of culture, of history. Unlike the magnet it has no (discounting psycho-kinesis) appreciable effect on iron. Now every science must construct its own object (*T*) in thought. But it does not follow from the fact that its thought of its real object (*F*) must be constructed in and by (and exists only in) thought that the object of its investigations is not independently real. (Indeed it was to mark the point, and the associated ambiguity in the notion of an object of knowledge, that I distinguished in Chapter 1 between transitive and intransitive objects.)

Now whereas few people nowadays, at least outside the ranks of professional philosophers, would hold that a magnetic field is a construction of thought, the idea that society is remains quite widely held. Of course in the case of society the grounds for this view are liable to consist in the idea that it is constituted (in some way) by the thought of social actors or participants, rather than, as in the case of the magnetic field, the thought of observers or theorists (or perhaps, moving to a more sophisticated plane, in some relationship – such as that of Schutzian 'adequacy',[3] accomplished perhaps by some process of dialogue or negotiation – between the two). And underlying that idea, though by no means logically necessary for it,[4] is more often than not the notion that society just consists (in some sense) in persons and/or their actions. Seldom does it occur to subscribers to this view that an identical train of thought logically entails their own reducibility, via the laws and principles of neurophysiology, to the status of inanimate things!

In the next section I am going to consider the claims of this naïve position, which may be dubbed *social atomism*, or rather of its epistemological manifestation in the form of *methodological individualism*,[5] to provide a framework for the explanation of social phenomena. Of course, as already mentioned in Chapter 1, if I am to situate the possibility of a non-reductionist naturalism on transcendental realist lines, then I must establish not only the autonomy of a possible sociology, but the reality of any objects so designated. That is to say, I must show that societies are complex real objects irreducible to simpler ones, such as people. For this purpose, merely to argue against methodological individualism is insufficient. But it is necessary. For if methodological individualism were correct, we could dispense entirely with this chapter, and begin (and end) our inquiry into the human sciences with a consideration of the properties, be they rationally imputed or empirically determined, of the individual atoms themselves: that is, of the amazing (and more or less tacitly gendered) homunculus man.

Against Individualism

Methodological individualism is the doctrine that facts about societies, and social phenomena generally, are to be explained solely in terms of facts about individuals. For Popper, for example, 'all social phenomena, and especially the functioning of social institutions, should be understood as resulting from the decisions etc. of human individuals . . . we should never be satisfied by explanations in terms of so-called "collectives"'.[6] Social institutions are merely 'abstract models' designed to interpret the facts of individual experiences. Jarvie has even committed himself to the linguistic thesis that '"army" is just the plural of "soldier" and all statements about the army can be reduced to statements about the particular soldiers comprising it'.[7] Watkins concedes that there may be unfinished or half-way explanations of large-scale phenomena in terms of other large-scale phenomena, such as of inflation in terms of full employment(!),[8] but contends that one will not have arrived at so-called rock-bottom (ultimate?) explanations of such phenomena until one has deduced them from statements about the dispositions, beliefs, resources and interrelations of individuals.[9] Specifically, social events are to be explained by deducing them from the principles governing the behaviour of the 'participating' individuals and descriptions of their situation.[10] In this manner, methodological individualism stipulates the *material* conditions for adequate explanation in the social sciences to complement the *formal* ones laid down by the deductive–nomological model.

Now when one considers the range of predicates applicable to individuals and individual behaviour – from those that designate properties, such as shape and texture, that people possess in common with other material things, through those that pick out states, such as hunger and pain, that they share with other higher animals, to those that designate actions that are, as far as we know, uniquely characteristic of them – the real problem appears to be not so much that of how one could give an individualistic explanation of social behaviour, but that of how one could ever give a non-social (i.e., strictly individualistic) explanation of individual, at least characteristically human, behaviour![11] For the predicates designating properties special to persons all presuppose a social context for their employment. A tribesman implies a tribe, the cashing of a cheque a banking system. Explanation, whether by subsumption under general laws, advertion to motives and rules, or redescription (identification), always involves irreducibly social predicates.

Moreover, it is not difficult to show that the arguments adduced in support of methodological individualism cannot bear the weight placed upon them. Thus comparison of the motives of a criminal with the procedures of a court indicates that facts about individuals are not necessarily either more observable or easier to understand than social facts; while comparison of the concepts of love and war shows that those applicable to individuals are not necessarily either clearer or easier to define than those that designate social phenomena.

Significantly, the qualifications and refinements proposed by methodological individualists weaken rather than strengthen their case. Thus the admission of ideal types, anonymous individuals *et al.*, into the methodological fold weakens the force of the ontological considerations in favour of it, while allowing 'half-way' and statistical explanations undercuts the epistemological ones. Moreover, the examples cited of supposedly genuinely 'holistic' behaviour, such as riots and orgies,[12] merely reveal the poverty of the implicit conception of the social. For, upon analysis of their oeuvre, it turns out that most individualists regard 'the social' as a synonym for 'the group'. The issue for them then becomes that of whether society, the whole, is greater than the sum of its constituent parts, individual people. And social behaviour then becomes explicable as the behaviour of groups of individuals (riots) or of individuals in groups (orgies).

Now I am going to argue that this definition of the social is radically misconceived. Sociology is not concerned, as such, with large-scale, mass or group behaviour (conceived as the behaviour of large numbers, masses or groups of individuals). Rather it is concerned, at least paradigmatically, with the persistent *relations* between individuals (and groups), and with the relations between these relations (and between such relations and nature and the products of such relations). In the simplest case its subject-matter may be exemplified by such relations as between capitalist and worker, MP and constituent, student and teacher, husband and wife. Such relations are general and relatively enduring, but they do not involve collective or mass behaviour as such in the way in which a strike or a demonstration does (though of course they may help to explain the latter). Mass behaviour is an interesting social-psychological phenomenon, but it is not the subject-matter of sociology.

The situation is made ironic by the fact that the more sophisticated individualists formally concede that relations may play a role in explanation. Why then the passion? I think that it must be explained, at least in part, by their predilection for a species of substantive social explanation, which they mistakenly believe to be uniquely consonant with political liberalism. As Watkins candidly puts it: 'Since Mandeville's *Fable of the Bees* was published in 1714, individualistic social science, with its emphasis on unintended consequences, has largely been a sophisticated elaboration on the simple theme that, in certain situations, selfish private motives [i.e. capitalism] may have good social consequences and good political intentions [i.e. socialism] bad social consequences'.[13] There is in fact one body of social doctrine, whose avatars include utilitarianism, liberal political theory and neo-classical economic theory, which does conform to individualistic prescriptions, on the assumption that what is in effect a generalized aggregation problem can be solved. According to this model reason is the efficient slave of the passions[14] and social behaviour can be seen as the outcome of a simple maximization problem, or its dual, a minimization one: the application of reason, the sole identifying characteristic of human beings, to desires (appetites and aversions in Hobbes) or feelings (pleasure and pain, in Hume, Bentham and Mill) that may be regarded as neurophysiologically given. Relations play no part in this model; and this model, if it applies at all, applies as much to Crusoe as to socialized humanity – with the corollary expressed by Hume that 'mankind is much the same at all times and places',[15] simultaneously revealing its ahistorical and a priori biases.

The limitations of this approach to social science should by now be well known. To say that people are rational does not explain *what* they do, but only at best (that is, supposing that an objective function could be reconstructed for their behaviour and empirically tested independently of it) *how* they do it. But rationality, setting out to explain everything, very easily ends up explaining nothing. To explain a human action by reference to its rationality is like explaining some natural event by reference to its being caused. Rationality then appears as an a priori presupposition of investigation, devoid of explanatory content and almost certainly false. As for neo-classical economic theory, the most developed form of this tendency in social thought, it may be best regarded as a normative theory of efficient action, generating a set of techniques for achieving given ends, rather than as an explanatory theory capable of casting light on actual empirical episodes: that is, as a praxiology,[16] not a sociology.

Besides its championship of a particular explanation form, individualism derives plausibility from the fact that it seems to touch on an important truth, awareness of which accounts for its apparent necessity: namely the idea that society is made up or consists of – and only of – people. In what sense is this true? In the sense that the material presence of social effects consists only in changes in people and changes brought about by people on other material things – objects of nature, such as land, and artefacts, produced by work on objects of nature. One could express this truth as follows: *the material presence of society = persons and the (material) results of their actions*. It is this truth that individualists have glimpsed, only to shroud it with their apologetic shifts.

It is evident that there is at work in methodological individualism a sociological reductionism and a psycho- (or praxio-) logical atomism, determining the content of ideal explanations in exact isomorphy with the theoretical reductionism and ontological atomism fixing their form.[17] It thus expresses particularly starkly the couple defining the method and object of investigation (viz. sociological individualism and ontological empiricism) which I earlier (in Chapter 1) suggested structure the practice of contemporary social science.

Now the *relational* conception of the subject-matter of sociology may be contrasted not only with the *individualist* conception, illustrated by utilitarian theory, but with what I shall call the 'collectivist' conception, best exemplified perhaps by Durkheim's work, with its heavy emphasis on the concept of the group. Durkheim's group is not of course Popper's. It is, to invoke a Sartrean analogy, more like a fused group than a series.[18] In particular, as an index of the social, it is characterized by the possession of certain emergent powers, whose justification will be considered below. Nevertheless, the key concepts of the Durkheimian corpus, such as *conscience collective*, organic v. mechanical solidarity, anomie, etc., all derive their meaning from their relationship to the concept of the collective nature of social phenomena. Thus, for Durkheim, to the extent at least that he is to remain committed to positivism, enduring relationships must be reconstructed from collective phenomena; whereas on the realist and relational view advanced here collective phenomena are seen primarily as the expressions of enduring relationships. Note that, on this conception, not only is sociology not essentially concerned with the group, it is not even essentially concerned with behaviour.

If Durkheim combined a collectivist conception of sociology with a positivist methodology, Weber combined a neo-Kantian methodology with a still essentially individualist conception of sociology. His break from utilitarianism is primarily at the level of the form of action or type of behaviour he is prepared to recognize, not at the level of the unit of study. It is significant that just as the thrust contained in Durkheim's isolation of the emergent properties of the group is checked by his continuing commitment to an empiricist epistemology, so the possibilities opened up by Weber's isolation of the ideal type are constrained by his continuing commitment to an empiricist ontology. In both cases a residual empiricism holds back, and ultimately annuls, a real scientific advance.[19] For it is as futile to attempt to sustain a concept of the social on the basis of the category of the group, as it is to attempt to sustain a concept of necessity on that of experience. Marx did, I think, make an attempt to combine a realist ontology and a relational sociology.[20] One can thus schematize four tendencies in social thought as in Table 2.1.

Table 2.1   Four Tendencies in Social Thought

	Method	*Object*
Utilitarianism	empiricist	individualist
Weber	neo-Kantian	individualist
Durkheim	empiricist	collectivist
Marx	realist	relational

N.B. Concepts of method (social epistemology) underpinned by general ontology; concepts of object (social ontology) underpinned by general epistemology.

It should be noted that as the relations between the relations that constitute the proper subject-matter of sociology may be *internal*, only the category of *totality* can, in general, adequately express it. Some problems stemming from this will be considered below. But first I want to consider the nature of the connection between society and the conscious activity of people.

On the Society/Person Connection

It is customary to draw a divide between two camps in sociological theory: one, represented above all by Weber, in which social objects are seen as the results of (or as constituted by) intentional or meaningful human behaviour; and the other, represented by Durkheim, in which they are seen as possessing a life of their own, external to and coercing the individual. With some stretching the various schools of social thought – phenomenology, existentialism, functionalism, structuralism, etc. – can then be seen as instances of one or other of these positions. And the varieties of Marxism can then also be neatly classified. These two stereotypes can be represented as in the diagrams below.

Model I: The Weberian stereotype   **Model II:** The Durkheimian stereotype
'Voluntarism'   'Reification'

Now it is tempting to try and develop a general model capable of synthesizing these conflicting perspectives, on the assumption of a dialectical interrelationship between society and people. I want to discuss a plausible variant of such a model, advocated most convincingly by Peter Berger and his associates.[21] Its weaknesses will, I think, enable us to work our way to a more adequate conception of the relationship between society and people, as well as to better display the errors of the conventional stereotypes.

According to the Berger model, which I shall call Model III, society forms the individuals who create society; society, in other words, produces the individuals, who produce society, in a continuous dialectic. Model III can be represented as below.

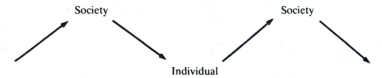

Model III: The 'Dialectical' conception
'Illicit Identification'

According to the protagonists of this model 'social structure is not characterizable as a thing able to stand on its own, apart from the human activity that produced it'.[22] But equally, once created, 'it is encountered by the individual [both] as an alien facticity [and] . . . as a coercive instrumentality'.[23] 'It is *there*, impervious to his wishes . . . other than [and resistant to] himself.'[24] This scheme thus seems able to do justice both to the subjective and intentional aspects of social life and to the externality and coercive power of social facts. And thus to avoid at once any voluntaristic implications of the Weberian tradition and any reification associated with the Durkheimian one. For a categorial distinction is now drawn between natural and social facts, in that the latter, but not the former, depend essentially upon human activity.

Thus, while agreeing with Durkheim that 'the system of signs I use to express my thoughts, the system of currency I employ to pay my debts, the instruments of credit I utilize in my commercial relations, the practices followed in my profession, etc., function independently of my use of them',[25] the advocates of this model regard such systems, instruments and practices as *objectivations* that, under certain conditions, take on an alienated form. According to them, objectivation is 'the process whereby human subjectivity embodies itself in products that are available to oneself and one's fellow men as elements of a common world'[26] and alienation is 'the process whereby the unity of the producing and its product is broken'.[27] Thus languages, forms of political and economic organization, and cultural and ethical norms are all ultimately embodiments of human subjectivity. And any consciousness which does not see them as such is necessarily reified. Reification must, however, be distinguished from *objectivication*, which is defined as 'the moment in the process of objectivation in which man establishes distance from his producing and its product, such that he can take cognizance of it and make of it an object of his consciousness',[28] and is regarded as necessary to any conceivable social life.

On Model III, then, society is an objectivation or externalization of human beings. And human beings, for their part, are the internalization or reappropriation in consciousness of society. Now I think that this model is seriously misleading. For it encourages, on the one hand, a voluntaristic idealism with respect to our understanding of social structure and, on the other, a mechanistic determinism with respect to our understanding of people. In seeking to avoid the errors of both stereotypes, Model III succeeds only in combining them. People and society are not, I shall argue, related 'dialectically'. They do not constitute two moments of the same process. Rather they refer to radically different kinds of thing.

Let us consider society. Return for a moment to Durkheim. It will be recalled that, reminding us that the member of a church (or let us say, the user of a language) finds the beliefs and practices of his or her religious life (or the structure of his or her language) ready-made at birth, he argues that it is their existence *prior* to his or her own that implies their existence *outside* themselves, and from which their coercive power is ultimately derived.[29] Now if this is the case and the social structure, and the natural world in so far as it is appropriated by human beings, is always *already made*, then Model III must be corrected in a fundamental way. It is still true to say that society would not exist without human activity, so that reification remains an error. And it is still true to say that such activity would not occur unless the agents engaging in it had a conception of what they were doing (which is of course the fundamental insight of the hermeneutical tradition). But it is no longer true to say that agents *create* it. Rather one must say: they *reproduce* or *transform* it. That is, if society is always already made, then any concrete human praxis, or, if you like, act of objectivation can only modify it; and the totality of such acts sustain or change it. It is not the product of their activity (any more, I shall argue, than human action is completely determined by it). Society stands to individuals, then, as something that they never make, but that exists only in virtue of their activity.

Now if society pre-exists the individual, objectivation takes on a very different significance. For it, conscious human activity, consists in work on *given* objects and cannot be conceived as occurring in their absence. A moment's reflection shows why this must be so. For all activity presupposes the prior existence of social forms. Thus consider *saying, making* and *doing* as characteristic modalities of human agency. People cannot communicate except by utilizing existing media, produce except by applying themselves to materials which are already formed, or act save in some or other context. Speech requires language; making materials; action conditions; agency resources; activity rules. Even spontaneity has as its necessary condition the pre-existence of a social form with (or by means of) which the spontaneous act is performed. Thus if the social cannot be reduced to (and is not the product of) the individual, it is equally clear that society is a necessary condition for any intentional human act at all.

Now the necessary pre-existence of social forms suggests a radically different conception of social activity from that which typically informs discussion of the society/person connection. It suggests an essentially Aristotelian one, in which the paradigm is that of a sculptress at work, fashioning a product out of the material and with the tools available to her. I shall call this the *transformational model of social activity*. It applies to discursive as well as to non-discursive practices; to science and politics, as much as to technology and economics. Thus in science the raw materials used in the construction of new theories include established results and half-forgotten ideas, the stock of available paradigms and models, methods and techniques of inquiry, so that the scientific innovator comes to appear in retrospect as a kind of cognitive *bricoleur*.[30] To use the Aristotelian terms, then, in every process of productive activity a material as well as an efficient cause is necessary. And, following Marx, one can regard social activity as consisting, analytically, in *production*, that is in work on (and with), entailing the transformation of, those material causes. Now if, following Durkheim, one regards society as providing the material causes of human action, and following Weber, one refuses to reify it, it is easy to see that both society and human praxis must possess a *dual character*. Society is both the ever-present *condition* (material cause) and the continually reproduced *outcome* of human agency. And praxis is both work, that is, conscious *production*, and (normally unconscious) *reproduction* of the conditions of production, that is society. One could refer to the former as the *duality of structure*,[31] and the latter as the *duality of praxis*.

Let us turn now to people. Human action is characterized by the striking phenomenon of intentionality. This seems to depend upon the feature that persons are material things with a degree of neurophysiological complexity which enables them not just, like the other higher-order animals, to initiate changes in a purposeful way, to monitor and control their performances, but to monitor the monitoring of these performances and to be capable of a commentary upon them.[32] This capacity for second-order monitoring also makes possible a retrospective commentary upon actions, which gives a person's account of his or her own behaviour a special status, which is acknowledged in the best practice of all the psychological sciences.

The importance of distinguishing categorically between people and societies, and correspondingly between human actions and changes in the social structure, should now be clear. For the properties possessed by social forms may be very different from those possessed by the individuals upon whose activity they depend. Thus one can allow, without paradox or strain, that purposefulness, intentionality and sometimes self-consciousness characterize human actions but not transformations in the social structure.[33] The conception I am proposing is that people, in their conscious activity, for the most part unconsciously reproduce (and occasionally transform) the structures governing their substantive activities of production. Thus people do not marry to reproduce the nuclear family or work to sustain the capitalist economy. Yet it is nevertheless the unintended consequence (and inexorable result) of, as it is also a necessary condition for, their activity. Moreover, when social forms change, the explanation will not normally lie in the desires of agents to change them that way, though as a very important theoretical and political limit it *may* do so.

I want to distinguish sharply, then, between the genesis of human actions, lying in the reasons, intentions and plans of people, on the one hand, and the structures governing the reproduction and transformation of social activities, on the other; and hence between the domains of the psychological and the social sciences. The problem of how people reproduce any particular society belongs to a linking science of 'socio-psychology'. It should be noted that engagement in a social activity is itself a conscious human action which may, in general, be described either in terms of the agent's reason for engaging in it or in terms of its social function or role. When praxis is seen under the aspect of process, human choice becomes functional necessity.

Now the autonomy of the social and the psychological is at one with our intuitions. Thus we do not suppose that the reason why garbage is collected is necessarily the garbage collector's reason for collecting it (though it depends upon the latter). And we can allow that speech is governed by the rules of grammar without supposing either that these rules exist independently of usage (reification) or that they determine what we say. The rules of grammar, like natural structures, impose *limits* on the speech acts we can perform, but they do not *determine* our performances. This conception thus preserves the status of human agency, while doing away with the myth of creation (logical or historical), which depends upon the possibility of an individualist reduction. And in so doing it allows us to see that necessity in social life operates in the last instance via the intentional activity of agents. Looked at in this way, then, one may regard it as the task of the different social sciences to lay out the structural conditions for various forms of conscious human action – for example, what economic processes must take place for Christmas shopping to be possible – but they do not describe the latter.

The model of the society/person connection I am proposing could be summarized as follows: people do not create society. For it always pre-exists them and is a necessary condition for their activity. Rather, society must be regarded as an ensemble of structures, practices and conventions which individuals reproduce or transform, but which would not exist unless they did so. Society does not exist independently of human activity (the error of reification). But it is not the product of it (the error of voluntarism). Now the processes whereby the stocks of skills, competences and habits appropriate to given social contexts, and necessary for the reproduction and/or transformation of society, are acquired and maintained could be generically referred to as *socialization*. It is important to stress that the reproduction and/or transformation of society, though for the most part unconsciously achieved, is nevertheless still an *achievement,* a skilled accomplishment of active subjects, not a mechanical consequent of antecedent conditions. This model of the society/person connection can be represented as below.

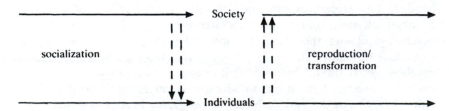

Model IV: The Transformational Model of the Society/Person Connection

Society, then, provides necessary conditions for intentional human action, and intentional human action is a necessary condition for it. Society is only present in human action, but human action always expresses and utilizes some or other social form. Neither can, however, be identified with, reduced to, explained in terms of, or reconstructed from the other. There is an ontological hiatus between society and people, as well as a mode of connection (viz. transformation) that the other models typically ignore.

Notice that on Model I there are actions, but no conditions; on Model II conditions, but no actions; on Model III no distinction between the two. Thus in Durkheim, for example, subjectivity tends to appear only in the guise of the interiorized form of social constraint. But it should be equally clear, against voluntarism, that real subjectivity requires conditions, resources and media for the creative subject to act. Such material causes may be regarded, if one likes, as the results of prior objectivations. But they are, in *any* act, analytically irreducible and actually indispensable all the same. The 'given' component in social action can never be reduced to zero, analysed away. This conception of the society/person connection thus implies a radical transformation in our idea of a non-alienating society. For this can now no longer be conceived as the immaculate product of unconditioned ('responsible') human decisions, free from the constraints (but presumably not the opportunities) inherited from its past and imposed by its environment. Rather it must be conceived as one in which people self-consciously transform their social conditions of existence (the social structure) so as to maximize the possibilities for the development and spontaneous exercise of their natural (species) powers.

It should be noted that Model IV, as a result of its emphasis on material continuity, can sustain a genuine concept of *change*, and hence of *history*.[34] This is something that neither Model III nor the methodological stereotypes it attempts to situate as special cases can do. Thus Model III appears to involve continuous recreation, with genuine novelty, seemingly entailing incomplete social formation, something of a mystery. On the Weberian stereotype change reduces to contrast, and on the Durkheimian it can only be explained by advertion to exogenous variables. Model IV, moreover, generates a clear criterion of historically significant events: viz. those that initiate or constitute ruptures, mutations or more generally tranformations in social forms (such as Dalton's training as a meteorologist or the French Revolution).

Some Emergent Properties of Social Systems

Now if social activity consists, analytically, in production, that is in work on and the transformation of given objects, and if such work constitutes an analogue of natural events, then we need an analogue for the mechanisms that generate it. If social structures constitute the appropriate mechanism-analogue, then an important difference must be immediately registered – in that, unlike natural mechanisms, they exist only in virtue of the activities they govern and cannot be empirically identified independently of them. Because of this, they must be social products themselves. Thus people in their social activity must perform a double function: they must not only make social products, but make the conditions of their making, that is reproduce (or to a greater or lesser extent transform) the structures governing their substantive activities of production. Because social structures are themselves social products, they are themselves possible objects of transformation and so may be only relatively enduring. Moreover the differentiation and development of social activities (as in the 'division of labour' and 'expanded reproduction' respectively) implies that they are interdependent; so social structures may be only relatively autonomous. Society may thus be conceived as an articulated ensemble of such relatively independent and enduring generative structures; that is, as a complex totality subject to change both in its components and their interrelations. Now, as social structures exist only in virtue of the activities they govern, they do not exist independently of the conceptions that the agents possess of what they are doing in their activity, that is, of some theory of these activities. Because such theories are themselves social products, they are themselves possible objects of transformation and so they too may be only relatively enduring (and autonomous). Finally, because social structures are themselves social products, social activity must be given a social explanation, and cannot be explained by reference to non-social parameters (though the latter may impose constraints on the possible forms of social activity).

Some ontological limitations on a possible naturalism may be immediately derived from these emergent social properties, on the assumption (to be vindicated below) that society is *sui generis* real:

1. Social structures, unlike natural structures, do not exist independently of the activities they govern.
2. Social structures, unlike natural structures, do not exist independently of the agents' conceptions of what they are doing in their activity.
3. Social structures, unlike natural structures, may be only relatively enduring (so that the tendencies they ground may not be universal in the sense of space–time invariant).

These all indicate real differences in the possible objects of knowledge in the case of the natural and social sciences. (The internal complexity and interdependence of social structures do not mark a *necessary* difference from natural ones.) They are not of course unconnected, though one should be wary of drawing conclusions of the sort: 'Society exists only in virtue of human activity. Human activity is conscious. Therefore consciousness brings about change'. For (a) social changes need not be consciously intended and (b) if there are social conditions for consciousness, changes in it can in principle be socially explained. Society, then, is an articulated ensemble of tendencies and powers which, unlike natural ones, exist only as long as they (or at least some of them) are being exercised; are exercised in the last instance via the intentional activity of human beings; and are not necessarily space–time invariant.

I now want to turn to the ontological status of societies. I have argued elsewhere that living things determine the conditions of applicability of the physical laws to which they are subject, so that their properties cannot be reduced to the latter; that is, that emergence characterizes both the natural and the human worlds[35] (and that this is consistent with what may be termed a 'diachronic explanatory reduction', that is, a reconstruction of the historical processes of their formation out of 'simpler' things). Now if, as I shall show in Chapter 3, intentional action is a necessary condition for certain determinate states of the physical world, then the properties and powers that persons possess in virtue of which intentionality is correctly attributed to them are real. Similarly, if it can be shown that but for society certain physical actions would not be performed, then employing the causal criterion set out in Chapter 1, one is justified in asserting that it is real.

Now I think that Durkheim, having established the *autonomy* of social facts using the criterion of *externality*, in effect employed just such a criterion to establish their *reality*, in invoking his other criterion of *constraint*:

> I am not obliged to speak French with my fellow-countrymen nor to use the legal currency, but I cannot possibly do otherwise. If I tried to escape this necessity, my attempt would fail miserably. As an industrialist I am free to apply the technical methods of former centuries, but by doing so I should invite certain ruin. Even when I free myself from these rules and violate them successfully, I am always compelled to struggle with them. When finally overcome, they make their constraining power felt by the resistance they offer.[36]

Durkheim is saying in effect that but for the range of social facts, particular sequences of sounds, movements of bodies, etc., would not occur. Of course, one must insist, against Durkheim, that the range of social facts depends upon (though it is irreducible to) the intentional activity of human beings. The individualist truth that people are the only moving forces in history – in the sense that nothing happens, as it were, behind their backs; that is, everything that happens, happens in and through their actions – must be retained. Moreover, social structures must be conceived as in principle *enabling*, not just coercive. Nevertheless, in employing a causal criterion to establish the reality of social facts, Durkheim observed perfectly proper scientific practice – though it must be recognized that one is here dealing with a most peculiar kind of entity: a structure irreducible to, but present only in its effects.

Although Durkheim used a causal criterion to establish the reality of social facts, on a collectivist conception of sociology, the same criterion can be employed (with more epistemological consistency) to establish their reality on a relational one. (There is no special difficulty, as for example the concept of spin in physics shows, in ascribing reality to relations on a causal criterion.) Indeed, given the openness of the world within which its phenomena occur, it is only if a non-empirical object is specified for it that sociology's theoretical autonomy can be definitely secured – a point dramatically illustrated by the pitfalls into which Weber's definition of sociology,[37] which logically includes worship (because other-orientated) but excludes prayer, plunges it.

What is the connection between the tranformational model of social activity developed in the previous section and the relational conception of sociology advanced in the second section? The relational conception does not of course deny that factories and books are social forms. Nor does it insist that the rules of grammar (or the generative complexes at work in other spheres of social life) are, or must be conceived as, relations. But it maintains that their being *social*, as distinct from (or rather in addition to) material objects, and their consisting in *social* rules, as distinct from purely 'anankastic' ones[38] (which depend upon the operation of natural laws alone), depends essentially on, and indeed in a sense consists entirely in, the relationships between people and between such relationships and nature (and the products and functions of such relationships) that such objects and rules causally presuppose or entail.

It is not difficult to see why this must be so. For it follows from the argument of the previous section that social structures (a) be continually reproduced (or transformed) and (b) exist only in virtue of, and are exercised only in, human agency (in short, that they require active 'functionaries'). Combining these desiderata, it is evident that we need a system of mediating concepts, encompassing both aspects of the duality of praxis, designating the 'slots', as it were, in the social structure into which active subjects must slip in order to reproduce it; that is, a system of concepts designating the 'point of contact' between human agency and social structures. Such a point, linking action to structure, must *both* endure and be immediately occupied by individuals. It is clear that the mediating system we need is that of the *positions* (places, functions, rules, tasks, duties, rights, etc.) occupied (filled, assumed, enacted, etc.) by individuals, and of the *practices* (activities, etc.) in which, in virtue of their occupancy of these positions (and vice versa), they engage. I shall call this mediating system the position-practice system. Now such positions and practices, if they are to be individuated at all, can only be done so *relationally*.

It follows as an immediate consequence of this that the initial conditions in any concrete social explanation must always include or tacitly presuppose reference to some or other social relation (however the generative structures invoked are themselves best conceived). And it is, I suggest, in the (explanation of the) differentiation and stratification, production and reproduction, mutation and transformation, continual remoulding and incessant shifting, of the relatively enduring relations presupposed by particular social forms and structures that sociology's distinctive theoretical interest lies. Thus the transformational model implies a relational interest for sociology. And it suggests in terms of that interest a way of differentiating sociology from the other social sciences (such as linguistics, economics, etc.), which, however, logically presuppose it.

It should be noted that neither individuals nor groups satisfy the requirement of continuity derived from the reapplication of Durkheim's criterion (of externality or pre-existence) for the autonomy of society over discrete moments of time. In social life only relations endure.[39] Note also that such relations include relationships between people and nature and social products (such as machines and firms), as well as interpersonal ones. And that such relations include, but do not all consist in, 'interactions'. (Thus contrast the relationship between speaker and hearer in dialogue with the deontic relationship between citizen and state.) Finally, it is important to stress that from the standpoint of the social sciences, though not necessarily either that of the psychological sciences or of historical explanation, the relations one is concerned with here must be conceptualized as holding between the positions and practices (or better, positioned-practices), not between the individuals who occupy/engage in them.[40]

One advantage of the relational conception should be immediately apparent. It allows one to focus on a range of questions, having to do with the *distribution* of the structural conditions of action, and in particular with differential allocations of: (a) productive resources (of all kinds, including for example cognitive ones) to persons (and groups) and (b) persons (and groups) to functions and roles (for example in the division of labour). In doing so, it allows one to situate the possibility of different (and antagonistic) interests, of conflicts *within* society, and hence of interest-motivated transformations in social structure. In focusing on distribution as well as exchange, the relational conception avoids the endemic weakness of (market) economics. And in allowing conflicts within society as well as between society and the individual, it remedies the chronic failing of (orthodox) sociology, preoccupied as that was (and indeed still is) with the 'Hobbesian problem of order'.[41]

Marx combined an essentially relational conception of social science and a transformational model of social activities with the additional premise – of historical materialism – that it is material production that ultimately determines the rest of social life.[42] Now, as is well known, although it can be established a priori that material production is a necessary condition for social life, it cannot be proved that it is the ultimately determining one. And so, like any other fundamental conceptual blueprint or paradigm in science, historical materialism can only be justified by its fruitfulness in generating projects encapsulating research programmes capable of generating sequences of theories, progressively richer in explanatory power. Not the least of the problems facing historical materialism is that, although considerable progress has been made in particular areas of explanation, the blueprint itself still awaits adequate articulation. (One has only to think of the problem of reconciling the thesis of the relative autonomy of the superstructures with that of their determination in the last instance by the base to be reminded of this.)[43]

It is doubtful if any topic in philosophy has been more dogged by dogma that that of internal relations. The doctrine that all relations are external is implicit in the Humean theory of causality, where it is enshrined in the notion of the contingency of the causal connection. But it has been accepted by virtually the whole orthodox (empiricist and neo-Kantian) tradition in the philosophy of science. Conversely, rationalists, absolute idealists and mistresses of the arts of Hegelian and Bergsonian dialectics have usually subscribed to the equally erroneous view that all relations are internal. Here again, a major philosophical difference cuts across the Marxist/non-Marxist divide. Colletti and Ollman[44] represent only the most recent, and particularly extreme, variants of positions already fully articulated within Marxism at least as far back as Hilferding and Dietzgen. Now it is essential to recognize that some relations are internal, and some are not. Moreover, some natural relations (such as that between a magnet and its field) are internal, and many social relations (such as that between two cyclists crossing on a hilltop) are not. It is in principle an open question whether or not some particular relation, in historical time, is internal.

A relation R_{AB} may be defined as *internal* if and only if A would not be what it *essentially* is unless B is related to it in the way that it is. R_{AB} is *symmetrically internal* if the same applies also to B. ('A' and 'B' may designate universals or particulars, concepts or things, including relations.) The relation bourgeoisie–proletariat is symmetrically internal;

traffic warden–state asymmetrically internal; passing motorist–policeman not (in general) internal at all. The fact that it is an epistemically contingent question as to whether or not some given relation is internal is obscured by the condition that when one knows what a thing's essential nature is, one is then often in a position to give a real definition of it; so that it will then appear to be analytic that *B* is related to it in the way that it is. But of course real definitions are not plucked a priori out of hats, spun out of thought alone. Rather they are produced a posteriori, in the irreducibly empirical process of science.[45]

It is vital to appreciate that there can be no presumption of explanatory equality between the *relata* of an internal relationship. Thus capitalist production may dominate (determine the forms of) exchange, without the latter ceasing to be essential for it. Internally related aspects may command, as it were, differential causal force. Or, to put it another way, *ontological depth* or stratification, defined causally, is consistent with *relational internality*, including symmetry, that is, existential parity. Indeed it is characteristic of the social sphere that surface structure is necessary for deep, just as *langue* is a condition of *parole* and intentionality of system.

Now most social phenomena, like most natural events, are *conjuncturally* determined and, as such, in general have to be explained in terms of a multiplicity of causes.[46] But, given the epistemic contingency of their relational character, the extent to which their explanation requires reference to a *totality* of aspects, bearing internal relations to one another, remains open. However, even a superficially external relationship, such as that between Breton fishermen and the owners of the shipwrecked tanker *Amoco Cadiz* may, given the appropriate focus of explanatory interest, permit (or necessitate) a totalization revealing, for example, the relationships between forms of economic activity and state structure. This ever-present possibility of discovering what is a (potentially new) totality in a nexus accounts for the chameleon-like and 'configurational'[47] quality of a subject-matter which is not only always changing but may (in this respect, like any other) be continually redescribed. Now although *totalization* is a process in thought, totalities are *real*. Although it is contingent whether we require a phenomenon to be understood as an aspect of a totality (depending upon our cognitive interests), it is not contingent whether it *is* such an aspect or not. Social science does not create the totalities it reveals, although it may itself be an aspect of them.

It has always been the special claim of Marxism to be able to grasp social life as a totality, to display it, in Labriola's words, as 'a connection and complexus',[48] whose various moments may of course be asymmetrically weighted, primed with differential causal force. And Marxism has claimed to be able to do so in virtue of a theory of history, specifying *inter alia* the mode of articulation of the moments of that totality or instances of the social structure. The theory of history can only be judged by historical materials. But can anything be said, in the light of the foregoing analysis, about the intentions, if not the results, of this project?

Our analysis indicates a way of conceptualizing the relationship between the special social sciences (such as linguistics, economics, politics, etc.), sociology, history and a totalizing theory of society such as that ventured by Marxism. If history is above all the science of the 'past particular' and sociology is the science of social relations, the various social sciences are concerned with the structural conditions for (that is, the generative complexes at work in the production of) particular types of social activity. Of course, given the interdependence of social activities, hypostatization of the results of such particular analyses must be most assiduously avoided. Moreover, as external conditions may be internally related to the generative mechanisms at work in particular spheres of social life, the special sciences logically presuppose a totalizing one, which, on the transformational model, can only be a theory of history. If sociology is concerned with the structures governing the relationships which are necessary, in particular historical periods, for the reproduction (and transformation) of particular social forms, its *explananda* are always specific; so there can be no sociology-in-general, only the sociology of particular historically situated social forms. In this way, sociology presupposes both the special sciences and history. But the relational conception entails that the *social* conditions for the substantive activities of transformation in which agents engage can only be *relations* of various kinds. And the transformational model entails that these activities are essentially *productions*. The subject-matter of sociology is, thus, precisely: *relations of production* (of various kinds). Now if such relations are themselves internally related and subject to transformation, then sociology must either presuppose or usurp the place of just such a totalizing and historical science of society as Marxism has claimed to be. In short, to invoke a Kantian metaphor,[49] if Marxism without detailed social scientific and historical work is empty, then such work without Marxism (or some such theory) is blind.

On the Limits of Naturalism

In the third section I argued that the pre-existence of social forms is a necessary condition for any intentional act, and I showed how such pre-existence entails a transformational model of social activities. In the previous section I derived a number of ontological limits on naturalism, as emergent features of societies, and vindicated the notion of their *sui generis* reality. I now want to complete my argument by showing how, given that societies exist and have the properties (derived from the transformational model) that they do, they might become possible objects of knowledge for us.

It will be recalled that the major ontological limits on the possibility of naturalism turn on the activity-, concept-, and space–time-dependence of social structures (see (1) to (3) on p. 38). Before considering how social science is possible despite, or rather (as I shall attempt to show) because of, these features, differentiating its subject-matter from nature, I want to consider two other types of limit of naturalism, which may be characterized as epistemological and relational respectively.

Society, as an object of inquiry, is necessarily 'theoretical', in the sense that, like a magnetic field, it is necessarily unperceivable. As such it cannot be empirically identified independently of its effects; so that it can only be known, not shown, to exist. However, in this respect it is no different from many objects of natural scientific inquiry. What does distinguish it is that not only can society not be identified independently of its effects, it does not *exist* independently of them either. But however strange this is from an ontological point of view,[50] it raises no special epistemological difficulties.

The chief epistemological limit on naturalism is not raised by the necessarily unperceivable character of the objects of social scientific inquiry, but rather by the fact that they only ever manifest themselves in open systems; that is, in systems where invariant empirical regularities do not obtain. For social systems are not spontaneously, and cannot be experimentally, closed. Now it is as easy to exaggerate the real methodological import of this point, as it is to underestimate its critical significance for the doctrines of received philosophy of science. For, as I have shown in detail elsewhere,[51] practically all the theories of orthodox philosophy of science, and the methodological directives they secrete, presuppose closed systems. Because of this, they are totally inapplicable in the social sciences (which is not of course to say that the attempt cannot be made to apply them – to disastrous effect). Humean theories of causality and law, deductive–nomological and statistical models of explanation, inductivist theories of scientific development and criteria of confirmation, Popperian theories of scientific rationality and criteria of falsification, together with the hermeneutical contrasts parasitic upon them, must all be totally discarded. Social science need only consider them as objects of substantive explanation.

The real methodological import of the absence of closed systems is strictly limited: it is that the social sciences are denied, in principle, decisive test situations for their theories. This means that criteria for the rational development and replacement of theories in social science must be *explanatory and non-predictive*. (Particularly important here will be the capacity of a theory (or research programme) to be developed in a non-*ad hoc* way so as to situate, and preferably explain, without strain, a possibility once (and perhaps even before) it is realized, when it could never, given the openness of the social world, have predicted it.) It should be stressed that this difference has in itself no ontological significance whatsoever. It does not affect the form of laws, which in natural science too must be analysed as tendencies; only the form of our knowledge of them. Moreover, because the mode of application of laws is the same in open and closed systems alike,[52] there is no reason to suppose that the mode of application of social laws will be any different from natural ones. And although the necessity to rely exclusively on explanatory criteria *may* affect the subjective confidence with which beliefs are held, if a social scientific theory or hypothesis has been *independently* validated (on explanatory grounds) then one is in principle just as warranted in applying it transfactually as a natural scientific one. Moreover, given that the problem is typically not *whether* to apply some theory *T* to the world, but rather *which* out of two or more theories, *T,T'*, to apply, the degree of our *relative* preference for one theory over another will not be affected by a restriction on the grounds with which that preference must be justified.

The fact that the subject-matter of the social sciences is both intrinsically historical and structured by relations of internal, as well as external, interdependency sets a constraint upon the kinds of permissible theory-construction. For it may, as argued in the previous section, necessitate reference in principle to conceptions of historically developing totalities. But it does not pose an additional difficulty, over and above the unavailability of closures, for the empirical testing of theories.[53] However, two significant limits on the possibility of meaningful *measurement* in the social sciences should be noted. The *irreversibility* of ontologically irreducible processes, comparable to entropy in the natural sphere, entails the necessity for concepts of qualitative rather than merely quantitative change.[54] But the *conceptual* aspect of the subject-matter of the social sciences circumscribes the possibility of measurement in an even more fundamental way.[55] For meanings cannot be measured, only understood. Hypotheses about them must be expressed in language, and confirmed in dialogue. Language here stands to the conceptual aspect of social science as geometry stands to physics. And precision in meaning now assumes the place of accuracy in measurement as the a posteriori arbiter of theory. It should be stressed that in both cases theories may continue to be justified and validly used to explain, even though *significant* measurement of the phenomena of which they treat has become impossible.

Now experimental activity in natural science not only facilitates (relatively)[56] decisive test situations, it enables *practical access,* as it were, to the otherwise latent structures of nature. And the malleability achieved in the laboratory may provide an invaluable component in the process of scientific discovery that the social sciences, in this respect, will be denied. However, our analysis of the relational and ontological limits will yield an analogue and a compensator respectively for the role of experimental practice in discovery.

The chief relational difference is that the social sciences are part of their own field of inquiry, in principle susceptible to explanation in terms of the concepts and laws of the explanatory theories they employ; so that they are *internal* with respect to their subject-matter in a way in which the natural sciences are not. This necessitates a precision in the sense in which their objects of knowledge can be said to be 'intransitive' (see Chapter 1). For it is possible, and indeed likely, given the internal complexity and interdependence of social activities, that these objects may be causally affected by social science, and in some cases not exist independently of it (as for example in the sociology of social science!). Conversely, one would expect social science to be affected or conditioned by developments in what it patently cannot exist independently of, viz. the rest of society. Thus, whereas, in general, in the natural world the objects of knowledge exist and act independently of the process of the production of the knowledge of which they are the objects, in the social arena this is not so. For the process of knowledge–production may be causally, and internally, related to the process of the production of the objects concerned. However, I want to distinguish such *causal interdependency,* which is a contingent feature of the processes concerned, from *existential intransitivity,* which is an a priori condition of any investigation and applies in the same way in the social, as the natural, sphere. For, although the processes of production may be interdependent, once some object O_t exists, if it exists, however it has been produced, it constitutes a possible object of scientific investigation. And its existence (or not), and properties, are quite independent of the act or process of investigation of which it is the putative object, even though such an investigation, once initiated, may radically modify it. In short, the concept of existence is univocal: 'being' means the same in the human as the natural world, even though the modes of being may radically differ. The human sciences, then, take intransitive objects like any other. But the categorial properties of such objects differ. And among the most important of these differences is the feature that they are themselves an aspect of, and causal agent in, what they seek to explain. It is vital to be clear about this point. For if it is the characteristic error of positivism to ignore (or play down) interdependency, it is the characteristic error of hermeneutics to dissolve intransitivity. As will be seen, both errors function to the same effect, foreclosing the possibility of scientific critique, upon which the project of human self-emancipation depends.

So far the case for causal interdependency has turned merely on the possibility of a relatively undifferentiated society/social science link. But the case for such a link may be strengthened by noting that just as a social science without a society is impossible, so a society without some kind of scientific, proto-scientific or ideological theory of itself is inconceivable (even if it consists merely in the conceptions that the agents have of what they are doing in their activity). Now if one denotes the proto-scientific set of ideas P, then the transformational model of social activity applied to the activity of knowledge-production suggests that social scientific theory, T, requiring cognitive resources, is produced, at least in part, by the transformation of P. The hypothesis under consideration is that this transformation will be vitally affected by developments in the rest of society, S.

It might be conjectured that in periods of transition or crisis generative structures, previously opaque, become more visible to agents.[57] And that this, though it never yields quite the epistemic possibilities of a closure (even when agents are self-consciously seeking to transform the social conditions of their existence), does provide a partial analogue to the role played by experimentation in natural science. The conditions for the emergence of a new social scientific theory must of course be distinguished from the conditions for its subsequent development and from the conditions for its permeation into the *Lebenswelt* of lived experience (or incorporation into social policy), though there are evident (and reciprocal) connections between them.[58] Thus it is surely no accident that Marxism was born in the 1840s or stunted under the combined effects of Stalinism, on the one hand, and Fascism, the Cold War and the 1945–70 boom, on the other;[59] or that sociology, in the narrow sense, was the fruit of the two decades before the First World War.[60]

It should be noted that because social systems are open, historicism (in the sense of deductively justified predictability) is untenable. And because of their historical (transformational) character, qualitatively new developments will be occuring which social scientific theory cannot be expected to anticipate. Hence for ontological, as distinct from purely epistemological, reasons, social scientific (unlike natural scientific) theory is *necessarily* incomplete. Moreover as the possibilities inherent in a new social development will often only become apparent long after the development itself, and as each new development is, in a sense, a product of a previous one, we can now see why it is that history must be continually rewritten.[61] There is a relational tie between the development of knowledge and the development of the object of knowledge that any adequate theory of social science, and methodology of social scientific research programmes, must take account of. In particular, Lakatosian judgements about the progressive or degenerating nature of research programmes[62] cannot be made in isolation from judgements about developments in the rest of society conditioning work in particular programmes.

I have argued that once a hypothesis about a generative structure has been produced in social science it can be tested quite empirically, although not necessarily quantitatively, and albeit exclusively in terms of its explanatory power. But I have so far said nothing about how the hypothesis is produced, or indeed about what its status is. Now in considering theory-construction in the social sciences it should be borne in mind that the putative social scientist would, in the absence of some prior theory, be faced with an inchoate mass of (social) phenomena, which she would somehow have to sort out and define. In systems, like social ones, which are necessarily open, the problem of constituting an appropriate (that is, explanatorily significant) object of inquiry becomes particularly acute. It becomes chronic if, as in empirical realism, lacking the concepts of the stratification and differentiation of the world, one is unable to think the irreducibility of transfactually active structures to events, and the effort, which is science, needed to reveal them. Undifferentiated events then become the object of purely conventionally differentiated sciences, producing a crisis of definitions and boundaries, the existence of a merely arbitrary distinction between a theory and its applications (or the absence of any organic connection between them) and, above all, a problem of verification – or rather falsification. For when *every* theory, if interpreted *empirically*, is false, no theory can ever be falsified.[63] Goldmann's claim that 'the fundamental methodological problem of any human science . . . lies in the division [*découpage*] of the object of study . . . [for] once this division has been made and accepted, the results will be practically predictable'[64] is then not at all surprising.

How, then, given the mishmash nature of social reality, is theory-construction accomplished in social science? Fortunately most of the phenomena with which the social scientist has to deal will already be identified, thanks to the *concept-dependent* nature of social activities, under certain descriptions. In principle, the descriptions or nominal definitions of social activities that form the transitive objects of social scientific theory may be those of the agents concerned, or theoretical redescriptions of them. The first step in the transformation $P \rightarrow T$ will thus be an attempt at a real definition of a form of social life that has already been identified under a particular description. Note that in the absence of such a definition, and failing a closure, any hypothesis of a causal mechanism is bound to be more or less arbitrary. Thus in social science attempts at real definitions will in general precede rather than follow successful causal hypotheses – though in both cases they can only be justified empirically, viz. by the revealed explanatory power of the hypotheses that can be deduced from them.

Our problem, then, is shifted from that of how to establish a non-arbitrary procedure for generating causal hypotheses to that of how to establish a non-arbitrary procedure for generating real definitions. And here a second differentiating feature of the subject-matter of the social sciences should be recalled – the *activity-dependent* nature of social structures, viz. that the mechanisms at work in society exist only in virtue of their effects. In this respect society is quite distinct from other objects of scientific knowledge. But note that, in this, it is analogous to the objects of philosophical knowledge. For just as the objects of philosophical knowledge do not exist apart from the objects of scientific knowledge, so social structures do not exist apart from their effects. So, I suggest that in principle as philosophical discourse stands to scientific discourse, so a discourse about society stands to a discourse about its effects. Moreover in both cases one is dealing with conceptualized activities, whose conditions of possibility or real presuppositions the second-order discourse seeks to explicate. However there are also important differences. For in social scientific discourse one is concerned not to isolate the a priori conditions of a form of knowledge as such, but the particular mechanisms and relations at work in some identified sphere of social life. Moreover its conclusions will be *historical*, not formal; and subject to empirical test, as well as various a priori controls.[65]

Now the substantive employment of an essentially apodeictic procedure should occasion us no surprise. For transcendental arguments are merely a species of which retroductive ones are the genus, distinguished by the features that their *explanandum* consists in the conceptualized activities of agents and, as becomes an arena characterized by a multiplicity of causes, that they isolate necessary not sufficient conditions for it. But in view of this homology are we not in danger of collapsing the philosophy/science distinction upon which Ĭ insisted in Chapter 1? No. For the syncategorematic (or, as it were, only proxy-referential) character of the nevertheless irreducible discourse of philosophy (discussed in Chapter 1) has to be contrasted with the directly referential character of social scientific discourse. Hence, though in both cases there are two levels of discourse, in social science there are two levels of reality (social structures, and their effects), whereas in philosophy there is just one, viz. that investigated by science itself. Of course in both cases more than one set of conditions will normally be consistent with the activity concerned, so that supplementary considerations will be needed to establish the validity of the analysis. But in social science, wherever possible, such considerations will include the provision of independent empirical grounds for the existence (and postulated mode of activity) of the structural mechanisms concerned, whereas, in philosophy, in the nature of the case, this is impossible. Thus a scientific (or substantive) transcendental argument may be distinguished from a philosophical (or formal) one according to the autonomous reality (or lack of it) of the object of the second-order discourse, the way (or rather immediacy) with which reference to the world is secured, and the possibility or otherwise of a posteriori grounds for the analysis.

Our deduction of the possibility of social scientific knowledge, from the necessary pre-existence of social forms for intentional action, illustrates the formal use of a transcendental procedure. The results of such an analysis may be used both as a critical grid for the assessment of existing social scientific theories and as a template for adequate conceptualizations of social scientific *explananda*. Marx's analysis in *Capital* illustrates the substantive use of a transcendental procedure. *Capital* may most plausibly be viewed as an attempt to establish what must be the case for the experiences grasped by the phenomenal forms of capitalist life to be possible; setting out, as it were, a pure schema for the understanding of economic phenomena under capitalism, specifying the categories that must be employed in any concrete investigation. I have already suggested that for Marx to understand the essence of some particular social phenomenon is to understand the social relations that make that phenomenon possible. But the transformational model suggests that, to understand the essence of social phenomena as such and in general, such phenomena must be grasped as productions; so that the relations one is concerned with here are, above all, relations of production.

Now the minor premise of any substantive social scientific transcendental argument will be a social activity as conceptualized in experience. Such a social activity will be in principle *space–time-dependent*. And in the first instance of course it will be conceptualized in the experience of the agents concerned. It is here that the hermeneutical tradition, in highlighting what may be called the conceptual moment in social scientific work, has made a real contribution. But it typically makes two mistakes. Its continuing commitment to the ontology of empirical realism prevents it from seeing the following:

1. The *conditions* for the phenomena (namely social activities as conceptualized in experience) exist *intransitively* and may therefore exist independently of their appropriate conceptualization, and as such be subject to an unacknowledged possibility of historical transformation.
2. The *phenomena* themselves may be *false* or in an important sense inadequate (for example, superficial or systematically misleading).

Thus what has been established, by conceptual analysis, as necessary for the phenomena may consist precisely in a level (or aspect) of reality which, although not existing independently of agents' conceptions, may be inadequately conceptualized or even not conceptualized at all. Such a level may consist in a structural complex which is really generative of social life but unavailable to direct inspection by the senses or immediate intuition in the course of everyday life. It may be a tacit property of agents (such as knowledge of a grammar) utilized in their productions; or a property of the relationships in which agents stand to the conditions and means of their productions, of which they may be unaware. Now such a transcendental analysis in social science, in showing (when it does) the historical conditions under which a certain set of categories may be validly applied, *ipso facto* shows the conditions under which they may not be applied. This makes possible a second-order critique of consciousness, best exemplified perhaps by Marx's analysis of commodity fetishism.[66] Value relations, it will be remembered, are real for Marx, but they are historically specific social realities. And fetishism consists in their transformation in thought into the natural, and so ahistorical, qualities of things. An alternative type of transformation is identified by Marx in the case of idealistic (rather than naturalistic) explanations of social forms, such as money in the eighteenth century, 'ascribed a conventional origin' in 'the so-called universal consent of mankind'.[67] The homology between these two types of substantive mystification and the metatheoretical errors of reification and voluntarism should be clear.

But, as Geras has pointed out,[68] Marx employed another concept of mystification, in which he engages in what one may call a first-order critique of consciousness – in which, to put it bluntly, he identifies the phenomena themselves as false; or, more formally, shows that a certain set of categories is not properly applicable to experience at all. This is best exemplified by his treatment of the wage form, in which the value of labour power is transformed into the value of labour – an expression which Marx declares to be 'as imaginary as the value of the earth', 'as irrational as a yellow logarithm'.[69] Once more, this mystification is founded on a characteristic category mistake – that, intrinsic to the wage–labour relation, of reducing powers to their exercise, comparable to confusing machines with their use. One can also see this categorial error as an instance of the reduction of efficient to material causes, as Marx's critique of the Gotha Programme[70] turns on the isolation of the contrary mistake.

Thus, contrary to what is implied in the hermeneutical and neo-Kantian traditions, the transformation $P \rightarrow T$ both (1) isolates real but non-empirical and not necessarily adequately conceptualized conditions and (2) consists essentially, as critique, in two modes of conceptual criticism and change. Now the appellation 'ideology' to the set of ideas *P* is only justified if their *necessity* can be demonstrated: that is, if they can be explained as well as criticized. This involves something more than just being able to say that the beliefs concerned are false or superficial, which normally entails having a better explanation for the phenomena in question. It involves, in addition, being able to give an account of the *reasons* why the false or superficial beliefs are *held* – a mode of explanation without parallel in the natural sciences. For beliefs, whether about society or nature, are clearly social objects.

Once this step is taken then conceptual criticism and change pass over into social criticism and change, as, in a possibility unique to social science,[71] the object that renders illusory (or superficial) beliefs necessary comes, at least in the absence of any overriding considerations, to be criticized in being explained; so that the point now becomes, *ceteris paribus*, to change it. Indeed in the full development of the concept of ideology, theory fuses into practice, as facts about values, mediated by theories about facts, are transformed into values about facts. The rule of value-neutrality, the last shibboleth in the philosophy of the social sciences, collapses, when we come to see that values themselves can be false.

At the beginning of this section I distinguished epistemological and relational limits on naturalism from the ontological ones immediately derived from the transformational model of social activity. But a moment's reflection shows that these limits may be derived from that model too. For the historical and interdependent character of social activities implies that the social world must be open, and the requirement that social activity be socially explained implies that social science is a part of its own subject-matter. Similarly, it is not difficult to see that the application of the transformational model to beliefs and cognitive material generally implies commitment to a principle of epistemic relativity,[72] and that this lends to moral and political argument in particular something of a necessarily transitional and open character.[73]

Our deduction of the possibility of naturalism in the social sciences is complete, although we have still to explore an important range of consequences of it. Society is not given in, but presupposed by, experience. However, it is precisely its peculiar ontological status, its transcendentally real character, that makes it a possible object of knowledge for us. Such knowledge is non-natural but still scientific. The transformational model implies that social activities are historical, interdependent and interconnected. The law-like statements of the social sciences will thus typically designate historically restricted tendencies operating at a single level of the social structure only. Because they are defined for only one relatively autonomous component of the social structure, and because they act in systems that are always open, they designate tendencies (such as for the rates of profit on capitalist enterprises to be equalized) which may never be manifested, but which are nevertheless essential to the understanding (and the changing) of the different forms of social life, just because they are really productive of them. Society is not a mass of separable events and sequences. But neither is it constituted by the concepts that we attach to our physiological states. Rather it is a complex and causally efficacious whole – a totality, which is being continually transformed in practice. As an object of study it can neither be read straight off a given world nor reconstructed from our subjective experiences. But, although empirical realism cannot think it, in this respect at least it is on a par with the objects of study in the natural sciences too.

Social Science as Critique: Facts, Values and Theories

The generally accepted, and in my opinion essentially correct, interpretation of Hume, is that he enunciated what has – at least since Moore's *Principia Ethica* – become an article of faith for the entire analytical tradition, namely that the transition from 'is' to 'ought', factual to value statements, indicatives to imperatives, is, although frequently made (and perhaps even, like eduction, psychologically necessary), logically inadmissible.[74] I want to argue that, on the contrary, it is not only acceptable but mandatory, provided only that minimal criteria for the characterization of a belief system as 'ideological' are satisfied.

For the anti-naturalist tradition in ethics, then, there is a fundamental logical gulf between statements of what *is* (has been or will be) the case and statements of what *ought* to be the case. It follows from this, first, that no factual proposition can be derived from any value judgement (or, more generally, that any factual conclusion depends upon premises containing at least (and normally more than) one factual proposition); and second, that no value judgement can be derived from any factual proposition (or, more generally, that any value conclusion depends upon premises containing at least one value judgement). Accordingly, social science is viewed as neutral in two respects: first, in that its propositions are logically independent of, and cannot be derived from, any value position; second, in that value positions are logically independent of, and cannot be derived from, any social scientific proposition. I shall write these two corollaries of 'Hume's Law' as follows:

(1) $V \nrightarrow F$
(2) $F \nrightarrow V$

It is important to keep (1) and (2) distinct. For it is now often conceded that the facts are in some sense tainted by, or contingent upon, our values. But whatever doubt is cast upon (1), (2) is still deemed canonical. That is, it is still held that the findings of social science are consistent with any value-position; so that even if social science cannot be value-free, social values remain effectively *science-free*. It is of course accepted that science may be used instrumentally in the pursuit of moral ideals, political goals, etc., but science cannot help to determine the latter. We remain free in the face of science to adopt any value-position. 'Keep Science out of Politics (Morality, etc.)' could be the watchword here.

My primary argument is against (2). But I reject (1) as well; that is, I accept the thesis of the value-dependency of (social) facts, and will consider it first. It will be seen, however, that without a rejection of axis (2) of the dichotomy, criticism directed at axis (1), or its implications, must remain largely ineffectual. And my aim will be to show how theory, by throwing into relief the (ever-diminishing) circle in which facts and values move, can presage its transformation into an (expanding) explanatory/emancipatory spiral.

(1) has been criticized from the standpoint of the subjectivity of both (a) the *subject* and (b) the *object* of investigation (as well as, more obliquely, in the hermeneutical, critical and dialectical traditions from the standpoint of (c) the *relationship* between the two). Thus to consider (a) first, it has been argued that the social values of the scientist (or the scientific community) determine (i) the selection of problems; (ii) the conclusions; and even (iii) the standards of inquiry (for example by Weber, Myrdal and Mannheim respectively).

(i) is often treated as uncontroversial; in fact, it embodies a serious muddle. It is most usually associated with Weber's doctrine that although social science could and must be *value-free*, it had nevertheless to be *value-relevant*.[75] Crudely summarized, Weber's position was that because of the infinite variety of empirical reality, the social scientist had to make a choice of what to study. Such a choice would necessarily be guided by his or her values, so that s/he would choose to study precisely those aspects of reality to which s/he attached cultural significance, which thereby became the basis for the construction of 'ideal-types'. Now this is doubly misleading. For, on the one hand, the natural world is similarly complex; and, on the other, aspects of the work of the natural sciences are equally motivated by practical interests. In fact, one needs to make a distinction between the pure and the applied (or practical) natural sciences. In pure science choice of the properties of an object to study is motivated by the search for explanatory mechanisms;[76] in applied science it may be motivated by the industrial, technological, medical or more generally socio-cultural significance of the properties. Thus while it is practical interests which determine which out of the infinite number of possible compounds of carbon are studied,[77] it is theoretical interests which motivate the identification of its electronic structure. Weber's neo-Kantianism misleads him into substituting the distinction *natural/social* for the distinction *pure/applied*. There is nothing in the infinite variety of the surface of the social cosmos to necessitate a difference in principle in the structure of the search for explanatory mechanisms. Nor, *pace* Habermasians, is an interest in emancipation something with which one has to *preface* that search, although, as I shall argue shortly, explanatory social science necessarily has emancipatory implications.[78] At a deeper level, any doctrine of value-relevance (or knowledge-constitutive-interests) also suffers from the defect that it leaves the *source* of the values (or interests) unexplained.

(ii) is altogether more powerful. The underlying notion at work is that social science is so inextricably 'bound up' with its subject-matter that its interest in it will affect, and (if some concept of objectivity – relational or otherwise – is retained) distort, its perception, description or interpretation of it. Examples of such affecting/distorting are readily available.[79] It is clear that (ii) rests on an epistemological premise, viz. that of the internality of social science with respect to its subject-matter, together with a psychological or sociological one, asserting the practical impossibility of making the analytical separation the positivist enjoins on the social scientist. And it posits, with respect to the claim made in (1) above, an *interference* between the subject's interests in the object and its knowledge of it.

Now it is vital to distinguish three ways in which such interference could operate. It could operate *consciously* (as in lying); it could operate *semi-consciously* (as in the wishful thinking of the incurable optimist or the special pleading of a pressure group); or it could operate *unconsciously* (whether or not it can become accessible to consciousness). It is only the third case that raises serious difficulties for (1). I want to distinguish the case where the conclusions of such an unconscious mode of 'interference' are *rationalizations* of motivation from the case where they constitute *mystifications* (or ideologies) of social structure. In either case the interference may be regarded as necessary or as contingent upon a particular set of psychic or social circumstances.

Recognition of the phenomena of rationalization and mystification as the effects of unconscious interference enables us to pinpoint the error in an influential 'solution' to the problem of 'value-bias', authorized *inter alia* by Myrdal.[80] On this solution, recognizing that value-neutrality is impossible, all the social scientist needs to do is state his or her own value assumptions fully and explicitly at the beginning of some piece of work so as to put the reader (and possibly also the writer) on their guard. It is not difficult to see that this solution begs the question. For it presupposes that X knows what his or her values are; that is, it presupposes that s/he has the kind of knowledge about him- or herself that *ex hypothesi*, in virtue of unconscious interference, s/he cannot have about society. Now for X to have such knowledge about him- or herself, s/he would have had to become fully conscious of the formerly unconscious mode of interference, in which case a statement of value assumptions is *unnecessary*, because objectivity is now possible. Conversely, if X is not conscious of the (unconscious) mode of interference, then any statement of his or her (professed) value assumptions will be *worthless*. Moreover, one cannot say in general whether any such statement will be more or less misleading. (Thus consider, for instance, what often follows professions of the kind 'I'm not prejudiced about . . .' or 'I'm a tolerant sort of person/true liberal/ good democrat . . .') *Mutatis mutandis*, similar considerations apply in the case of conscious and semi-conscious modes of interference: avowals are either unnecessary or potentially misleading.

(iii) posits a relativity in the methodological norms secreted by different conceptual schemes or paradigms, together with a value-dependence of such conceptual schemes of the sort already discussed under (ii). I want to consider it *pari passu* with the general problem of relativism, of which it is just a special case. Two objections to relativism are regularly trotted out: first, that it is self-refuting; second, that it denies what we do in fact do, for example translate, make cross-cultural comparisons, etc.[81]

The argument for the self-refuting character of relativism is easily refuted. The argument asserts that if all beliefs are relative, then there can be no good grounds for relativism; hence one has no reason to accept it. Conversely, if one has reason to accept it, then at least one belief is not relative; so that relativism is false. Now this argument confuses two distinct theses (which are indeed typically confused by pro- as well as anti-relativists). The first is the correct thesis of *epistemic relativity*, which asserts that all beliefs are socially produced, so that all knowledge is transient, and neither truth-values nor criteria of rationality exist outside historical time. The other is the incorrect thesis of *judgemental relativism*, which asserts that all beliefs (statements) are equally valid, in the sense that there can be no (rational) grounds for preferring one to another. Denying the principle of epistemic relativity inevitably entails embracing some type of epistemological *absolutism* (which, by a short route, invariably results in some kind of idealism), while acceptance of judgemental relativism inevitably leads to some or other form of *irrationalism*. Epistemic relativity is entailed both by ontological realism[82] and by the transformational conception of social activity: it respects a distinction between the sense and reference of propositions, while insisting that all speech acts are made in historical time. Such a principle neither entails nor (even if any were logically possible) gives grounds for a belief in the doctrine of judgemental relativism. On the contrary, it is clear that if one is to act at all there must be grounds for preferring one belief (about some domain) to another; and that such activity in particular practices is typically codifiable in the form of systems of *rules*, implicitly or explicitly followed.

The anti-relativist argument may now be refuted. Epistemic relativism is a particular belief (about the totality of beliefs). Like any belief (including its contrary), it arises under, and is (analytically) only comprehensible, and therefore only acceptable, under definite historical conditions. Epistemic relativism is certainly comprehensible to us. And it is clear that there are in fact excellent grounds, both transcendental and empirical, for accepting it, and denying its contrary. (Of course if, on some inter-galactic voyage, we were to unearth some 'World 3' or world of timeless forms, in which it could be shown that our knowledge had been all the while participating, then we should certainly revise this judgement and accept some form of absolutism!)

Turning to the second objection to relativism, the undeniable fact that we can translate, etc., no more proves the existence of neutral languages or absolute standards than our interaction with lions proves that they can talk.[83] Whorf's hypothesis is not refuted by the existence of appropriate bilinguals (or it could never have been consistently formulated); any more than the *psychological* capacity of a physicist to understand both Newtonian and Ensteinian theory indicates that they are not *logically* incommensurable; or our ability to see a drawing as either a duck or a rabbit shows that there must be a way of seeing it as both at once. I will return to the special problems raised by the notion of our understanding other cultures and other times in Chapter 4.

Arguments of type (b) turn not on the 'value-bias' of social science, but on the 'value-impregnation' of its subject-matter. They typically depend upon the fact that the subject-matter of social science is itself in part constituted by, or indeed just consists in, values or things to which the agents themselves attach (or have attached for them) value, that is, objects of value. Presumably no one would wish to deny this. The point only becomes a threat to (1) if it is established that the value-dependency of the subject-matter of social science makes it impossible or illegitimate to perform the required analytical separation in social scientific discourse. (For it is clear that one might be able to describe values in a value-free way.) If one represents the subject-matter of social science by S_1 and social science by S_2, as in the diagram opposite, the claim is that the nature of S_1 is such that, in virtue of its value-

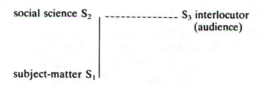

impregnation, either no description in L_2 satisfies (1), or at least the best or most adequate scientific description in L_2 does not satisfy (1). (This may be held to be a necessary, normal or occasional state of affairs.)

The significance of the fact that one is here concerned with questions of *descriptive* (and more generally scientific) *adequacy* may best be introduced by considering a famous example of Isaiah Berlin's. Thus compare the following accounts of what happened in Germany under Nazi rule: (α) 'the country was depopulated'; (β) 'millions of people died'; (γ) 'millions of people were killed'; (δ) 'millions of people were massacred'. All four statements are true. But (δ) is not only the most evaluative, it is also the best (that is, the most precise and accurate) description of what actually happened. And note that, in virtue of this, all but (δ) generate the wrong perlocutionary force. For to say of someone that he died normally carries the presumption that he was *not* killed by human agency. And to say that millions were killed does not imply that their deaths were part of a single organized campaign of brutal killing, as those under Nazi rule were. This point is important. For social science is not only *about* a subject matter, it is *for* an audience. That is, it is always in principle a party to a triadic relationship, standing to an actual or possible interlocutor (S_3) as a potential source of (mis-/dis-) information, explanation, justification, etc. Now I want to argue that, even abstracting from perlocutionary considerations, criteria for the scientific adequacy of descriptions are such that in this kind of case only the (δ) statement is acceptable.

If one denotes some social phenomenon in S_1 as 'P_1', then the most adequate description of P_1 in L_2 will be that description – let us call it D^*_2 – (with whatever evaluative components it incorporates) entailed by that theory T^* (formulated in L_2) with the *maximum explanatory power* (including of course the power, wherever possible, to explain descriptions of P_1 in S_1). In general the attainment of hermeneutic adequacy is a necessary but not a sufficient condition for generating the appropriate description D^*_2. Indeed if the hermeneutically adequate description is D°_2 and its target in L_1 is D°_1, then whether or not $D^*_2 = D^\circ_2$ is contingent. And the susceptibility of D°_1 to scientific *critique* is exactly reflected in the *process* of description, explanation and re-description that, as has been noted in Chapter 1, characterizes scientific activity at any one level or stratum of reality. (This process is of course implicit in the transformational model, with the relevant ruptural point being the identification of the operative explanatory structure.) Such a process respects the *authenticity* of $D°_1$, but does not regard it as an incorrigible datum.[84] So that although the achievement of *Verstehen* is, in virtue of the concept-dependence of social structures, a condition for social science, the process of social science does not leave the initial descriptions – either in L_2 or in principle in L_1 – intact. In short, just as natural science has no foundations, there are no foundations of social knowledge – scientific or lay.

It is important to note that commitment to a principle of hermeneutic adequacy as a moment in social science is not only consistent with a subsequent critique of the *verstehende* description, it itself stands in need of supplementation by semiotic analysis. For the hermeneutic mediation of meanings (or fusion of horizons) must be complemented by consideration of the question posed by semiotics as to how such meanings (horizons, etc.) are produced. (Of course such a question must itself be expressed in a language, so that the process mediation-analysis is an iterative one.) Now if, following Saussure, one regards meanings as produced by, as it were, cutting into pre-existing systems of difference,[85] then in science our cut must be made so as to maximize total explanatory power. And another type of critique – a *metacritique* of L_1 – becomes possible if it can be shown that L_1 (or some relevant subsystem of it) is such that the adequate representation of P_1 in L_1 is impossible. This concern with the production of meaning corresponds exactly to the attentiveness shown in the natural sciences to the construction of instruments and equipment; so that one can say that if the hermeneutic moment corresponds (with respect to the conceptual aspect of social life) to observation, then the semiotic one corresponds to instrumentation in the empirical work of the natural sciences.

Now of course it does not follow that commitment to a principle of hermeneutic adequacy will automatically result in the replication in L_2 of the evaluative components in $D°_1$; nor does the production of $D°_2$ itself imply any value commitment. The question is rather whether the scientifically adequate description D^*_2 breaks the rule of value-neutrality. Where it constitutes a critique of $D°_1$ it does so necessarily. For to show that agents are systematically deluded about the nature of their activity is (logically) impossible without passing the judgement that $D°_1$ is false; and '$D°_1$ is false' is not a value-neutral statement. Strictly speaking, this is sufficient for the purposes of our argument. For we require only to show that S_1 is such that in social science value-neutral descriptions are not always possible. But it is worth dwelling on the point in its more general aspect. Our problem is to utilize the powers of L_2 so as to maximize our understanding in L_2 of S_1. L_2 is the only language we can use. And the terms we use to describe human behaviour will be terms which function *inter alia* regulatively and evaluatively in S_2: these are the only terms we can, without parody or satire, use; and we cannot dislocate them from their living context without misrepresenting as lifeless the context they are employed to describe. Hence just as to define a foetus as an unborn human being is already to load the debate on abortion in a certain way, so to attempt to construct an index of fascism comparable to that of anaemia[86] is both absurd (because the elements of a fascist state are internally related) and value-laden (because it functions so as to remove from our purview, in science, precisely that range of its implications internally related to objects that we value, such as human life). In short, not to call a spade a spade, in any human society, is to misdescribe it.

Positivist dogma (1) must thus be rejected both on the grounds that it ignores the subject's interest in the object and on the grounds that the nature of the object is such that criteria for descriptive (and more generally scientific) adequacy entail at least the possibility of irreducibly evaluative descriptions. Criticism of (1) however leaves the questions of the determination, and non-instrumental justification, of values unresolved. Moreover, by making facts partially dependent upon values (and leaving value-choice undetermined) a seemingly inevitable element of arbitrariness is introduced into the scientific process. Indeed there seems no reason why, in the light of our special interests, we should not generate whatever facts we please. In order to forestall such a radical conventionalism, let us cross to the other side of the divide, viz. (2), and see if science has any implications for values; if one can break into the circle here. Before offering my own account of the matter, I want to discuss two recent attempts to break down the fact/value distinction along the axis denied in (2).

Charles Taylor, in an important article,[87] shows clearly how theories (or 'explanatory frameworks') do in fact secrete values. The structure of his argument may be represented as follows:

(3) $T \leftrightarrow F \rightarrow V$

Unfortunately, however, by failing to specify any criterion for choosing between theories, he leaves himself open to the interpretation that one should choose that theory which most satisfies our conception of what 'fulfills human needs, wants and purposes';[88] rather than that theory which, just *because it is explanatorily most adequate* and capable *inter alia* of explaining illusory beliefs about the social world, best allows us to situate the possibilities of change in the value direction that the theory indicates. He thus merely displaces, rather than transcends, the traditional fact/value dichotomy. Alternatively, one might attempt to interpret Taylor as arguing that one ought to opt for the theory that secretes the best value-position, because theories tend to be acted upon and human needs are the independent (or at least chief) variable in social explanation.[89] But this involves a dubious set of propositions, including a substantive scheme of explanation with voluntaristic implications.

Searle's attempted derivation of 'ought' from 'is', where the critical 'is' statement is a statement describing institutional facts (that is, facts constituted by systems of rules), turns on the existence of a series of connections between saying 'I promise', being under an obligation and it being the case that one ought to do what one is under an obligation to do.[90] The structure of Searle's argument may be represented as:

(4) $I.F. \rightarrow V$

It has been criticized (for example by Hare) on the grounds that the institutional facts upon which it rests merely encapsulate general moral principles, and (for example by Flew) on the grounds that the mere utterance of words does not imply the kind of commitment that alone warrants a normative conclusion. Now it is certainly the case that the mere fact that one acts within an institution in such a way that one's action would not be possible but for its constitutive rules, does not imply a moral (as distinct from a motivational, or purely instrumental) commitment to it. Otherwise it would be logically impossible to be a socialist within a capitalist society, or a libertarian within a totalitarian one. Promising is an institution within a network of institutions which one might decide, on moral grounds,[91] either to opt out of or merely 'play' (sincerely or insincerely). A society of discursive intelligences where promising is regarded rather as Americans regard cricket, is, although perhaps not very attractive, certainly conceivable – in a way in which a society not subject to norms of truth, consistency and coherence is not. To derive a morally unrevocable (*ceteris paribus*) 'ought' from an 'is' one has to move from premises which are constitutive of purely factual discourse, which are transcendentally necessary.

My argument, it is important to note, does not permit a simple inference from facts to values. It turns, rather, on the capacity of a *theory* to explain false consciousness, and in particular on the capacity of a theory to allow the satisfaction of minimal criteria for the character-ization of a system of beliefs as *ideological*. (Fuller criteria will be elaborated in the appendix to this chapter.) Now it will be remembered that I argued in the last section that one is only justified in characterizing a set of ideas P as 'ideological' if both (a) P is false, that is, one possesses a superior explanation for the phenomena in question; and (b) P is more or less contingently (conjuncturally) necessary, that is, one possesses an explanation of the falsity of the beliefs in question. It should be noted that the necessity one is dealing with here may only be the necessity for *some* illusion, rather than any *particular* one; and that, where (as in the case of myths about nature) *different* theories are required for the satisfaction of (a) and (b), they must at least be consistent with one another. One can write these criteria as follows:

(a) $T > P$
(b) $T \exp I (P)$

Now to criticize a belief as false is *ipso facto* not only to criticize any action or practice informed or sustained by that belief, but also anything that necessitates it. In social science this will be precisely the object that renders illusory (or superficial) beliefs, along any of the dimensions of mystification already indicated in the last section, necessary. The structure of my argument may be represented as:

(5) $T > P. \; T \exp I (P) \rightarrow - V (O \rightarrow I (P))$

Of course this only entails the imperative 'change it' if change is possible and in the absence of overriding considerations. But that is the case with *any* valuation (for example, smoking is harmful).[92]

If, then, one is in possession of a theory which explains why false consciousness is necessary, one can pass immediately, without the addition of any extraneous value judgements, to a negative evaluation of the object (generative structure, system of social relations or whatever) that makes that consciousness necessary (and, *ceteris paribus*, to a positive evaluation of action rationally directed at the removal of the sources of false consciousness). Might it not be objected, however, that the fact/value distinction only breaks down in this way because one is committed to the prior valuation that truth is a good, so that one is not deriving a value judgement from entirely factual (natural) premises? But that truth *is* a good (*ceteris paribus*) is not only a condition of moral discourse, it is a condition of any discourse at all. Commitment to truth and consistency apply to factual as much as to value discourse; and so cannot be seized upon as a concealed (value) premise to rescue the autonomy of values from factual discourse, without destroying the distinction between the two, the distinction that it is the point of the objection to uphold.

Given that clear paradigms exist of the form of explanation represented by (5), can a case be made out for supposing such an explanation-form to be transcendentally necessary? Now it is evident that there can be no action without beliefs, and no beliefs save by work on or with other beliefs, so that judgements of falsity are transcendentally necessary. Further, it is clear that it is only if an agent can *explain* a belief that s/he can set out to rationally *change* it, in the case where it is not susceptible to direct criticism. Now if beliefs are not to be given a totally voluntaristic explanation; if they are at all recalcitrant – like the rest of the social structure (as is implied by their internality to it); or if a sociology of knowledge is to be possible and necessary (and one is already implicit in lay practice); then the form of ideological explanation schematized in (5) is *a condition of every rational praxis*. Put informally, the possibility of coming to say to another or oneself 'now this is why you (*I*) erroneously believe such-and-such' is a presupposition of any rational discourse or authentic act of self-reflection at all.

Ceteris paribus, then, truth, consistency, coherence, rationality, etc., are good, and their opposites bad, precisely because commitment to them are conditions of the possibility of discourse in general. Now it is certainly the case that to say of some belief *P* that it is illusory is *ceteris paribus* (henceforth *CP*) to imply that it is detrimental to the achievement of human goals and the satisfaction of human wants. But it is not *because* of this, on the argument I have advanced, that *P* is bad. Of course science is not the only human activity, or the most important (in an explanatory sense). Further, just as the values it encapsulates may be undermined in certain kinds of societies, so they may be overridden by other values. However, such overriding cannot consistently be argued to be either necessarily or even normally warranted. Moreover it is only by reference to social scientific (and psychological) theories that an infinite regress of values can be avoided and questions of ultimate values resolved (as of course in practice they always – implicitly or explicitly – are). Different 'highest-order' explanatory theories will contain their own conception of what kinds of social organization are possible and of what human beings essentially are (or can become). The most powerful explanatory theory, by situating the greatest range of real (non-Utopian) possibilities, will increase our rational autonomy of action. But it is a mistake of the greatest magnitude to suppose that, in Laplacean fashion, it will tell us what to do. The most powerful explanatory theory in an open world is a non-deterministic one.

Aside from this, science, although it can and must illuminate them, cannot finally 'settle' questions of practical morality and action, just because there are always – and necessarily – social practices besides science, and values other than cognitive ones; because, to adapt a famous metaphor of Neurath's, while we mend the boat, we still need to catch fish in the sea. On the other hand, once we break from the contemplative standpoint of traditional epistemology and conceive human beings as engaged in practical and material activity, and not just thinking and perceiving, it becomes difficult to see how (2) could have held philosophers in thrall for so long. For we can certainly derive technical imperatives from theoretical premises alone (subject to a *CP* clause).[93] Moreover, to criticize a belief or theory is *ipso facto* to criticize any action informed, or practice sustained, by that belief or theory, so that even at level (a) of (5) we pass directly to practical imperatives. But to stop there is to halt at 'that kind of criticism which knows how to judge and condemn the present, but not how to comprehend it'.[94] To move beyond such criticism we need to reveal the object that makes false consciousness necessary, in a moment – level (b) of (5) – which I have called 'critique'. Once we have accomplished this, we have then done as much as science alone can do for society and people. And the point becomes to transform them.

APPENDIX

A Note on the Marxist Concept of Ideology

It is not my intention here to provide a full treatment of the Marxist concept of ideology, but rather merely to consider two problems associated with it. The first concerns the location of ideology (and science) within the topography of historical materialism; the second concerns the criteria for the characterization of beliefs as 'ideological', and specifically for distinguishing ideology from science.

A. Sciences and Ideologies in Historical Materialism

In the work of the mature Marx the concept of ideology has a double designation: on the one hand, it is assigned to the superstructure to be explained in terms of the base; and on the other, it forms part of the analysis of the base itself, most notably in the figure of commodity fetishism. Now this double designation, not to say schism, in the thematization of the concept of ideology within Marxism itself reflects a historical fact of some importance. Marx inaugurated two distinct research programmes: an economic theory, or critique, of the capitalist mode of production, elaborated above all in *Capital*; and a theory of history, historical materialism, sketched, for example, in the famous 1859 Preface and put to work in a few justly celebrated conjunctural analyses. But he never satisfactorily integrated the two. (One symptom of this is the absence, in his mature work, of any theory of capitalist *society*.) And it was left to Engels, and subsequent Marxists, following their own intuitions and Marx's clues, to try to resolve the problems engendered by this original cleavage within Marxism.

Foremost among such problems is of course that of reconciling the thesis of the relative autonomy and specific efficacy of the various superstructures (however individuated and enumerated) with that of their determination in the last instance by the base (however identified and defined) – see n. 43 below. In general terms Marxists have long recognized two errors: *idealism*, dislocation of a superstructure from the base (or the totality); and *reductionism* (or economism), reduction of a superstructure to a mechanical effect or epiphenomenon of the base (or to an expression of the totality). Now if one places science within society, as one surely must, these opposed errors can be identified in the works of Althusser in the mid-1960s (in his so-called 'theoreticist' phase) and of the early Lukács respectively. Thus for Althusser science is effectively *completely* autonomous,[95] while for Lukács it tends to be merely an *expression* of (the reification intrinsic to) capitalist society.[96] Lysenkoism, in which science is conceived as a mechanical function of the economic base, is an *economistic* variant of reductionism.[97]

This problem of simultaneously avoiding economic reductionism and theoretical idealism has a direct counterpart on the plane of ideology. For, on the one hand, there is, in *Capital*, a theory of false or superficial economic ideas, which cannot just be extrapolated (without detailed independent investigations) into a general theory of ideas-in-capitalist-society. And, on the other hand, if historical materialism is to mark any advance over empiricist sociology and historiography, it must presumably provide a framework for accounting for legal, political, cultural, religious, philosophical and scientific ideas as well as economic ones. Specifically, I want to suggest that (1) ideas cannot just be lumped together and assigned in an undifferentiated bloc to the category of superstructure; and (2) all activity, including purely economic activity, necessarily has an ideational component or aspect (as the Ist Thesis on Feuerbach implies), that is to say, it is unthinkable except in so far as the agent has a conception of what s/he is doing and why s/he is doing it (in which of course s/he may be mistaken). The critique of idealism developed in *The German Ideology* consists: firstly, in the rejection of the Hegelian notion of the autonomous existence of the ideal;[98] and secondly, in the assertion of the primacy of the material over the ideal.[99] But however precisely the latter claim is to be interpreted, Marx can hardly be plausibly committed to a materialist inversion of Hegel on the first count, viz. as asserting the autonomous existence of the material in social life. Thus the crude distinction economic base/ideological superstructure must be rejected and replaced instead by a conception of the *different ideologies* associated with the *different practices*, including both scientific practices and the practices identified, in any particular formation, as basic. Of course these ideologies will stand in various relations to one another, and sometimes reveal striking homologies and straightforward functionalities. But this way of looking at ideologies leaves open their nature and relations for substantive scientific investigation. Moreover, it allows both that the various practices may have different, and varying, degrees of autonomy from the base; and that in some cases (physics, technology, literature, warfare) the practices concerned may have relatively autonomous bases of their own.[100]

In its classical tradition, Marxism has conceived ideologies as systems of false beliefs, arising in response to the objective conditions of material existence and as playing an essential role in reproducing (and/ or transforming) social relations of production. Typically, moreover, it has opposed ideology to science; and science has been conceived, at least by Marx, Engels and Lenin, as a weapon in the emancipation of the working class. Ideology is categorially false consciousness, grounded in the existence of a particular historically contingent form of (class) society and serving the interests of a system of domination (at root, class domination) intrinsic to it. Now, as Poulantzas has noted, the only fully worked out theory of ideology in Marxism is in Marx's critique of political economy; so it is to this that we must turn in considering what is involved in the Marxist notion of a critique, and the counterposition of ideology to science.

B. Science v. Ideology in the Critique of Political Economy

I suggest that a system of beliefs *I* may be characterized as 'ideological', within this conceptual lineage, if and only if three types of criteria – which I shall call critical, explanatory and categorial – are satisfied. To consider the *critical* criteria first, in order to designate *I* as 'ideological' one must be in possession of a theory (or a consistent set of theories) *T* which can do the following:

1. Explain most, or most significant, phenomena, under its own descriptions, explained by *I* (under *I*'s descriptions, where these are 'incommensurable' with those of *T*).
2. Explain in addition a significant set of phenomena not explained by *I*.

To satisfy the *explanatory* criteria for the designation of *I* as 'ideological', *T* must be able to do the following:

3. Explain the reproduction of *I* (that is, roughly, the conditions for its continued acceptance by agents) and, if possible, specify the limits of *I* and the (endogenous) conditions for its transformation (if any), specifically:
   3'. In terms of a real stratification or connection (that is, a level of

structure or set of relations) described in *T* but altogether absent from or obscured in *I*.

4. Explain, or at least situate, itself within itself.

Finally, to satisfy the *categorial* criteria for the designation of *I* as 'ideological', *I* must be *unable* to satisfy either of the following:

5. A criterion of scientificity, specifying the minimum necessary conditions for the characterization of a production as scientific; or
6. A criterion of domain-adequacy, specifying the minimum necessary conditions for a theory to sustain the historical or social (or whatever) nature of its subject-matter.

And *T* must be able to satisfy both.

(1) and (2) explicate the sense in which T is cognitively superior to *I*.[101] But (3') assigns to T a specific type of cognitive superiority. It possesses an ontological depth or totality that *I* lacks. (3) demarcates social scientific from natural scientific explanation. The condition that beliefs about phenomena, as well as phenomena, are to be explained derives from the internality of social theories with respect to their subject-matter (see p. 47). And this of course also indicates the desirability of the satisfaction of a criterion of reflexivity, viz. (4). It should perhaps be stressed that one is *only* justified in characterizing a system of beliefs as 'ideological' if one is in possession of a theory that can explain them. The categorial criteria (5) and (6) presuppose of course that *T*, or some metatheory consistent with it, specifies the appropriate conditions (as has been done here in Chapters 1 and 2 respectively). For Marx classical political economy satisfied (5), but not properly speaking (6), in virtue of the category mistakes, such as that of fetishism, in which it was implicated. But vulgar economy did not even satisfy (5). Finally, it should be noted that, traditionally, theoretical ideologies have been distinguished from the forms of consciousness they reflect, or rationalize (or otherwise defend); so that within the analysis of any '*I*' an internal differentiation with respect to discursive level will be necessary. Now let us put this formal apparatus to work on *Capital*.

Capital is subtitled 'a critical analysis of capitalist production'. It is at one and the same time a critique of bourgeois political economy; a critique of the economic conceptions of everyday life that, according to Marx, bourgeois political economy merely reflects or rationalizes; and a critique of the mode of production that renders these conceptions necessary for the agents engaging in it. It is the structure of this triple critique that provides the key to the analysis of ideology in Marx's mature economic writings.

For Marx vulgar economy merely reflects the phenomenal forms of bourgeois life. It does not penetrate to the essential reality that produces these forms.[102] But it is not just laziness or scientific 'bad faith' that accounts for this. For the phenomenal forms that are reflected or rationalized in ideology actually mask the real relations that generate them. As Godelier has put it: 'it is not the subject who deceives himself [nor, one might add, is it any other subject – be it individual, group or class], but *reality* [that is, the structure of society] that deceives [or better, produces the deception in] him'.[103] Marx's project is thus to discover the mechanisms by which capitalist society necessarily appears to its agents as something other than it really is; that is, of its specific opacity. And inasmuch as he succeeds in this task, showing these forms to be both false *and* necessary, *Capital's* status as a triple critique is explained (and its right to its subtitle fully justified).

I noted above (p. 52) how fetishism, by *naturalizing* value, *dehistoricizes* it. Its social function is thus to conceal the historically specific class relationships that underlie the surface phenomena of circulation and exchange. Now the wage form, in confusing the value of labour and the value of labour power, reduces *powers* to their *exercise*. Its social function is thus to conceal the reality, in the process of capitalist production, of unpaid labour (the source of surplus value). And as Marx says, 'if history took a long time to get to the bottom of the mystery of wages, nothing is easier than to understand the necessity, the *raison d'être* of this phenomenon'.[104] So both the value and wage forms, on which Marx's critique of political economy turn, involve characteristic, and (within the context of Marx's theory) readily explicable, category mistakes.

Now once one accepts that phenomenal forms are necessary to the functioning of a capitalist economy (that is, once one rejects a crude materialistic inversion of the Hegelian notion of the autonomy of the ideal), one can set out the following schema, adapted from an article by John Mepham.[105]

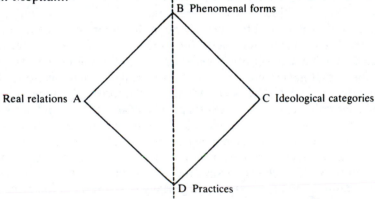

Real relations, *A*, characteristically located by Marx in the sphere of production, generate phenomenal forms, *B*, characteristic of the spheres of circulation and exchange, which in turn are reflected in the categories of ideological discourse, *C*, which sustain and underpin such ordinary commercial practices as buying and selling, wage-negotiating, etc., at *D*. These are in turn, of course, necessary for the reproduction of the real relations *A*. The dotted line through *BD* denotes, as it were, the cut of everyday life. Marx's analysis typically moves retroductively from *B* to *A*, enabling a critique of *C* and informing practice at *D*. Moreover the analysis, in isolating the conditions for the phenomenal forms in a mode of production necessitating forms which are false (as in the case of the wage form) or systematically misleading (as in the case of the value form), *ipso facto*, without the intervention of any value judgements (other than those bound up in the assessment of the cognitive adequacy of the theory and *a fortiori* its superiority over bourgeois political economy), issues in a negative valuation of that mode of production. In discovering that the source of consciousness is such that it is false, Marx automatically discredits that source, while simultaneously showing how that consciousness may yet be necessary. It follows from this also that, although a critique in Marx's sense is at once transcendentally and subversively critical, Marxist science is subversive in virtue of its cognitive power alone.

Finally, it should be noted that Marx's analysis of political economy reveals not only a gap between how an object is and how it appears to be, but a 'contradiction', which I shall call a 'Colletti contradiction',[106] between the way it presents itself in experience and the way it really is. This is not just because analysis reveals a level of structure and set of relations not manifest to experience (or bourgeois ideology), which it does (see criterion (3') above), but which does not justify reference to a 'contradiction'. Nor is it only because the very forms in which social life presents itself to experience embody fundamental category mistakes (such as the presentation of the social as natural in fetishism or the 'interpellation' of individuals as free agents in their constitution as subjects).[107] Rather it is because, through the theorem of the necessity of phenomenal forms for social life, they are themselves internally related to (that is, constitute necessary conditions for) the essential structures that generate them. On Marx's analysis, social reality is shot through with such Colletti contradictions. Paradoxically, however, far from confirming Colletti's diagnosis of 'two Marx's'[108] it is precisely the existence of just one – the scientist – that explains this. (For were criticism to be separable from analysis there would be no problem, and no contradictions of this type.) Moreover it is important to stress that such contradictions, which involve merely the necessary co-existence in social reality of an object and a categorially false presentation of it, can be *consistently described*, as indeed can the more straightforward logical kind present in the thought of every mathematics student. Colletti's transcendental idealism misleads him into viewing the principle of non-contradiction, conceived as a regulative ideal for thought, as a constitutive principle of thinkable reality. But of course where, as in social life, thought is itself part of social reality, there are bound to exist logical contradictions in reality. And if thought does not constitute (and so completely exhaust) social reality, there are bound to exist mis-representations of reality in reality. And among such misrepresentations will be some which are necessary for what they misrepresent. Now if such misrepresentations are themselves generated by what they mis-represent it will *seem* as if one has just moved in a circle, that one has a simple case of the identity of opposites here. But of course this is not so. For at each moment in the analysis concept and object remain distinct; and the relations involved are causal, not logical. Such a relation is still characterizable as one of 'contradiction', in virtue of the misrepresen-tation involved. But because one of the *relata* consists in a (misrepre-sented) real object, the contradiction is not internal to thought, as in the dialectics of both Plato and Hegel. And because the *relata* are necessary for each other, they do not stand in a purely contingent, external relationship to one another, as in a Newtonian conflict of forces or a Kantian *Realrepugnanz*.[109] So that if one chooses to use the term 'dialectical', in deference to custom but in opposition to history, to refer to *such* oppositions, it seems advisable to preface it, to indicate its specificity, by some such term as 'Marxian'.

NOTES

1. See *A Realist Theory of Science*, 1st edn (Leeds 1975), 2nd edn (Hassocks and New Jersey 1978), esp. ch. 1 sec. 4.
2. K. Marx, *Grundrisse* (Harmondsworth 1973), p. 265.
3. See, for example, A. Schutz, 'Common-Sense and Scientific Interpretations of Human Actions', *Collected Papers* 1 (The Hague 1967), or 'Problems of Interpretative Sociology', reprinted from *The Phenomenology of the Social World* (London 1967) in A. Ryan (ed.), *The Philosophy of Social Explanation* (Oxford 1973).
4. As is evinced by the possibility of absolute idealism as the ontological ground for idealist sociologies (often, and arguably necessarily, combined with individualism – for example Weber or Dilthey – or collectivism – for example Durkheim or, say, Lévi-Strauss – in the work of a single author). See also T. Benton, *Philosophical Foundations of the Three Sociologies* (London 1977), p. 85, n. 11.
5. See the specific analogy drawn by J.W.N. Watkins between methodo-logical individualism in social science and mechanism in physics in 'Ideal Types and Historical Explanation', *British Journal for the Philosophy of Science* 3 (1952), reprinted in A. Ryan (ed.), *op. cit.*, p. 90, and 'Historical Explanation in the Social Sciences', *British Journal for the Philosophy of Science* 8 (1957), reprinted as 'Methodological Individualism and Social

Tendencies' in *Readings in the Philosophy of the Social Sciences*, M. Brodbeck (ed.) (London 1970), p. 270.

6. K. R. Popper, *The Open Society and its Enemies* 2 (London 1962), p. 98.

7. I. Jarvie, 'Reply to Taylor', *Universities and Left Review* (1959), p. 57.

8. J. W. N. Watkins, 'Methodological Individualism', p. 271.

9. *Loc. cit.*

10. J. W. N. Watkins, 'Ideal Types', p. 88.

11. See A. Danto, *Analytical Philosophy of History* (Cambridge 1965), ch. 12, and S. Lukes, 'Methodological Individualism Reconsidered', *British Journal of Sociology* 19 (1968), reprinted in A. Ryan (ed.), *op. cit.*

12. See J. W. N. Watkins, 'Ideal Types', p. 91 and 'Methodological Individualism', p. 273.

13. *Ibid.*, p. 278.

14. D. Hume, *A Treatise on Human Nature* (Oxford 1967), p. 415.

15. D. Hume, *Essays Moral and Political* 2 (London 1875), p. 68. Although this paradigm is perhaps for the first time clearly articulated by Hume, it is significant that in his thought, unlike many who followed him, it is counterbalanced by a stress on certain intrinsically social sensibilities, most notably sympathy, and an interest in history – both characteristic of the Scottish Enlightenment generally (see, for example, G. Davie, *The Democratic Intellect* (Edinburgh 1961)). Indeed for Hume it is precisely sympathy among the 'constant and universal principles of human nature' that provides the ground for our interest in history. See, for example, *Enquiries* (Oxford 1972), p. 223.

16. See S. Kotarbinski, 'Praxiology', *Essays in Honour of O. Lange* (Warsaw 1965).

17. See, for example, J. W. N. Watkins, 'Ideal Types', p. 82, n. 1.

18. J.-P. Sartre, *Critique of Dialectical Reason* (London 1976), bk. 2, ch. 1 and bk 1, ch. 4.

19. There are of course non-, and even anti-individualist tendencies in Weber's thought – see, for example, R. Aron, *Philosophie critique de l'histoire* (Paris 1969). Similarly there are non- and (especially in *The Elementary Forms of Religious Life*) anti-positivist strains in Durkheim's thought – see, for example, S. Lukes, *Durkheim* (London 1973), and R. Horton, 'Lévy-Bruhl, Durkheim and the Scientific Revolution' in *Modes of Thought*, R. Finnegan and R. Horton (eds.) (London 1973). My concern here is only with the *dominant* aspects.

20. See, for example, R. Keat and J. Urry, *Social Theory as Science* (London 1975), ch. 5; and B. Ollman, *Alienation* (Cambridge 1971), esp. chs. 2 and 3. Of course there are positivist and individualist elements in Marx's work as well.

21. See especially P. Berger and S. Pullberg, 'Reification and the Sociological Critique of Consciousness', *New Left Review* 35 (1966) and P. Berger and T. Luckmann, *The Social Construction of Reality* (London 1967).

22. P. Berger and S. Pullberg, 'Reification', pp. 62–3.

23. *Ibid.*, p. 63.

24. *Loc. cit.*

25. E. Durkheim, *The Rules of Sociological Method* (New York 1964), p. 2.

26. P. Berger and S. Pullberg, 'Reification', p. 60.

27. *Ibid.*, p. 61.

28. *Ibid.*, p. 60.

29. E. Durkheim, *The Rules of Sociological Method*, pp. 1–2.

30. See C. Lévi-Strauss, *The Savage Mind* (London 1966), ch. 1.

31. See A. Giddens, *New Rules of Sociological Method* (London 1976), p. 121; and J. Lyons, *Chomsky* (London 1970), p. 22.
32. See R. Harré and P. Secord, *The Explanation of Social Behaviour* (Oxford 1972), esp. ch. 5.
33. Mentalistic predicates may play a legitimate role in the explanation of social changes either as a result of their literal use to refer to processes of conscious choice, deliberation, etc., or as a result of their metaphorical use to refer to the effects of teleonomic processes or homeostatic systems. See, for example, A. Giddens, 'Functionalism: après la lutte', *Studies in Social and Political Theory* (London 1977), esp. p. 116, or A. Ryan, *The Philosophy of the Social Sciences* (London 1970), pp. 182–94. But on the whole, persons make a bad model for societies (and vice versa).
34. Marx, perhaps, comes closest to articulating this conception of history:

    History is nothing but the succession of the separate generations, each of which exploits the materials, the capital funds, the productive forces handed down to it by all preceding generations, and thus, on the one hand, continues the traditional activity in completely changed circumstances and, on the other, modifies the old circumstances with a completely changed activity (K. Marx and F. Engels, *The German Ideology* (London 1965), p. 65).

    The epistemic distance established in Model IV between society and people also indicates, at least schematically, a way in which substance can be given to the celebrated Marxian proposition that 'people make history, but not under conditions of their choice'. The 'people' here must of course be understood not just as acting idiosyncratically, but as expressing the definite and *general* interests and needs of particular strata and classes, where these are defined in the first instance by their differential relationships (of possession, access, etc.) to the productive resources constituting structural conditions of action. These productive resources in turn must be conceptualized generically so as to include *in principle*, for example, political and cultural resources as well as purely economic ones.

35. See *A Realist Theory of Science*, p. 113. See also M. Polanyi, *The Tacit Dimension* (London 1967), ch. 2.
36. E. Durkheim, *The Rules of Sociological Method*, p. 3.
37. See M. Weber, *Economy and Society* (New York 1968), p. 4.
38. See G. H. von Wright, *Norm and Action* (London 1963), p. 10.
39. Of course populations are continuous and provide a biological basis for social existence. But their social attributes, whether analysed stochastically or not, must be explicated on either relational or collectivist lines. And so they cannot provide the required social substrate without begging the question we are concerned with here.
40. Cf. Marx:

    I paint the capitalist and landlord in no sense *couleur de rose*. But here individuals are dealt with only in so far as they are personifications of economic categories, embodiments of particular class-relations and class-interests. My standpoint, from which the evolution of human society is viewed as a process of natural history, can no less than any other make the individual responsible for relations whose creature he socially remains, however much he may subjectively raise himself above them (*Capital*, 1 (London 1970), p. 10).

41. See especially T. Parsons, *The Structure of Social Action* (New York 1959), pp. 89–94 and *passim*.
42. According to Marx human beings 'begin to distinguish themselves from animals as soon as they begin to *produce* their means of subsistence' (*The German Ideology*, p. 31).

> The first premiss of all human existence and therefore of all history [is] the premiss . . . that men must be in a position to live in order to be able to 'make history'. But life involves before anything else eating and drinking, a habitation, clothing and many other things. The first historical act is thus the production of the means to satisfy these needs, the production of material life itself (*ibid.*, p. 39).

> The 'first historical act' must of course be understood in an analytical, not chronological, sense. Cf. also: 'In all forms of society it is a determinate production and its relations which assigns every other production and its relations their rank and influence. It is a general illumination in which all other colours are plunged and which modifies their specific tonalities. It is a special ether which defines the specific gravity of everything found within it' (*Grundrisse*, p. 107).

43. The problem for Marxism has always been to find a way of avoiding both economic (or worse technological) reductionism and historical eclecticism, so that it does actually generate some substantive historiographic propositions. It is a problem of which both Marx and Engels were aware. Thus as Engels was at pains to stress:

> According to the materialist conception of history, the economy is the ultimately determining element in history. [But] if someone twists this into saying that it is the *only* determining [one], he thereby transforms that proposition into a meaningless, abstract, senseless phrase. The economic situation is the basis, but the various elements of the superstructure . . . also exercise their influence upon the course of events . . . and in many cases preponderate in determining their form. There is an interaction of all these elements in which, amid the endless host of accidents, the economic movement finally asserts itself as necessary (F. Engels, Letter to J. Bloch, 21 Sept. 1890, *Marx–Engels Selected Works* 2 (London 1968), p. 692).

> But how is one to conceptualize this ultimate necessity? Marx provides a clue. Replying to an objection he concedes that 'the mode of production of material life dominates the development of social, political and intellectual life generally . . . is very true for our time, in which material interests preponderate, but not for the Middle Ages, in which Catholicism, nor for Athens or Rome, where politics, reigned supreme'. But Marx contends: 'this much [also] is clear. That the Middle Ages could not live on Catholicism, nor the Ancient World on politics [alone]. On the contrary, it is the economic conditions of the time that explain why here politics and there Catholicism played the chief part' (*Capital* 1, p. 81). Althusser has attempted to theorize this insight by saying that it is the economy that *determines* which relatively autonomous structure is the *dominant* one. See L. Althusser, *For Marx* (London 1969), especially chs. 2 and 6, and L. Althusser and E. Balibar, *Reading Capital* (London 1970).

44. See especially L. Colletti, 'Marxism and the Dialectic', *New Left Review* 93 (1975), and B. Ollman, *op. cit.*
45. See *A Realist Theory of Science*, esp. pp. 173–4. See also Marx's distinction between the 'method of presentation', which he characterizes 'as if a

priori', and the (a posteriori) 'method of inquiry' in *Capital*, 1, p. 19.

46. *Ibid.*, esp. ch. 2, sec. 6.

47. See N. Elias, 'The Sciences: Towards a Theory', *Social Processes of Scientific Development*, R. Whitley (ed.) (London 1974).

48. A. Labriola, *Essays on the Materialistic Conception of History* (Chicago 1904).

49. I. Kant, *Critique of Pure Reason*, N. Kemp Smith (trans.) (London 1970), B74/A51.

50. But is the notion of a 'field' that exists only in virtue of its effects any stranger, or prima-facie more absurd, than the combination of the principles of wave and particle mechanics in elementary micro-physics, which is now reckoned a commonplace?

51. See *A Realist Theory of Science*, app. to ch. 2.

52. *Ibid.*, ch. 2, sec. 4.

53. There is no problem about the empirical testing of theories of phenomena which are internally related (although there is a problem, which can only be resolved intra-theoretically, about the appropriate specification or individuation of the different aspects or parts). For the locus of the empirical is the observable, and discrete observable items can always be described in ways which are logically independent of one another. Hence even if social scientific theories can only be compared and tested *en bloc*, they can still be tested empirically. Thus because, say, 'capital' cannot be empirically identified and even if, as argued by Ollman (*op. cit.*), 'capital' cannot be univocally theoretically defined (or even conceptually stabilized), it does not follow that *theories* of capital cannot be empirically evaluated. The problem of the best individuation may then be resolved by considering which individuation is implied by (or necessary for) that theory which has the best causal grip on reality.

54. See, for example, N. Georgescu-Roegen, *The Entropy Law and the Economic Process* (Cambridge, Mass. 1971), esp. ch. 2.

55. See, for example, A. Cicourel, *Method and Measurement in Sociology* (New York 1964), esp. ch. 1.

56. See, for example, P. Duhem, *op. cit.*, pp. 180–90.

57. If correct, this has an analogue in the conscious technique of 'Garfinkel-ling' in social psychology – see, for example, H. Garfinkel, *Studies in Ethnomethodology* (New Jersey 1967) – and perhaps also in the role played by psychopathology in the development of a general psychology. See also A. Collier, *R. D. Laing: The Philosophy and Politics of Psychotherapy* (Hassocks 1977), p. 132.

58. Consider, for example, the way in which the mass unemployment of the 1930s not only provided the theoretical dynamo for the Keynesian innovation, but facilitated its ready acceptance by the relevant scientific community.

59. See P. Anderson, *Considerations on Western Marxism* (London 1976), for an extended discussion.

60. See, for example, G. Therborn, *Science, Class and Society* (London 1976), ch. 5, sec. 3.

61. See H. Lefebvre, 'What is the Historical Past?', *New Left Review* 90 (1975), esp. pp. 33–4.

62. See I. Lakatos, 'Falsification and the Methodology of Scientific Research Programmes', *Criticism and the Growth of Knowledge*, I, Lakatos and A. Musgrave (eds.) (Cambridge 1970).

63. See *A Realist Theory of Science*, p. 132. Cf. the notorious 'unfalsifiability'

of economic theories. See, for example, E. Grunberg, 'The Meaning of Scope and External Boundaries of Economics', *The Structure of Economic Science*, S. Krupp (ed.) (New Jersey 1966).

64. L. Goldmann, *Marxisme et sciences humaines* (Paris 1970), p. 250. See also Gadamer's strictures on statistics: 'such an excellent means of propaganda because they let facts speak and hence simulate an objectivity that in reality depends on the legitimacy of the questions asked' (*Truth and Method*, p. 268).

65. For example, the transformational model of social activity implies that it is a necessary condition for any adequate social theory that the theory be consistent with the reproduction (and/or transformation) of its object, and preferably that it should be able to specify the conditions under which such reproduction (and transformation) occurs. See, for example, M. Hollis and E. Nell, *Rational Economic Man* (Cambridge 1975), esp. ch. 8 for a criticism of neo-classical economic theory along these lines.

66. See *Capital*, 1, ch. 1. Such a critique bears a formal analogy to Kant's *Dialectic*. See D. Sayer, 'Science as Critique: Marx vs Althusser', *Issues in Marxist Philosophy*, J. Mepham and D. Ruben (eds.) (Hassocks 1979).

67. *Capital*, 1, pp. 90–1.

68. N. Geras, 'Essence and Appearance: Aspects of Fetishism in Marx's *Capital*', *New Left Review* 65 (1971), reprinted as 'Marx and the Critique of Political Economy', *Ideology in Social Science*, R. Blackburn (ed.) (London 1972), p. 297.

69. See *Capital*, 1, p. 537 and *Capital*, 3, p. 798 respectively.

70. K. Marx, 'Critique of the Gotha Programme', *Selected Works* (London 1968), p. 319.

71. See R. Edgley, 'Reason as Dialectic', *Radical Philosophy* 15 (Autumn 1976).

72. See, for example, S. B. Barnes, *Interests and the Growth of Knowledge* (London 1977), esp. ch. 1.

73. See, for example, J. Brennan, *The Open Texture of Moral Concepts* (London 1977), esp. pt. 2.

74. *Treatise*, esp. pp. 469–70. See R. Hare, *Freedom and Reason* (Oxford 1963), p. 108.

75. See M. Weber, *The Methodology of the Social Sciences* (Chicago 1949), esp. pp. 72–6.

76. See *A Realist Theory of Science*, p. 212.

77. See, for example, J. Slack, 'Class Struggle Among the Molecules', *Counter Course*, T. Pateman (ed.) (Harmondsworth 1972).

78. See Engels to Lafargue, 11 Aug. 1884: 'Marx rejected the "political, social and economic ideal" you attribute to him. A man of science has no ideals, he elaborates scientific results, and if he is also politically committed, he struggles for them to be put into practice. But if he has ideals, he cannot be a man of science, since he would then be biased from the start'; quoted in M. Godelier, 'System, Structure and Contradiction in *Capital*', *Socialist Register* (1967), reprinted in R. Blackburn (ed.), *op. cit.*, p. 354, n. 43. Of course what Engels omitted to mention was the possibility that Marx's scientific results might *imply* a political commitment.

79. For example G. Myrdal, *The Political Element in the Development of Economic Theory* (London 1953), or N. Chomsky, 'Objectivity and Liberal Scholarship', *American Power and the New Mandarins* (London 1969).

80. See, for example, G. Myrdal, *Value in Social Theory* (London 1959), p. 120.
81. See, interestingly, K. Mannheim, *Ideology and Utopia* (London 1960), pp. 300–1.
82. See *A Realist Theory of Science*, p. 249.
83. See L. Wittgenstein, *Philosophical Investigations* (Oxford 1963), p. 223.
84. A. Giddens, in an important work, *New Rules of Sociological Method*, p. 16, p. 161 and *passim*, systematically confuses the fact that the sociologist must utilize the cognitive resources of the agents under investigation in order to generate adequate descriptions of their conduct with the idea of their incorrigibility. He thus relapses into the pre-relativistic notion of incorrigible foundations of knowledge – despite an attempt to distinguish such incorrigible data from their representations as 'commonsense' (*ibid.*, p. 158). This is akin to trying to disentangle sense-data from their physical object implications. For such cognitive resources do not exist save in the form of beliefs such as 'X is voting, praying, stealing, working, etc.', embodying factual and theoretical presuppositions about the activities under question. It is thus not surprising that Giddens only sees the relationship between S_2 and S_1 as one of 'slippage' (*ibid.*, p. 162), potentially compromising, moreover, to S_2. But the relationship $S_2 \rightarrow S_1$ is not just of slippage, but potentially one of critique; and such a critique is far from neutral in its implications. For though slaves who fully comprehend the circumstances of their own subordination do not thereby become free, such an understanding is a necessary condition for their rational self-emancipation. Conversely their master has an interest in their remaining ignorant of the circumstances of their slavery. Knowledge is asymmetrically beneficial to the parties involved in relations of domination. Moreover, quite generally, explanatory knowledge increases the range of known possibilities and so *ceteris paribus* tilts the 'ideological balance-of-forces' against conservatism and the status quo (quite apart from its other effects). It is thus quite wrong to regard social science as *equally* 'a potential instrument of domination' as of 'the expansion of the rational autonomy of action' (*ibid.*, p. 159).
85. See, for example, R. Coward and J. Ellis, *Language and Materialism* (London 1977), p. 41.
86. According to Nagel, any threat to the value-neutrality of social science can be blocked by rigorously distinguishing between *appraising* value judgements which 'express *approval* or *disapproval* either of some moral (or social) ideal or of some action (or institution) because of commitment to such an ideal' and *characterizing* value judgements which 'express an *estimate* of the degree to which some commonly recognized (and more or less clearly defined) type of action, object or institution is embodied in a given instance' – E. Nagel, *The Structure of Science* (London 1961), p. 492. Thus the judgement that a person is anaemic on the basis of a red blood cell count is a characterizing one; while the judgement that anaemia is undesirable is an appraising one (*loc. cit.*). There are several problems with this counter. Firstly, it is unclear why Nagel calls a characterizing judgement a value judgement at all. In effect the characterizing/appraising distinction just transposes the very fact/value one in question. Secondly, Nagel treats social reality as unproblematic and social science as approximating the deductive model. He thus fails to see that while the atomic resolution of theoretically defined concepts may be plausible in the

case of some externally related natural phenomena, it is totally inapplicable to the reconstruction of social phenomena comprised of internally related elements. Institutions, such as the monarchy, and systems, for example of morality, either exist (and so must be grasped) *in toto* or they do not exist at all. Of course there are fuzzy boundaries and borderline cases, and descriptions require empirical testing. However, the occurrence of qualitative changes and the conceptual aspect of social reality limit the possibility of significant quantification in social science. Moreover, to confuse the empirical checking out of our descriptions in L_2 and the properties of *that* process, with what such descriptions describe (in S_1), and the properties *they* possess, is to commit the verificationist fallacy.

87. C. Taylor, 'Neutrality in Political Science', *Philosophy, Politics and Society*, 3rd Series, P. Laslett and W. Runciman (eds.) (Oxford 1967), reprinted in A. Ryan (ed.), *op. cit.*

88. *Ibid.*, p. 161.

89. See, for example, *ibid.*, pp. 145–6, p. 148 and *passim*.

90. See J. R. Searle, 'How to Derive "Ought" from "Is"', *Philosophical Review* 73 (1964) and *Speech Acts* (Cambridge 1969), ch. 8.

91. For example if one believed that it was morally wrong to commit oneself and others to action in the future.

92. See, for example, R. Swinburne, 'The Objectivity of Morality', *Philosophy* 51 (1976).

93. See R. Edgley, *Reason in Theory and Practice* (London 1969), esp. 4.11.

94. K. Marx, *Capital*, 1, p. 505.

95. See N. Geras, 'Althusser's Marxism: An Assessment', *New Left Review* 71, reprinted in *Western Marxism: A Critical Reader*, G. Stedman Jones *et al.* (London 1977).

96. See G. Stedman Jones, 'The Marxism of the Early Lukács', *New Left Review* 70, reprinted in G. Stedman Jones *et al.*, *op. cit.*

97. See D. Lecourt, *Proletarian Science?* (London 1977).

98. The key to Hegelian philosophy, which enables it to achieve its philosophical coup. viz. the reconciliation of the Kantian antinomies, is precisely the realization by consciousness, in the form of the absolute spirit, that its object is in the end nothing other than itself. This involves precisely the denial of the *autonomous* existence of matter; that is, of its existence except as one moment in the development of Geist, the self-realization of the absolute idea. For Marx, in contrast, 'neither thought nor language . . . form a realm of their own, they are only *manifestations* of actual life' (*The German Ideology*, C. Arthur (ed.) (London 1974), p. 118), so that 'consciousness can never be anything else than conscious existence' (*ibid.*, p. 47).

99. This notion cannot be explicated here. But among its standard implications are the following ideas: (1) that the economic, and beneath that, the biological and ultimately the physical – see S. Timpanaro, *On Materialism* (London 1975) – set boundary conditions for the non-economic; (2) that the economic partly – and over – determines the non-economic; (3) that ideas must be explained at least in part by something other than ideas – something which need not be material but must be 'materialized' in order to exist as a social object; (4) that all social phenomena are intransitive (in the sense of p. 47); (5) that all social phenomena require a material substrate and/or possess a material referent.

100. See, for example, N. Stockman, 'Habermas, Marcuse and the *Aufhebung*

of Science and Technology', *Philosophy of the Social Sciences* 8 (1978), and T. Eagleton, *Criticism and Ideology* (London 1976), on the material bases of science and literature respectively.

101. The currently fashionable rejection of the criterion of false consciousness by those who wish to define ideology solely by reference to its serving 'concealed' interests or its embodying 'unnecessary' domination pre-supposes that it might be possible to detect those interests or its role without a theory capable of explaining the phenomena that the ideological theory did. It thus presupposes that the conditions under which the *I*-theory holds are irrelevant to its explanation; and hence either that it is groundless or that one can study it in isolation from its grounds.

102. 'The vulgar economists' way of looking at things stems . . . from the fact that it is only the direct form of manifestation of relations that is reflected in their brains and not their inner connections' (letter from Marx to Engels, 27 June 1867, *Marx–Engels Selected Correspondence* (Moscow 1956)). 'Vulgar economy actually does no more than interpret, systematize and defend in doctrinaire fashion the conceptions of agents of bourgeois production who are entrapped in bourgeois production relations' (K. Marx, *Capital*, 3, p. 817). 'In opposition to Spinoza, it believes that "ignorance is sufficient reason"' (K. Marx, *Capital*, 1, p. 307).

103. M. Godelier, 'System, Structure and Contradiction in *Capital*', *Socialist Register* (1967), reprinted in R. Blackburn (ed.), *op. cit.*, p. 337.

104. K. Marx, *Capital*, 1, p. 540. Dealing with the transformation of the value of labour power into that of labour in consciousness, Marx says 'this phenomenal form which makes the real relation invisible, and indeed shows the exact opposite of that relation, forms the basis for all the juridical notions of both labourer and capitalist, of all the mystifications of the capitalist mode of production, of all its illusions as to liberty, of all the apologetic shifts of the vulgar economists' (*loc. cit.*). Moreover, whereas 'the value of labour appears directly and spontaneously as a current mode of thought, the [value of labour power] must first be discovered by science. Classical political economy nearly touches the true relations of things, without, however, consciously formulating it. This it cannot do so long as it sticks to its bourgeois skin' (*ibid.*, p. 542).

105. J. Mepham, 'The Theory of Ideology in *Capital*', *Radical Philosophy* 2 (1972), p. 18.

106. After L. Colletti, *op. cit.*

107. See, for example, L. Althusser, 'Ideology and Ideological State Apparatuses', *Lenin and Philosophy* (London 1971), pp. 160ff. It should be noted that these category mistakes are corrigible in analysis, so that Marković's paradox, viz. that an account of social reality as reified (etc.) must itself embody reified elements (see M. Marković, 'The Problem of Reification and the *Verstehen–Erklären* Controversy', *Acta Sociologica* 15 (1972)) does not vitiate Marxism.

108. L. Colletti, *op. cit.*, especially pp. 21–2.

109. See *ibid.*, p. 6.

Chapter 3

Agency

Introduction

In Chapter 2 I showed how the properties that societies possess might make them objects of knowledge for us. A key step in the development of the argument consisted in the demonstration of the ontological irreducibility of societies to people. I now want to consider how we can come to have knowledge of people.

In considering the properties that people possess that might make them objects of knowledge for us, I shall once more be concerned to demonstrate the existence of certain fundamental features or powers, establish their irreducibility to simpler or more basic ones, and show how it is in virtue of the existence and exercise of these powers that an autonomous science – in this case of psychology – is possible. The powers most naturally invoked here are those that involve consciousness, that is, those states of persons in virtue of which mentalistic predicates are applicable. And my aim here again will be to consider the extent to which the hypothesis of naturalism, viz. that there are generative structures, knowable to us, producing the manifest phenomena (in this case of consciousness), can be vindicated – in the domain now of the psychological sciences. This question can be transposed to the one familiar to philosophers as: '*Can reasons be causes*?' For the category of reasons, though not free from ambiguity, is that in terms of which we most naturally couch explanations for human conduct; and generative structures are, analytically, causal. It is my aim here to provide an affirmative answer to that question. Such an answer is of course already presupposed by the argument of Chapter 2 in which the reality of social forms was established by reference to their causal efficacy in affecting states of the material world, as mediated through intentional human agency. So that in this way I will also be completing the argument of the previous chapter.

It may be helpful if I indicate my position at the outset. I am going to argue that intentional human behaviour is caused, and that it is always caused by reasons, and that it is only because it is caused by reasons that it is properly characterized as intentional. The agent (and others) may or may not be aware of the reasons that cause his/her intentional behaviour. Now any explanation of the reasons that form the immediate (naturalistic) explanations of human actions may necessarily have recourse both to psychological mechanisms, unavailable to conscious-ness, and to non-psychological (e.g., physiological and sociological) ones. So although a stratified science of psychology is possible, its objects act in open systems co-determined by the effects of non-psychological mechanisms. Moreover, the mechanisms delineated as 'psychological' may be radically non-homogeneous and affected by the operation of non-psychological mechanisms; so that there can be no presumption that a unified, or say ahistorical, science of psychology is possible.

I shall commence my defence of naturalism here by more or less dogmatically asserting the existence of certain powers, postponing their elucidation until later. The argument of the second and third sections establishes, against idealism, the *reality* of these powers, and the argument of the fourth and fifth sections establishes, against materialism and behaviourism, their *irreducibility* to purely physical operations and overt behaviour respectively, so vindicating the autonomy of psychology as the putative science (or ensemble of sciences) of mind. In the last section I shall consider the status and limits of intentional human agency.

An entity x may be said to possess a *mind* at time t if and only if it is the case that it possesses at t the capacity either to acquire or to exercise the acquired ability to creatively manipulate symbols.[1] In this chapter I intend to show that the capacities that constitute mind, as so conceived, are properly regarded as causal, and that mind is a *sui generis* real emergent power of matter, whose autonomy, though real, is neverthe-less circumscribed.

The concept of a *person*, in its normal employment, is a unitary concept of an entity to which both of two types of predicates (material and psychological) are applicable.[2] As persons *act*, it seems obvious that the powers one should first pay attention to here are those which are implicated in the notion of a person's *activity*. Now *praxis*, doing or acting, typically consists in causally intervening in the natural (material) world, subject to the possibility of a reflexive monitoring of that intervention. These two aspects of praxis are of course reflected in our material and psychological predications respectively. But note that the first aspect is both logically and temporally (both phylogenetically and ontogenetically) prior to the second. The capacity for a reflexive self-monitoring of one's own causal interventions in the world, to be aware of one's own states of awareness during one's activity (to monitor the monitoring of one's activity), is intimately connected with our pos-session of a language, conceived as a system of signs apt for the production and communication of information. For any entity *x* that lacked the capacity to refer to its own states of consciousness (and to interiorize references to itself in the third person) could not *use* those states of consciousness for the production and communication of information, and so could not be said to possess a language. Conversely any *x* which could so use its states of consciousness must possess the capacity to make its own past and anticipated states of awareness the present objects of its awareness. Such reflexivity over time would seem, then, to be a necessary condition for any discursive (non-intuitive) intelligence. And given our actual linguistic (and paralinguistic) skills, it enables a simultaneous, retrospective or anticipatory commentary[3] upon our actual or imagined causal interventions in the world, typically expressed in the media of sound, mark and gesture. Both intervention and commentary are, of course, always the situated doings of agents at places in time.

Now human activity is in fact a more or less continous stream in time of such (more or less deliberate, more or less routine) causal intervening in the world, subject to the continuing possibility of reflexive self-awareness, only analytically separable into *episodes*. But to talk of such a stream as one of human activity itself presupposes an analytical distinction in the total biography of our bodies. For besides our praxes, that is, (α) the things that we do, there are (β) the things that happen to us. It is customary to restrict the term 'action' to the former. 'And the problem arises: what is left over if I subtract the fact that my arm goes up from the fact that I raise my arm?'[4] It is natural to answer that in the latter case 'I intended it' and to say that a piece of behaviour is only properly described as an action, as distinct from a mere movement, if I intended something I did in or by it; if, that is, it is *intentional* under some description. Now the same action may be redescribed, correctly, in terms of its effects (results and consequences), which may or may not be intentional. Thus I may flick a switch to turn on a light, to illustrate a philosophical point, blowing a fuse, so annoying my host, but also alerting a prowler, etc. This is the familiar 'accordion effect' of action – in which, in a single action, a number of different acts (some intentional, some not) are performed. Acts, then, are what are done in or by actions. There is in general no single correct description of an action, independent of context and descriptive purposes, of it as an act of a particular type. But there is always in principle a correct decision as to whether a piece of behaviour is an action or not (turning on whether it is intentional under some description or not). Moreover, it is clear that there must be some things that we just do ('basic acts')[5] and do not do by doing other things or, given that action is a process in time, we could never do anything at all. But it is not clear that there is any one class of acts that *must* be basic. Thus 'trying to move a limb' can sometimes describe an action.[6] However it would seem that if a piece of behaviour is correctly described as a basic act then it must also be the case that it be performed intentionally. Now it is important to note that an action can, like any other event, be misdescribed; and by the agent, as well as by an observer. Thus perlocutionary characterizations of human agency (characterizations of what is done *by* it)[7] are always liable to be reversed or superseded in the 'pile of debris' wrought by the accordion effects of actual history.[8] But even illocutionary characterizations (that is, characterizations of what is done *in* an action) in terms of basic-action-kinds by the agents concerned are corrigible. Thus a long-suffering patient may sincerely believe that s/he is trying to move a limb, and yet s/he may be merely, as one says, 'going through the motions'.

When a reason is cited in explanation of a human action any of a whole variety of mental items may be invoked. But, at least typically, it seems that in any such explanation both cognitive and conative considerations are involved – in that if a cognitive item, such as a belief, is mentioned, a conative one, such as a desire, is presupposed, and vice versa.[9] Now the particular concept of causality at work will clearly be vital in any assessment of the causal status of reasons (of whatever type). When something is cited as a cause it is, I think, most typically being viewed as that factor which, in the circumstances that actually prevailed, 'so tipped the balance of events as to produce the known outcome'.[10] Clearly such a concept is non-Humean and generative. But any full transcendental realist defence of the naturalistic status of reason explanations will need to show not only that reason explanations function in our discourse in a causal kind of way, but that reasons are analogous to the causal structures of nature and that empirical knowledge of them is possible. My strategy in this project will be first to rebut the arguments that have led philosophers to deny that reasons can be causes; next to show why if, *inter alia*, they are to discharge their explanatory function (that is, if naturalism is to be possible here), they must be causes; then to sketch a model designed to show how reasons may plausibly be construed as causes and how it is, just in virtue of those powers of people in virtue of which reasons come to be possessed, maintained and exercised, that knowledge of them is possible.

Agents, Reasons and Causes I: Objections to Naturalism

Why, then, is it denied that reasons can be causes?

1. The *teleological argument* turns on certain alleged logical differences

between teleological explanations, to which reason explanations are assimilated, and casual ones. Thus contrast (a) '*X* occurs for the sake of *Y*' and (b) '*X* causes *Y*'. It is contended that in (a): (i) the focus of interest is *X*, (ii) *X* is consistent with the non-occurrence of *Y* and (iii) a change in *Y* will bring about a change in *X*; whereas in (b) the reverse of all these propositions holds. (i) seems arbitrary. Ordinary causal explanations, as well as teleological ones, are defeasible in open systems, so that (ii) fails. But (iii) fails also. For a change in *Y* will only bring about a change in *X* if, as in the case of a thermostat, the desired end-state is represented by a place in a series temporally prior to *X*, say *W*, in which case (i) fails as well. Thus teleological explanations are most naturally construed as a species of ordinary causal explanation, where the cause is, in the case of reasons, some antecedent state of mind.

2. *Vicious regress arguments* of the sort elaborated by Melden and Ryle, though specifically directed against 'acts of the will', can be generalized in an attempt to show that human actions cannot have any causes of a mentalistic type. Now to have a reason for an action I do not have to have a reason for that reason. Moreover possession of a reason should not in general be construed as an action, but rather as a disposition or state. And the possession of a reason for an action can itself be sufficient for that action, when appropriate circumstances materialize. Thus if I am a German social democrat, I do not have to wait upon a further reason to vote SPD on polling day – I just exercise my reason in voting. So at no possible point of application does a vicious regress in fact arise.

3. Behaviourism replaces introspectionism as a non-solipsistic empirical realist theory of mind. As such, *behaviourist arguments* are not designed to show that reasons cannot be causes, but rather either that the category of reasons is altogether otiose, or that reasons are not mental causes but redescriptions of overt behaviour. Now even *if* it were the case that the only grounds for ascribing reasons were overt behavioural ones (and that these could be identified in a way which did not already presuppose mentalistic predicates),[11] it would not follow that reasons (a) were not mental or (b) could not be efficient causes of behaviour. To suppose the former is to commit the 'verificationist' fallacy of confusing what a claim is about with our grounds for making it. To suppose the latter is to commit the 'essentialist' fallacy of holding that the only real causes are ultimate ones (a position that inexorably makes *all*, not just mentalistic, causal claims unverifiable). Appeals to ordinary usage are at best indecisive. And behaviour, no less than speech, has first to be *interpreted* in terms of a language in order to give grounds for a causal claim. But as such interpretation is, or depends upon, a

mental act or process, a behaviourist analysis of behaviourist practice is impossible.

4. A *verstehende argument*, from the meaningful or intelligible nature of reasons, is often advanced to show that they cannot be causes. Now inasmuch as the epistemological claim is made that the natural world cannot be made, in a scientific redescription and explanation of it, intelligible, then it must be rejected. But inasmuch as the ontological claim is made that the social world is already constituted as meaningful, prior to the application of scientific theory to it, then a clear difference between it and the natural world must be accepted.[12] However, the significance of this difference for the argument in question must be carefully considered. For the meaning of an action such as 'chopping wood' or 'saying "hullo"', that is, its correct identification as an act of a particular type in a particular language and culture, is always and in principle independent of the intention with which it is on some particular occasion, by some particular agent, performed.[13] (This is not of course to deny the importance of a hermeneutic understanding of the language or culture for the correct *identification* of the latter.) Now the immediate *explananda* of reason explanations are intentional acts.[14] And it is a necessary condition for an act to be correctly described as intentional that the agent *believes* (perhaps unconsciously) it to possess some quality that is *desired* or more generally wanted (again perhaps unconsciously). Thus that which one wants to discover in what a reason explanation allows one immediately to explain is not its correct social meaning, but the trait or quality that the agent believes his/her action to possess (which could be called actor's meaning). And the explanation will typically proceed by reconstructing the set of beliefs which led the agent to want to perform an action manifesting that quality. That the reason for the behaviour is itself a belief (or set of beliefs) differentiates it from *physical* causes, which are not beliefs and can only be the objects of beliefs; but does not suffice to show that such reasons cannot be causes. For that a stronger argument is required.

5. The *logical connection argument* is generally regarded as the strongest in the anti-causalist's battery. It contends that (a) causes must be logically distinct from effects; but (b) reasons are not logically distinct from the actions they explain; so that (c) they cannot be their causes. Both premises are faulty. It is quite improper to talk of events, as distinct from their descriptions, being logically connected or not. Logic connects statements, not events, actions and the like, which are connected, when they are, by relations of natural necessity. Now, that to identify (or redescribe) a human action in terms of its cause should sometimes suffice to explain it in no way differentiates human actions from other natural events, which are

often redescribed in terms of their causes (for example, toast as burnt, a flash as lightning). Moreover, their identification in such a way that the description of the cause logically entails the description of the effect is exactly paralleled by the class of physical action statements (such as 'he drank the coffee') that underlie our ordinary attributions of causality.[15] But actions can also normally be redescribed independently of their reasons. 'Flicking the switch' is logically independent of 'turning on the light', but my *reason* for flicking the switch (for example, my desire to illuminate the room) is always and in principle independent of the successful performance of the act which is its intentional object.

The fact that the notion of wanting (or desiring or intending) to do *x* logically presupposes the notion of doing *x* (that intentionality presupposes agency; that one cannot just intend, one has to intend to do something, as Husserl and the phenomenological tradition have stressed) is exactly paralleled by the fact that the notion of a cause logically presupposes that of an effect (*x* cannot just be a cause, it has to be the cause of something).[16] So if one represents the former fact by saying that there is an internal connection between 'wanting to do *x*' and 'doing *x*', the latter fact must equally be represented by saying that there is an internal connection between 'causing *x*' and '*x*'. *Ceteris paribus* prolonged exposure to the sun results in sunburn, just as *ceteris paribus* (henceforth usually *CP*) my wanting to illuminate the room results in my turning on the light. Once set in motion a cause tends to issue in an effect that bears its trace and a reason in an action that the agent believes will fulfil or satisfy it.[17] This is a necessary or conceptual truth. But it is contingent, and up to science to discover, in any particular case, what the generative causes or reasons are. So where the logical connection theorist posits a radical dichotomy, one discovers instead exact parallels.

6. According to the next set of considerations, reasons and causes differentiate, not distinct kinds of events or happenings, but distinctive types of explanation. Typically, it is argued that to cite a reason is to talk at a different logical level, or as Waismann put it *language stratum*, from that at which one talks of the causes of natural events. This thesis has a distinctly Kantian air, and is compatible (as in Davidsonian 'anomalous monism')[18] with the idea that all events are governed by a closed deterministic system of (Humean) 'laws', that is, empirical invariances. In support of this position it is argued: (a) that criteria for identity are different in the case of human actions and bodily movements; (b) that the contexts in which reasons and causes are cited are logically discrepant; and (c) that there are fundamental differences in the conceptual structures of paradigms of the two modes of explanations.

(a) Now as, in general, open systems are characterized by both a plurality and a multiplicity of causes, the fact that the same bodily movement may be used to perform different actions, and that the same action may be performed with different bodily movements,[19] should hardly surprise us. It is a Humean myth to suppose that for any given event (under a particular description) there is a unique set of antecedent or concomitant conditions under which it is constantly conjoined. So one has no grounds here for saying that there is not a real difference between a human action and a mere bodily movement in that in the former (but not the latter) case a determinate set of reasons figures among its causes.

(b) turns on the fact that reasons are typically offered in justificatory contexts.[20] Now it would seem to be a necessary condition for any adequate justification R of an action A_t that R was the reason why the agent performed that action at t. And it is difficult to see how this claim can be explicated without making use of the notion of R causing it. Behind (b), however, lies a consideration of some importance in explicating the nature of reasons. For in contradistinction from other causes, we *appraise* reasons *qua* beliefs for consistency, truth, coherence, etc. And we appraise them in particular from a certain standpoint, necessitated by the irreducibility of intentionality – that of their suitability for believing (accepting) and acting upon. I shall call this standpoint that of the *axiological imperative*. Such appraisals of beliefs are necessitated by the condition that what I am to do can never be reduced to, or discovered by scrutiny of the antecedents of, what I will do.[21] For what I will do will happen not in spite, but *because*, of any decisions, etc., I take (and more generally, the beliefs and purposes I have). Thus the appropriate picture of the agent's situation is not one of two series: one (S_1) in which it is determined what is going to happen, and the other (S_2) in which the agent has plans and beliefs, desires and intentions, and generally cogitates his/her life. Of course if this picture was appropriate there would be a problem of how, if S_1 existed (irrespective of the degree of our access to it), there was any room for S_2. But there is only one series, ontologically speaking, and it is continuous with S_2. And it is an error of the greatest magnitude to suppose that what is going to happen in the future is (epistemically) determined before it is (ontologically) caused.[22] For, when it is caused, it will be caused by the action of bodies, preformed, complex and structured, possessing powers irreducible to their exercise, endowed with various degrees of self-regulation (and transformation), in thoroughgoing interaction with one another, and subject to a flow of contingencies that can never be predicted with certainty. The future is open. As for human agents, it is contingent that they exist and have the powers that they do. But given that they do, they cannot help but co-determine it.

Consider now the arguments grouped around (c). Compare the paradigms (α) 'I raised my arm' with (β) 'my arm went up'. In the future tense (α) expresses an intention, (β) a prediction. The answer to the question 'why' in (α) will be a story about reasons, purposes and the like, in (β) one about reflexes, nerves and muscles, for which the agent, in contrast with the former case, clearly has no special or privileged authority. These differences are then taken to show that one is dealing with a difference in category, or level of discourse, here. Now undoubtedly they do show that, in our conceptual system, we differentiate actions from mere movements and reasons from (physical) causes. But they do not show how, or on what criteria, such a differentiation is made; or indeed how it could be made unless actions were regarded (paradigmatically) as the class of bodily movements with reasons as their causes. For the language-stratum theorist must logically be committed to some form of epiphenomenalism or double aspect theory, in which the intentional level is conceived as the anomalous causal effect or a taxonomic redescription of (some elements at) the neurophysiological level. In any event, it is clear that, on language-stratum theory, reasons cannot affect the sequence of physical events that actually occur: they hover, as it were, in a noumenal cloud, like the smoke over the factory[23] or motes above the stream,[24] above and unconnected to whatever it is that actually happens, being as irrelevant to the latter as the colour of a machine is to its functioning, 'a lyric cry in the midst of business',[25] playing no real-generative role in the life of women and men.

Given this, two problems arise. Firstly, in any given context where it is deemed that reason explanations are appropriate, there can be no grounds independent of subjective preference (or its socialized form, custom or convention) for preferring one reason explanation to another. And note that, in virtue of this, both the agent's special authority and his/her responsibility collapses. If we choose to give the agent's explanation prima-facie credibility this is just a fact about our charitable liberal culture: it is not because the agent really does or might know more about what motivated him/her to perform one bodily movement (say kicking) rather than another (say kissing). And if we choose to hold him/her responsible for his/her bodily movements, this is again a fact about our intolerant moralistic culture: it is not because the bodily movement was produced in part by some state of mind of his/hers. (For were it to be, one would of course have to count such a state of mind a cause.)

Secondly, in virtue of what are reason explanations deemed

appropriate at all? For no more than those motes above the stream do reasons co-determine the states of the world. Given this, there is as much sense in trying to discover an agent's reason for his/her heartbeat as there is for his/her voting behaviour – the bodily movements are as little and as much determined by reasons in both sets of cases: that is to say, not at all. Our actual habits – of investigation, ascription and persuasion – appear as wishful illusions; and, if apparently motivated behaviour or its consequences are regarded as undesirable, the only way to alter them is by operating on the purely physical causes of the bodily movements concerned.[26]

It can thus be seen that, denied ontological purchase on the phenomenal world of bodily movements and physical happenings, both the status of reason explanations in general, and the particular reasons adduced in explanation, must ultimately appear as arbitrary, and the practices that depend upon them as illusory. Indeed, in the end, the very distinction on which the language-stratum theorist pitches his brief, between things that we do (α), like catching buses, and things that happen to us (β), like catching colds, becomes impossible to sustain. For it is only if we are the cause of some but not other of our bodily movements that such a contrast can be maintained; and that we can properly be said to act at all.

For the transcendental realist there is no problem in sustaining such a contrast, and such a concept. For in the (α), but not the (β) case, the agent's reasons are a necessary condition for the bodily movements that occurred, in the straightforward sense that had the agent not possessed them (and unless the bodily movements were overdetermined) they would not have occurred.[27] So that reasons are appropriately and correctly invoked in the former but not the latter case, and the source of the agent's special authority readily explained.

It should be stressed that to grant causal status to reasons necessitates no exemption to (or break in) natural laws. Indeed intentional human actions may best be regarded as setting initial and boundary conditions for the operation of physical laws; and reasons, when they are efficacious, for the operation of neurophysiological ones. For, contrary to myth, laws are typically universal, in that they apply to all members of a kind, without being deterministic, in the sense of completely determining the behaviour of the members of that kind.[28]

Of course the paradigms (α) and (β) get modified in practice. Thus one has the ($\alpha\beta$) case where the agent seems to be the cause of the things that happen to him/her (as in the case of the accident-prone person) and the ($\beta\alpha$) case where the things that happen (or have happened) to an agent seem to be the cause of what s/he does (as in the case of Freudian parapraxes). But this only introduces the more general phenomenon of mind–body dependency or inter-influence. Thus for ages the sexes have acted on the assumption that people react differently to the same suggestion under the influence of different bodily states ($\bar{\beta}\alpha$). The notion of a psychosomatic illness marks the reverse dependency ($\bar{\alpha}\beta$). None of this helps the language-stratum theorist, however, who is committed to denying all forms of interaction, in virtue of the transcategorial causality it seemingly entails.

7. Finally, various *contrast arguments* are frequently marshalled in support of the above arguments. Thus it is asserted that laws are involved in causal, but not reason explanations, which are essentially particular; that reasons but not causes are dispositions or states, rather than events; that to identify reasons and causes is to confuse a person's grounds for acting with the physiological mechanisms producing his/her behaviour; that causality entails determinism which is incompatible with the idea of free (and/or responsible) agents, presupposed by reason explanations. I have no space to deal with these arguments separately. But enough should already have been said to indicate how they may be countered on transcendental realist lines.

Agents, Reasons and Causes II: Naturalism Vindicated

Having rejected the arguments designed to show that reasons cannot be causes, I now want to argue that they *must* be causes if (1) they are to discharge their explanatory function; (2) discursive thought is to be possible; and (3) in particular, the concept of agency is to be saved.

First, it is clear that a person may possess a reason R for doing A, do A and yet R not be the reason why s/he does it.[29] It is only if X does A *because* of R that we are justified in citing R as the reason for A_t. And there would seem to be no way of explicating the 'because' save in terms of causality. For unless the reason was, in context, a necessary condition for the physical movement that actually occurred CP then, as I have just argued, both the decision to invoke a reason explanation and the particular reason explanation given must appear as totally arbitrary. Like a good fairy-tale it may soothe and satisfy the listener, but it cannot explain. If and whenever they explain, then, reasons must be interpreted as causes, on pain of ceasing to explain at all.

I now want to argue that a distinction between *real* and *possible* reasons (R_r/R_p) is essential to any discursive life; that this distinction cannot be explicated save in terms of the causal efficacy of real reasons;

and that the criterion for attributing such efficacy consists in their effect on states of the physical world. In particular I want to maintain three theses:

T_1: any cognitive activity that takes thought as its object presupposes the possibility of the R_r/R_p distinction;

T_2: any cognitive activity that takes action as its object presupposes the causal efficacy of reasons; and

T_3: the criterion of causal efficacy is 'making a difference' to the state of affairs that would otherwise have prevailed in the material world.

T_3 is relatively uncontroversial. It is clearly in T_1 and/or T_2 that the anti-causalist is likely to suspect a fish.

The class of possible reasons includes thought and unthought ones; and the former includes contemplated, conjectured, imaginary, imagined, professed and attributed reasons, as well as (cutting across all but imaginary reasons) real ones. Consider the notion of *pretence*, a species of the wider concept play. It is ironical that Winch should point out (in a book dedicated to the proposition that the category of causality can have no application to the social life of human beings) that in order for there to be criteria for the correct application of rules one must be able to distinguish the case where an agent is *actually* following a rule from the case where he is merely *pretending* to.[30] But how can such a distinction be maintained, unless the former case is explicated in terms of the rule, through the reason it gives the agent for behaving (or 'carrying on') in one way rather than another, actually motivating, that is being causally responsible for (or generating), his behaviour, identified in the last instance through the interpretation of the sequence of sounds or marks the agent makes? Or consider the notion of *rationalization*, most naturally explicated in terms of an R_r/R_p distinction, the former again presupposing the category of causality. More generally such a distinction may be seen to be a condition of a whole gamut of mental activities and states, ranging from false avowals made under post-hypnotic suggestion[31] through self-deception and dissimulation to the very possibility of self-doubt. But it is not difficult to see that the more mundane possibility that one has incorrectly described some state of consciousness ϵ by '$T\epsilon$' is a condition of possibility of any discursive thought at all. For it must be possible to be in error and doubt (and to be in error and doubt about error and doubt, so that Cartesian doubt is no exception), to conjecture, hypothesize and learn about the states of mind of oneself and others not just for rational argument about those states (and *a fortiori* for a science of psychology). It must be possible to do so for the acquisition and development of a mentalistic vocabulary in the first place, and hence for *any* science or culture (which of course logically presupposes it). In this way the logical possibility of error about, misdescription and misrecognition of one's own state of awareness, and hence *inter alia* of one's reasons, is a condition of any reflexive intelligence. In consciousness reason and consciousness of reason remain distinct.[32] And it is doubly important to be on one's guard against any Cartesian collapse of the intransitive dimension here. For such a collapse would function at once to make an a posteriori psychology and a changing science impossible.

Turning to T_2, notice that unless a reason could function as a cause there would be no sense in a person evaluating (or appraising) different beliefs in order to decide how to act. For either a reason will make a difference to his/her behaviour or it will not. In the former case it counts as a cause. In the latter case it is logically redundant, and deliberation, ratiocination (and indeed thought generally) become practically otiose. Note that this argument applies in principle also to purely theoretical reasoning, where the agent is making up his/her mind what (or whether) to believe (disbelieve, entertain, consider the implications of, etc.). In short, any cognitive activity that takes action as its object or result (of whatever kind) presupposes the causal efficacy of reasons, in the sense of their making a possible difference to the physical states that will actually obtain.

Now it follows from T_1 and T_2 that any activity which purports to be both rational and practical, such as science (or more generally any praxis in the sense explicated in the first section), presupposes the causal efficacy of reasons. The anti-causalist must thus either concede defeat or abandon the phenomena (including all the recognizable practices of intellectual and practical life) or embrace some fantastic theory of pre-established harmony, where everything is so arranged by a Hand (or occurs as a result of some most providential improbability) that it always appears *just as if* reasons functioned as causes of happenings in the physical world.

I submit, then, that a real reason R may be defined as a reason possessed by some agent X at t which was causally efficacious in producing (bringing about) X's behaviour at t. A criterion for distinguishing intentional actions from mere bodily movements, and hence for elucidating the difference between the (α) and (β) paradigms quickly follows. In the former case a real reason (or complex of reasons) R is a necessary condition for the bodily movement M at t, in the sense that but for the possession and exercise of R, in the circumstances that actually prevailed, M would not have occurred at t, unless it was overdetermined.

Now it is clear that if the concept of human agency is to be sustained, it must be the case that *we* are responsible for some but not other of our bodily movements. And unless our responsibility is causal, agency follows in the wake of reason explanations and intentionality as just another fairy-tale. It might be thought that a conflict arises between agent– and reason–causality. But this is not so. For agents are defined in terms of their tendencies and powers, among which, in the case of human agents, are their reasons for acting.

Having argued that reasons must be causes, I now want to develop a sketch of an argument designed to show how, in relation to our normal concepts of reason and causality, reasons may be plausibly construed as causes; and how, in virtue of the properties of people set out in the first section, the a posteriori confirmation and disconfirmation of reason explanations is possible.

First, viewing a cause as a lever or a generative condition, consider the simple case where X tells Y that Z, to whom he is engaged, is having an affair with A. Now it would be absurd to deny that X's speech action was not the lever, trigger or stimulus condition for Y's subsequent behaviour (whatever that might be); in short, it would be absurd to deny that it was its cause. Note that X's is a separately identifiable act; and that this paradigm may be generalized to cover forms of behaviour other than speech.

The next step in the argument consists in appreciating that the reason does not have to be provided by someone else to function as the precipitating cause of a person's behaviour. In virtue of our second-order monitoring powers we can supply ourselves with reasons for acting, and in fact do so continually. Of course such reasons may be rationalizations. Thus *excuses* are typically the externalized form of a releasing condition for a course of action already 'set upon', grounded in terms of socially acceptable or psychologically undisturbing principles and norms. But the powers that make rationalization possible also permit its detection. More generally, the reason given by the agent is subject to two types of control: the control of *negotiation* in dialogue; and the control of *coherence* with the rest of the agent's behaviour.[33]

The third step in the argument involves coming to see that not just events, but states and dispositions may properly be said to be causes. Thus the *possession* of a reason, conceived as a more or less long-standing disposition or orientation to act in a certain way, may itself be a cause – as being a social democrat gives an agent a reason for voting Labour. We have now reached a level which accords with our normal concept of a reason. Such reasons are clearly distinct from actions: they are possessed even when unexercised, and only exercised under suitable conditions, for example on polling days. In general they have to be analysed normically, that is, as tendencies; and like any tendency manifest in open systems, they are defeasible in special circumstances (for example, illness) or under the pressure of countervailing reasons. Note that they have a degree of manifest generality, and are subject to independent controls, as in the second step above.

Given that the naturalistic intuitions of everyday life have been vindicated, the question must be asked to what extent such reasons can themselves be explained in terms of the explanatory theories of the human sciences. Now suppose X is a trade-unionist and votes Labour; his/her behaviour may be subsumed under the normic generalization G, 'trade-unionists tend to vote Labour'. But just as in the natural sciences generalizations such as Boyle's Law require explanation in terms of theories, such as the Kinetic one, so G itself stands in need of explanation. Supposing it is explained in terms of the theory T that people tend to vote according to their perception of their class interests; then, paralleling the stratification of the natural sciences, this theory of voting behaviour may itself be explained in terms of some higher-order (and more general) theory, such as of class structure, T'. Note, in a distinction of great importance, that T only explains why a trade-unionist such as X tends to vote Labour; it does not explain why X is (such) a trade-unionist. It is a social, not a psychological explanation: it explains the role, not the person. Of course there is also space for a theory of the acquisition and maintenance of such tendencies in specific social contexts by specific kinds of person; that is, for a social psychology that would connect X's voting behaviour to his/her psychic nature. (Such a social psychology is logically presupposed by the temporal extension of the social system over time.) And, if, as seems (*pace* Eysenck) unlikely, there were grounds for positing a direct link between the two, there would also be room for a psychology here.

Now naturalistic social and psychological theories may of course come both to redescribe actions (and beliefs) and to undermine their rationale. But in so doing they always preserve the intentional nature of the actions (on pain of rendering themselves redundant, by surrendering the phenomena to a purely physical explanation), and may as well often preserve the grounded nature of the beliefs. Thus critical theory may recharacterize some action in terms of its social or psychic function or role and situate the agent's beliefs (via the application of the concepts of ideology and rationalization) as not only false but more or less necessary (and so grounded). However, whereas social theory will in general save the intentional nature of the action under (at least some of) the agent's own descriptions, psychological theory may only be able to characterize an action as intentional under descriptions necessarily unavailable to the agent concerned. (That it can do so derives of course from the vast extension of the scope of intentionality opened up by the concept of the unconscious.) Conversely, the grounding of a false but necessary belief in psychological theory may be that of the mechanisms generating the lived reality of an illusion, whereas in social theory it may be that of the lived illusoriness of what is real. And with these differences may go necessary differences in the emancipatory strategies and roles of these two branches of the human sciences.

I now want to complete my vindication of naturalism here by considering the appropriate analysis of reasons, and in particular, the connection between the cognitive and conative components of their analysis. I have already argued that reasons must be analysed as tendencies. Now I suggest that if an agent's belief corresponds to a tendency possessed, a want corresponds to a tendency exercised and an action to its manifestation in some or other physical state of the world, whether or not the want is realized. On this account, then, though both a belief and a want are presupposed in any reason explanation, they operate, as it were, at different logical levels: in that whereas a belief requires something else (such as a desire) to be effective, a want (conceived just as a causally efficacious belief) is automatically manifested in action, in the appropriate circumstances. This is reflected in the fact that whereas a desire, want or intention cannot be specified except as a desire, etc., to do something, so logically presupposing a belief, a belief can be specified in isolation from any desire. In the simplest case the belief presupposed by a desire, etc., is the belief that the action will manifest the quality or trait (or produce the anticipated effect) to which the desire has become, as it were, attached. But this logical asymmetry depends upon an ontological (or axiological) differ-ence. For, once exercised, a reason does not have to wait upon anything else to be manifest in action. It is spontaneously manifest *CP* in the appropriate circumstances. When we have an efficacious reason, and appropriate circumstances materialize, then (whether or not we are aware of the reason), as Aristotle put it: 'straightaway we act'.[34]

Reasons, then, are beliefs. And the fact that beliefs can be specified, as it were, disinterestedly, that is, in isolation from any desire, partly accounts for the systematic ambiguity in the notion of a reason as both a ground for a proposition and an explanation for an action, and for the familiar contrast between reasons for and reasons why. But this account of the matter seems to leave a problem as to why beliefs should ever become attached to desires. Now the Newtonian Revolution in psychology consists in coming to see that people do not have to be pushed, prodded or stimulated into action. They act spontaneously. Or we could say that they are active by nature. The irreducibility of intentionality means that it is not *that*, but rather *what*, people do that is problematic. The motto on President Truman's desk, 'the buck stops here', expresses very well the force of what I earlier characterized as the axiological imperative. But in one respect it is misleading. For whereas decisions are discrete, and often lagged, in time, action or better activity occurs as a continuous stream, in which the volitional element can never be analysed away, so that there is no more mystery about why beliefs become wants (causally efficacious) than there is about how wants issue in actions. For the desires that transform beliefs into wants (interests and needs)[35] and so, *ceteris paribus*, into actions, are generated, like the beliefs themselves, in the course of the practical business of life. Will, for its part, may best be regarded as pure or unimpeded desire;[36] and desire correspondingly as will, which, encountering some obstacle, requires beliefs about the manner as well as the object of its satisfaction. In this sense Aristotle was correct: the conclusion of a practical syllogism is an action.

One does what one wants to (or intends) unless prevented. This is a necessary truth. And no further explanation of action as such is required. But it is contingent what it is that one actually intends, that is, what states of the world one desires to see realized; it is contingent whether one knows what one intends and whether what one intends is within one's power; and it is contingent, if they are, whether, when one acts, the desired states will actually be realized, and, if they are, what effect this will subsequently have upon our desires (for example, whether such a state will, as one says, actually 'satisfy' them).

Now the explanation of any particular action will consist in, or depend upon, the reconstruction of the generative matrix, that is, the network of effective beliefs that, in the prevailing circumstances, produced the action on the occasion in question. And if what distinguishes human action from the rest of the natural order is that it is caused by states of mind, and such states (as I shall shortly argue) are real, then one can formulate, as a presupposition of investigation in the domain of the human sciences, a principle of psychic ubiquity determinism: viz. that for every action (or belief) there is a set of real reasons, constituting its rationale, which explains it. Such a principle does not imply any commitment to the pattern of rational explanation, for in particular the beliefs may not only be false but inconsistent; nor does it imply any commitment to psychic actualism and it expresses, rather than violates, the principle of agency. Reasons, then, are beliefs rooted in the practical interests of life. And a person's essence consists just in what she is most fundamentally disposed to do (or become): that set of effective beliefs that determines her psychic (and behavioural) identity, and fixes her in her particularity as a kind.

If we owe to Husserl the insight that agency presupposes belief, we owe to Schutz the insight that it occurs as a continuous stream unless prevented (by special causes). Now, to Aristotle must belong the credit for seeing that there is no problem in passing from desires to actions (so that no existential dilemma can arise), for seeing that desires are spontaneously realized in action (or, to put it the other way round, that our continuing activity is automatically trained on the objects of our desires). And to Marx must belong the credit for seeing that there is no problem in getting from desires to beliefs as they both express, and arise in response to, the practical business of living. One can note in passing that neither is there any problem, at least in principle, in getting from theory to practice on this account. For as, on the argument of Chapter 2, it is explanatory power that determines the values informing (motivating) or rationalizing our activity, the discovery of a more powerful theory, although not automatically issuing in a change of practice (for obvious, non-voluntaristic, reasons), is bound to introduce an element of 'dissonance' into the generative matrix of action (which may of course result in repression of the discovery). In these circumstances, as Wittgenstein put it: 'we now see something different and can no longer go on naïvely playing [as before]'.[37] Finally, we must credit Freud with extending, through the concept of the unconscious, the range of application of the concepts of belief and desire, and hence of the scope of the pattern of the naturalistic explanation of human action that I have here been vindicating.[38]

Emergent Powers and Materialism I: Against Reductionism

It is plausible, if wrong, to think that societies are just collectivities of people, and that people in turn are just more or less complex things; so that the subject-matter of sociology is just (reducible to) that of psychology or some similar discipline, such as praxiology, systematizing the principles governing the behaviour of people, and that the subject-matter of psychology is just (reducible to) that of neurophysiology and ultimately physics, systematizing the principles governing the behaviour of inanimate matter. Now in Chapter 2 I argued, against methodological individualism, that society, as a real object of possible scientific study, possesses properties irreducible to those of people. Here I want to argue, against materialism – and more particularly that rigorous form of it known as 'central state materialism' (CSM, for short)[39] – that people possess properties irreducible to those of matter. My aim in attacking materialism is not to comfort any sort of spiritualism; but, on the contrary, precisely to defend the possibility of a science of psychology, and thus to complete my arguments of the second and third sections by showing that the powers traditionally associated with mind, which are invoked in reason explanations, are *sui generis* real, entailing *inter alia* the operation of radically new principles of organization.

Metaphysically, I shall be advocating a position that I will characterize as '*synchronic emergent powers materialism*' – SEPM for short. But I want to leave open the questions as to whether there is a bearer or substance whose powers they are; and, if there is, as to what its identity is. That is, it will remain possible that mind just is a complex or set of powers, as far as we know, historically emergent from and present only in association with (certain complex forms of) matter. But it will equally remain possible that there is a substance, whose nature is at present unknown, which is the bearer of those powers.[40] Now if the latter alternative is correct, viz. that mind consists in the powers of a *substance*, once more there are two alternatives: that that substance just is matter, in whose complex organization mind consists; and that that substance is of an immaterial kind. On the first possibility SEPM reduces to a form of materialism, which could be characterized as a stratified monism; on the second to a species of dualistic interactionism. The first is indicated by neurophysiological evidence;[41] the second by work on paranormal phenomena.[42] But it should be stressed that it is neither necessary nor possible, on the basis of the present limited and conflicting scientific data, to decide on the status of the powers, whose irreducibility I will here be concerned to demonstrate.[43]

SEPM may be contrasted not only with the ontological doctrine of materialism, which collapses mental powers to their physical basis or conditions of possibility, but also with the epistemological (or 'logical') doctrine of behaviourism, which collapses mental powers to their overt exercise or conditions of identification. CSM, seizing on the second category mistake, with its substitution of behaviour for mind, attempts to achieve a metaphysical economy by identifying those inner states responsible for outward behaviour with the physico-chemical workings of the brain, or more fully central nervous system.[44] It is thus a species of reductionism.

I have pointed out elsewhere that the notion of a reduction is ambiguous.[45] If it is asserted that *B* can be 'reduced' to *A* it may be being claimed merely (1) that *A* provides a *basis* for *B*; (2) that *A* *explains* *B*; or (3) that knowledge of *A* enables us to *predict* the behaviour of *B*. It is uncontroversial that the brain provides a basis, medium or vehicle of mental powers and that it is a condition of the possibility of their existence, exercise and identification (at least under normal, i.e., non-paranormal, conditions). But a distinction must be made in respect of the kind of explanatory reduction contemplated in (2). For a *diachronic explanatory reduction*, in which the processes of the formation of the higher-order entities are reconstructed and explained in terms of the principles governing the elements out of which they are formed, is compatible with *synchronic emergence*, on which the higher-order principles cannot be completely explained in terms of lower-order ones. Note that it is to the former that biologists are committed in investigating the origins of life (or engineers in constructing machines), but it is to the denial of the latter that the materialist is committed. My argument is for synchronic emergence, and is compatible with the possibility of a biological explanation of the genesis of mental processes. (3) presupposes, of course, a closure.

Now reductionism has often appealed to social scientists and psychologists as a way of overcoming their 'backwardness'. What the reductionists forget is that every historically successful example of a reduction (such as of chemistry to physics) has depended upon the prior existence of a well-developed body of knowledge in the domain of the to-be-reduced science which, in a reduction, is then 'explained'. But of course the very problem in the human sciences is that there is no such body of knowledge: so that there is nothing (or at least as yet very little) for a reduction to explain. So that as a programme for their development reductionism must fail. Even if, *per impossibile*, the ontological theses of individualism and materialism were true, epistemologically speaking, societies would first have to be identified and understood as societies and people as people before their explanatory reduction could be scientifically contemplated.

It is instructive to compare the reductions mooted by individualism and materialism, viz.:

(a) S_1 .... S_j social states $\downarrow M1$
(b) P_1 .... P_k psychological states $\downarrow CSM$
(c) N_1 .... N_l neurophysiological states

Despite disanalogies,[46] neither satisfies two general criteria for a successful (synchronic) explanatory reduction, viz.:

(C1): that it must be the case that the individuals of the two kinds cannot be said to occupy the same place at the same time and one not be a part of the other; and
(C2): that the terms of the two sciences either are at least partially intertranslatable or, if they possess well-developed independent taxonomies, overlap in at least some of their reference states.

C1 indicates that a reduction is in general possible because the lower-order entities occupy a different volume of space, either larger or more usually smaller. But this is clearly not the case with the reductions postulated here. Thus it makes no sense to locate an economy or set of beliefs at some point in space. Consideration of C2 shows another reason why, even if the theses of materialism and individualism were true, the possibility of a successful reduction of psychology or sociology would depend upon their prior development as autonomous sciences. For there is no way in which neurophysiological states $N_1 \ldots N_l$ could be identified as the correlates of psychological states $P_1 \ldots P_k$ except under psychological state-descriptions. In the same way actions would first have to be identified as economic, political, religious, etc., that is, under some social state-description, for their psychological correlates to be found. So that in both cases the to-be-reduced science (or 'reductandum') has taxonomic priority. But this only raises a more general problem. For it would seem that to identify the relevant P- and S- states, one needs to impute to the objects under study (people, societies) properties of a kind (such as in the P-case intentionality and consciousness, and in the S-case preformation and the properties derived from the transformational model in Chapter 2) whose imputation to the lower-order domain is not only literally senseless, but would vitiate the point of the contemplated reduction. Cybernetically, these differences are reflected in the fact that S-processes are typically teleonomic, P-processes teleological and N-processes mechanical. As for the possibility of referential overlap, reductionism encounters a double difficulty here. For not only is it the case that the same social or psychological states can be realized in a number, probably infinite, of different ways;[47] but (worse) the reverse, viz. multiple social or psychological correlates of psychological or physiological states, also seems to hold.[48] Now, on the first count, given the fact of categorial differentiation and the phenomenon of emergent causality (viz. that reference to an element at the higher-order level may be a contingently necessary condition for the explanation of what happens at the lower-order level), reductionism becomes irrelevant to the scientifically interesting questions as to why one S- (or P-) state rather than another is realized, and why it is realized in the particular P- (or N-) way it is. And, on the second count, given that the relations between the levels reveal not a degree of complexity in the functional organization of unchanging units, but instead a radical mismatch, no explanation of this mismatch (which is certainly on the agenda of the infant sciences of socio-psychology and psycho-physiology) can be achieved in the unilinear reductive kind of way posited in $M1$ and CSM. In sum, then, the programmes of explanatory reduction considered here suffer from individually and jointly insuperable problems of individuation, identification, categorial differentiation, emergent causality and referential disjuncture (multiple realization and mismatch).

It should be noted that it follows from the breakdown of the thesis of the symmetry of explanation and prediction in open systems that an explanatory reduction, even of a synchronic kind, does not entail a predictive one. However, the actualist at (2) is also committed to (3), in virtue of his presupposition of a closure.[49] In a moment I will show that a person's neurophysiology cannot constitute a closed system. But here it is important to appreciate that both the intelligibility of the natural process of evolution and the operation of machines presuppose a world in which, although everything happens in accordance with physical laws, what happens is not completely determined by them. There is no uniquely determined or predetermined path linking amoebae to humans. Relations of natural generation are not in general (logically) transitive. Thus it is not the case that because S_1 produced S_2 and S_2 produced S_3 that S_1 produced S_3 (if either the entities at S_2 possess emergent powers or the system in which S_3 is formed is open or the process is stochastic). Nor is it the case that the entities at S_3 are incapable of reacting back on the levels S_2 or S_1 out of which they were formed. Again, machines can only be explained by reference to their principles of organization. These principles, though they make use of and are constrained by physical laws, cannot be completely explained by them. The laws concerned have to be 'set' or 'organized'; just as, to step up a level, the hardware of a computer has to be 'programmed'.

Now if, as is the case with living things, reference to emergent properties is necessary for the explanation of states of the physical world then, employing the causal criterion for the ascription of reality set out in Chapter 1 (and already invoked in Chapter 2), we are justified in saying that such properties (and *a fortiori* their emergence) are real.[50] It is important to stress that if and only if it is the case that some event E would not have occurred, under the conditions that actually prevailed but for (the operation of) X, then we are justified in calling X a cause of E, whether or not we know the nature of the mechanism at work. Now the powers that make psychology possible cannot be seen or touched, tasted, smelled or heard. But their existence and exercise are all the same a condition of the possibility of any empirical science.

Emergent Powers and Materialism II:
In Defence of Transcategorial Causality

Having examined the problems involved in the reduction contemplated by CSM, I now want to demonstrate that it is a metaphysically untenable position. In particular it will be seen that it faces difficulties of *analysis* and in sustaining adequate concepts of *causality* and of social *interaction*. I shall argue that on consideration of these three sets of difficulties, CSM reduces to epiphenomenalism, parallelism and a pre-established harmony of monads respectively; that other theories, such as the double-aspect one, fare no better; and that only a synchronic emergent powers materialism is consistent with the phenomena, and *a fortiori* with the possibility of psychology as a science of mind.

The materialist claim is that: (I) mind (P-states) is nothing but, is identical with, (certain) physico-chemical operations of the brain, or central nervous system (some N-states).

Two naïve objections to (I) must be dismissed straightaway. Firstly, there is no problem about explaining the (apparent) phenomena of mind-body (*P-N*) interaction, because, upon analysis, it just reduces to a body–body (*N–N*) one. Secondly, there is no problem, in principle, in sustaining a distinction between conscious and non-conscious states, in that they are theoretically differentiable as different states of matter (in terms of which the phenomena of consciousness are to be explained). However, to suppose that some *N*-states are *P*-states requires criteria for the differentiation of those *N*-states, say N_p-states, which are mind-states from those *N*-states which are not; that is, it requires criteria for the differentiation of the mental from the purely physical. Cognitive processes would seem to be differentiated from non-cognitive ones in that they are at least typically (but not necessarily) *conscious, referential* (that is, about something) and *intentional*.

Now it would seem that for '*A*' and '*B*' to be identical it must be the case that what can be truly said about *A* can also be truly said about *B* (and vice versa). Given this, (I) reduces to the claim (I') that what can be truly said about *P*-states can be truly said about N_p-states. But this is patently false. For it cannot be said that brain processes are *about* anything, that they are meaningful, or that they are true or false, or that they are *of* or *for* something (as is the case of beliefs and desires respectively).[51] Thus the materialist claim *cannot* be that what can be truly said about *P*-states can equally be truly said about N_p-states.

Instead the materialist would seem to have to maintain either (IIa) (much more radically) that some things cannot be truly (and perhaps even that nothing can be truly) said about *P*-states; or (IIb) that N_p-states explain *P*-states (in an *X*-sense, to be explicated below), but that the languages in which the N_p- and *P*-states, viz. L_{np} and L_p, are referred to and discussed are radically incommensurable. (IIa) is absurd. For it is a necessary condition for any discursive intelligence that it should be able to refer and intend, explicate and judge. In this way mentalistic predicates are irreducible. And contrary to the claims of materialists,[52] it is only a non-reductionist metaphysics that can bring itself within its own world view. Moreover (IIa) is inconsistent with any thesis of identity. For *an illusion is not identical with what explains it* (which must be real). But this leads on immediately to (IIb). For it would seem that the '*X*-sense' must be explicated roughly as follows: *Np*-states explain *P*-states in such a way as to show that they are in fact identical, that is, that the N_p-states picked out in L_{Np} designate one and the same thing as the *P*-states picked out in L_p. Note that this makes a scientific discovery turn on a recategorization, whereas what happens in science is the opposite. That is, scientists discover that what is referred to as 'water' or 'a gene' is *in fact* composed of (or consists of nothing but) molecules of H_2O or DNA, where they possess independent criteria for the identification and/or description of the properties of the *explanandum*. Moreover such an explanatory recategorization in science does not deny, but depends upon, the notion of the higher-order (or *explanandum*) level and its properties being real. What is the case with (IIb)? Either (1) the *P*-states are real and they possess the kind of characteristics (of intentionality, etc.) ascribed to them, in which event CSM reduces to old-fashioned epiphenomenalism, which talk of identity only serves to obscure; or (2) the *P*-states are illusory, and their alleged characteristics (such as intentionality) unreal, in which event no identity can hold and CSM collapses. For if *P*-states are identical with the N_p-states they cannot be illusions, and if *P*-states are illusions they cannot be identical with the N_p-states that are held to explain them.[53] Thus the argument from analysis shows that, in Huxley's words 'we are either conscious automata or we are not automata at all'.

If CSM denies the irreducibility of *P*-states, epiphenomenalism of course denies their causal status. Now before showing the absurdity involved in the denial of the irreducible and causal status of (some) mind-states, I want to consider two familiar objections to any non-reductionist theory that posits causal interaction between *P*- and *N*-states: first, that for any causal interaction there must be a common medium, or cause and effect must share common properties;[54] and second, that if there are no such medium or properties, then what is being posited is an arbitrary and/or unscientific break in the 'chain of causes and effects'. The second objection, betraying the legacy of actualism, need not detain us long, as I have already dealt with it in the second section. SEPM requires no exemption from scientific laws; and the emergence it attributes to mind is entirely consistent with any adequate scientific ontology. Thus, again contrary to materialist propaganda,[55] if it is assumed (or, as it is, required) that neurophysiology effectively constitutes a closed system, then, with the temporary exception of a few astronomic contexts, it is woman that is being anointed as the exception in nature! The first objection is more strongly grounded in scientific intuitions and practice. For in general this would demand that where elements of two kinds seem to be systematically connected, as cause and effect, one discovers the nature of the mechanism that links (or underlies) them. However, that this demand is made does not mean that it can always be satisfied. Little does it worry purveyors of this objection that the lynchpin of the Newtonian system – gravity – did not satisfy it, and that it is not satisfied by the effects of magnetic fields on material things! Now it is certainly the case that such causality as holds between beliefs and matter must be conceived, in the absence of any knowledge of a connecting mechanism, as *transcategorial*. But transcategorial causality is no stranger to science. And provided there are ways of identifying and describing behaviour at the two levels in relative independence of one another, there is no reason why the properties of the cause level, and *a fortiori* the relations between the levels, should not be studied in accordance with the most rigorous canons of empirical science. To stress, we do not know *how* P-states affect N-states, but *that* they do is (I argued in the third section) apodeictically demonstrable, in that it is a condition of possibility of any practical or rational activity at all. Moreover we will never find out how P-states affect N-states unless we make the P-states the site of an autonomous science.[56]

Consider now a crucial ambiguity in the programme of CSM. For, wishing both to identify and explain mind in terms of the physico-chemical operations of the brain, one must ask: what, on any given occasion, explains these operations? Could it, at least in the N_p-case, be anything other than mind?[57] Leaving this on one side, it is clear that the materialist must be committed to the view that N-states are a necessary and sufficient condition for a person's overt behaviour, $O_1 \ldots \ldots O_t$. It may be granted that there is a difference in the type of N-state with which consciousness is associated. But it remains a contingent fact that for any determinate complex of N-states, say N_x, there is a particular state of consciousness, say P_k, associated with it. And in particular it must be the case that P_k does not influence behaviour O_s (and hence the effect that O_s has on the resultant state of nature) at all. For either consciousness is illusory or it is real, and if it is real and CSM is to retain any doctrinal substance, then it must be the case that N_x is necessary and sufficient for O_s; that is, that O_s would have occurred, given N_x, *whatever* the P-state associated with it. Thus the movement of my hand across the paper, the sequence of sounds issuing from my mouth, the motion of my legs across the room, the shutting of the window and the resultant frightening of a sparrow would all have occurred *just as they did* without their conscious concomitants, and indeed were they to have been associated with quite different (and opposite) ones. This extra-ordinary position is in fact of course nothing other than the old seventeenth-century theory of parallelism, according to which mind never intervenes in the physical world, but its history is, as it happens, so arranged and timed as to be in perfect synchrony with the history of our bodies, and in such a way that it seems to us that we are the cause of some but not other of its movements, which are – *mirabile dictu* – precisely those which we intend!

The definitive critique of CSM, as distinct from the affront to our intuitions yielded by considerations of analysis and causality, is provided by an argument which is both novel and simple. It is clear that the materialist is committed to the notion that for any psychological (N_p) state there is in principle a finite and determinate (though possibly non-unique) set of prior or concomitant neurophysiological states uniquely and completely determining it; so that a person's neurophysiology describes an effectively closed system. Now if this is the case we clearly cannot allow any *P*-state (conceived as both irreducible and real) causally to intervene in, or affect, the sequence of *N*-states in a person's body. How then is communication, or social interaction generally, possible? For suppose *B* says to *A* 'Pass the condiments' at tea and *A* does so, that is, performs action X_a. We must now suppose *either* (1) that X_a is uniquely determined by some set of physiological states N_1 ...... N_n such that X_a would have been performed without *B*'s speech action; *or* (2) that *B*'s speech action as interpreted by *A* was causally efficacious in bringing about X_a.

Now (2) involves a *P*-state of *B*'s as a part of a causal series between some prior *N*-state of *A*'s and X_a, and conversely a *P*-state of *A*'s as part of a causal series between some prior *N*-state of *B*'s and *B*'s subsequent action, X_b, of taking the condiments from *A*. Moreover as, discounting a line of last resort to be discussed below, there is no direct physical link (connection or medium) between *A* and *B*, one must allow that, in the case of interpersonal communication, mind affects matter.

Once this is accepted, we can then extend it to cover all the other normal cases of mind–body interaction, of agency (where mind puts matter in motion, we know not how) and of perception (where mind 'reads' matter).[58] That is, we can quite readily allow that a person's own *P*-states can be the cause of his or her own actions, that is, of some but not other of his or her movements. Was it strictly necessary to introduce other persons for the argument? No – provided that the socialized individual is set in the context of a natural world which is open. For, literally, if it rains, and *A* opens his/her umbrella or takes any other form of protective or evasive action, the deterministic chain of neurophysiological states is broken!

Surprisingly, perhaps, individualism – that other reductionist position in the philosophy of the human sciences – and, beneath that, epistemological solipsism and idealism appear as conditions of the plausibility of materialism. For materialism is only really plausible if one thinks of a single mind and a single body, in isolation from other persons and in abstraction from the rest of nature, and inquires into the manner of their connection. To deny causal interaction between *P*- and *N*-states becomes absurd when we remember that the normal venue for the exercise of our cognitive powers is in situations of social interaction, and paradigmatically (though of course not exclusively) in dialogue or communication. For clearly here the link between agents is not neuro-physiological, but *P*-ish, psychological and interpretative (hermeneutic). And to deny the phenomenon of agency becomes impossible when we recall that the normal setting for the exercise of our bodily powers is in interaction with, and transformation of, nature.

The line of last resort mentioned above is for the materialist to deny that the link between agents in communication is, or depends upon, anything other than purely physical laws (as for example in the more extreme versions of physicalistic behaviourism).[59] Of course what are interpreted in communication are physical phenomena, such as sounds. But it cannot be maintained that there is a direct link, unmediated by interpretation, between the sound and the ensuing physical action. For, setting aside the obvious fact that it is the interpretation put upon the sound, not the sound itself, that is causally responsible for the resultant behaviour, there is no one-to-one correlation between sounds and behaviour. This is shown, at the very least, by the existence of, and the possibility of learning, different languages (or less macroscopically, usages) *or*, alternatively, forms of life (that is, ways of behaving). It should be noted that even if a physicalistic behaviourist reduction could be carried out, this would not affect the argument establishing the openness of any one person's neurophysiology. And if a materialist is willing to concede this, then materialism loses all distinctiveness as a philosophical thesis, and reduces merely to a form of general Laplacean determinism.

Now the only alternative to (2) above, viz. (1), entails that X_a is determined by an antecedent set of physiological states, such that, had *B* not asked *A* to pass the condiments, she would still have done so. CSM now reduces to a form of Leibnizian pre-established harmony of monads, in which each person's neurophysiology is so synchronized with every other's that it appears *as if* they were talking and laughing, smiling and winking. And in which each person's neurophysiology is so synchronized with the nature of every other object that it appears *as if* they were fitting and turning, digging and building. If one is prepared to countenance this, in the name of science, then one might as well set all scepticism aside and accept that there are fairies at the bottom of the garden, and gnomes to boot!

'Double-aspect' theories, which provide a currently fashionable alternative to CSM, suffer from the defects of ambivalent ontological commitment. For either the mental attributes are real or they are not. If they are real, then double-aspect theory reduces to SEPM; and, if they are not, it reduces to a form of materialism. If, on the other hand, the question is ducked, then one is left without any non-subjective criterion for the imputation of the mental attributes in question, or even for the imputation of any mental attributes at all.

Suppose the relationship between *P*- and *N*-states is conceived, as is sometimes suggested, as analogous to that between meanings and sounds, such that *P*-states are the 'meanings' given by s/he who experiences them to some but not other of his/her *N*-states. Now it is the meanings of the words and sentences we utter and our intentions in uttering them that explain the particular sounds we make. So that if meanings are regarded as Spinozian attributes of sounds, their reality and causal efficacy as social objects must be admitted. And if the particular occasions of their production are not to be regarded as physically (and mechanistically) determined, then reasons as psychological objects must be granted reality and causal status too.

My defence of the possibility of a transcendental realist ontology in the domain of the psychological sciences is complete. The powers associated with mind are both real, that is, causally efficacious (see the second and third sections), and irreducible, that is, emergent from matter (see the fourth and fifth sections). But any full defence of the possibility of a transcendental realist psychology must be complemented by critiques of behaviourism, which could reduce powers to their exercise, and of praxiology, which would make our knowledge of them a priori.

In Chapter 2 it was seen that the pre-existence of social forms is a necessary condition for any intentional action, and that their reality is entailed by their causal power. Here it has been seen that intentionality, and more generally praxis (in the sense of any practico-rational activity), presuppose the causal efficacy of reasons (that is, beliefs and desires). Indeed an intentional action may be defined as an action which has a real reason for its cause. We now have criteria differentiating the social from the individual; and both (that is, the human) from the purely physical or material. And we have seen how a non-physicalist (i.e., non-reductionist) naturalism can be vindicated in both the social and the psychological branches of the human sciences.

Rational Explanation

Behaviourism is moribund, if not yet quite dead. But there is still considerable support for 'rational explanation' from all points of the philosophical compass. The model was originally proposed by writers sympathetic to the hermeneutical tradition as an alternative to the deductive–nomological one, emphasizing rational rather than natural necessity, the thing to do rather than the thing done, etc.[60] But it was subsequently appropriated by positivists and shown to conform to a deductive schema, with some or other principle of rationality taking the place of empirical covering laws.[61] Now the model of rational explanation, at least in its canonical positivist form, suffers from all the difficulties of the deductive–nomological model, in that it presupposes the ubiquity of closed systems (and hence *inter alia* the ahistoricity of phenomena). And in most of the patterns actually canvassed it even neglects the multiplicity of means and plurality of ends that typify most real-life action situations.[62] However, as an instantiation of mainstream praxiology, it also suffers from the problems endemic to that position. Thus it characteristically ignores the interdependence of means and ends and the temporal and explanatory primacy (in the sense of the third section of Chapter 2) of social practices over the intentional human actions that reproduce or transform them.

However, conceived as a mode of explanation in its own right, it involves a number of additional difficulties. First, it is *not exhaustive*. It only applies to *actions*, and to their explanation in terms of the properties (rational dispositions) of *agents* (and/or, given the requisite composition laws, collectivities or groups). Moreover it only applies to those actions which can be adequately reconstructed as the outcome of rational decision-making procedures, and hence to those agents who are at the time of, and in respect of, the action concerned 'rational'. Second, it appears to be either *circular* or *unnecessary*. For if there is, as has been claimed, no way of identifying the agent's beliefs and desires without imputing (at least a degree of) rationality, then it should not be treated as a quasi-empirical premise in a deductive explanation, but as a presupposition of investigation. Conversely, if such ways exist, then it is unclear why the principle is necessary. Third, if it is superimposed as a norm, it is at best *indecisive*. For there is no criterion of rationality which uniquely singles out a course of action as 'the thing to do'. Conversely, an infinite number of different sets of beliefs and desires is in principle consistent with the (rational) performance of the action. (This is of course but one aspect of the 'underdetermination of theory by experience'.) Hence, as a presupposition it *cannot be sufficient* for the identification of the generative belief-desire complex. Fourth, whether rationality is treated as a synthetic a priori assumption or an empirical hypothesis, it is manifestly *false*. There is no reason to believe that any, let alone all (or even most), historical individuals are rational all the time in any of the mooted senses of 'rationality';[63] and in fact there are excellent grounds for supposing the contrary. Finally, if rationality is allowed to be a *variable*, another element of indeterminacy is introduced, stemming from the possibility of showing the action to be more or less rational, apparently subject to our 'value-preferences'.

Three main issues are raised by these points: (1) the *falsity* of rationality as a general assumption; (2) the sense (or respect) in which it may nevertheless still be held to be *necessary*; and (3) the so-called problem of the '*indeterminacy of translation*'. Considering (1) I will in general restrict my remarks to 'consistency', which is normally – perhaps incorrectly – taken to be a necessary, if not a sufficient, condition for 'rationality'.

Now in science one chooses that explanation which (*inter alia* shows in its subject-matter the degree and type of inconsistency that) has the *greatest explanatory power simpliciter*. To suppose synthetic a priori that every belief or action has a rationale, that is, psychic ubiquity determinism (see p. 96), is merely to suppose that for every belief or action there is a set of real reasons which, in conjunction with other causes, explains it. It is to suppose that the action is in part the result of a causally efficacious (real) reason, and hence (normally) of some causally efficacious reasoning process. It is neither to suppose (idealistically) that reasons completely explain every action; nor to suppose (rationalistically) that any reasoning process (whether implicit or explicit, unconscious or preconscious) occurring prior to (and in the case of neurotic and automatic actions perhaps long before) the action is valid. If such a reasoning process occurs or has occurred, it figures in an explanation of the action in virtue of its causal efficacy, *not* in virtue of its validity. Just as real reasons may be false, real reasoning processes may be invalid. And the key point to appreciate is that one can adequately (and consistently) depict a contradictory situation; one can, and must, *make sense of nonsense* (incoherence);[64] and one can, and must, *consistently describe*, and explain, *inconsistencies*. There are conditions, and causes, of incorrect and correct reasoning:[65] both alike, quite symmetrically, must be subjected to scientific investigation.[66] Both the errors of thinking inconsistency ontologically impossible, and consistency epistemologically self-explanatory, must be avoided.

The inconsistencies that occur within reasoning processes may be either relatively unmotivated, as in most mathematical mistakes, or relatively motivated, as in most forms of neurotic behaviour. In both cases their identification presupposes a relatively consistent metatheory. But in the motivated case the fact that the reasoning is mistaken is essential to its explanation (that is, the mistake *qua* mistake is causally efficacious in producing the behaviour). Consider the unmotivated case. Would it not be absurd to suppose that every logical or mathematical mistake was the expression of some underlying rationale – in the sense of correct reasoning process? Note, to dispense with the a priori assumption of rationality is not *per se* to eliminate the possibility of deductively 'tight' explanations of phenomena. For, though one cannot deduce a mistake, one can certainly deduce its *occurrence*. It is vital to distinguish the reasoning process of theory from the reasoning process theory seeks to describe. As an example of a motivated mistake, consider Freud's 'Rat Man', who slimmed to get rid of his 'dick' (fat), when he really wanted to get rid of his cousin (Dick) – of whose relationship with his girl-friend he was jealous.[67] Now one can certainly see the symbolic point of the Rat Man's 'mistake'. However, one should note that Freud's explanation, and his general theory of primary processes, are consistent with the Rat Man's overeating, to become fat, that is, *like* his cousin Dick; so that it would be wrong to think that one can adequately reconstruct all neurotic behaviour as the product of 'symbolically valid' syllogisms with determinate premises. Moreover there are no grounds for supposing that it will be possible to give hermeneutically adequate reconstructions for all motivated errors. Thus we may have indisputable grounds for supposing an error to be motivated without knowing what the motivation is; and we may know what the motive is without its necessarily being intelligible to us.

In addition to inconsistencies within reasoning processes, the psychological sciences must consider the possibilities of: (a) inconsistencies between subjects at any moment of time; (b) inconsistencies within subjects and over time; (c) inconsistencies between the roles assumed and the activities performed by the same subject; and, more generally, (d) inconsistencies between levels of structure. (a) is of course a necessary condition for any discursive activity. (c) has been thoroughly explored by social psychologists. (b), which is highly indicated by psychological theory, casts serious doubt upon the traditional philosophical notions of the transcendental unity of the subject and of personal identity. A special case of (d) is rationalization, involving an inconsistency within a subject between how something really is and how it appears to be. When, as in typical instances of repression, the rationalization is both (contingently) necessary for and (conjuncturally) generated by what it rationalizes, one has a psychological analogue of the Colletti contradictions discussed in the appendix to Chapter 2. Man is not a monad. And contrary to the implications of the epistemic fallacy – the tacit identification of the conditions of thought and the real (achieved most securely in empirical realism) – inconsistencies of all these types not only occur, but are consistently explicable. Their explanation will normally be partly in terms of the existence and activity of the opposed tendencies of complex structured objects (in internal dislocation) and partly in terms of the 'interference' characteristic of open systems.[68] Since the objects one is dealing with here possess (or indeed consist in) *beliefs*, the inconsistencies will be (or include) *logical* ones. Consistency (and rationality generally), suitably qualified – for example by the requirements of the scientific imagination – is *at best* a regulative ideal for scientific description; it is not a material presupposition of investigation. That is to say, consistency relates to the transitive process of science-production as a norm, not to the intransitive realm of its objects as a condition.

What has been said so far presupposes that the identification of the agent's beliefs is unproblematic. But, turning to issue (2), this is just what is often denied. Thus it is claimed that there is no way in which beliefs (and desires) can be identified without imputing to the agent in question, or the society of which s/he is a member, a degree of rationality[69] or a measure of coherence,[70] just as (analytically) actions cannot be described without presupposing intentionality (under some description). Now one must immediately dismiss the naïve counter-objection to this claim: viz. that there are certainly such ways – for example, taking the actor's account seriously and cross-checking it for consistency with the rest of his or her behaviour and independently validated theoretical knowledge. For the account must already have been translated and the behaviour identified (in the language of the social scientist) for such operations to be possible; and it is precisely such translation/identification that is in question. This leads on immediately to (3). For it is clear that there is no way in which beliefs can be identified independently of meanings or vice versa. To make a decision about language is *ipso facto* to make a decision about the thoughts language expresses. Now the general resolution of this problem depends upon coming to see that this (dual) problem of identification cannot be separated from the problem of explanation. Thus one chooses that *translation which is explanatorily most adequate*, whether or not it is the most 'charitable' (that is, shows the greatest degree of convergence between the beliefs of the subject and object of investigation), in the context of what is *already known* about the organization of the society in question (and societies in general). Clearly this problem is only a special case of the para-hermeneutic problem of the correct identification of phenomena in science. And the process of deciding translations by setting descriptions (identifications) in the context of their own explanation is a continuous and iterative one, which *inter alia* may necessitate revisions in judgements (where they are explanatorily relevant) of the rationality of beliefs and actions in the object-domain under study. In the same way the general problem of the underdetermination of theory by experience is resolved by choosing the *theory which is phenomenally* (descriptively) *most adequate*, whether or not it is the simplest; that is, by locating possible explanations of phenomena in the context of (what is already known about) their own explanation. Again, where the phenomena are human, this may result in changing assessments of consistency, etc.

It follows from the conception of the society/person relationship developed in the third section of Chapter 2 that any given society has psychological conditions for its existence, since its reproduction depends upon human agency. Now human beings, like any other empirically given object, are fields of effects (though of course none the less real for that). So it would indeed be surprising (in view of the theoretical labour and practical ingenuity required elsewhere) if persons constituted themselves, just as they stood, as suitable objects for scientific inquiry. Moreover we have known since Freud that mind cannot be naïvely identified with consciousness (the 'tip of the iceberg) and that wo/man is both already a social product and from the start a physical organism. It seems reasonable to deduce from this that though a stratified science of psychology

(conceived as the science of mind, not behaviour) is possible, its autonomy will be circumscribed by sociology and physiology in particular.

It follows from the theoretical dislocation of society and persons and
the hypothesis of the stratification of mind that in the field of the human
sciences one is dealing, in opposition to sociological individualism and
psychological empiricism (or rationalism), with a *double decentring* – of
society from man, and of mind from consciousness. Now one effect of
the first decentring is that the category of the biological individual may
be an unsuitable designator for socio-psychological and social psychological analysis. For associated with each biological individual may be a
number of distinct and inconsistent social personas,[71] some connected,
and some not, to definite roles in the reproduction of society. This
situates the possibilities of role-conflict, various forms of alienation and
anomie, and more generally of a disjuncture between personal and
social identity[72] – that is, between what a person essentially *is* (or has
become) and what, in virtue of his or her social designation or 'station',
s/he is *obliged to be*. Corresponding to this distinction are two
characteristic patterns of explanation, modes of reason-giving, and
sources of existential crisis. Thus, there are things that agents do
because they want to and things that they do because such action is
expected of them;[73] reasons that express the genesis of actions and
reasons that account for those actions to others; 'crises' induced by a
disruption in psychic equilibrium and 'crises' induced by an alteration in
social relations. And the stratification of mind itself has two aspects: the
depth stratification of beliefs and the vertical integration of purposes. If
the stratification of beliefs defines a psyche, the integration of purposes
defines a project. The articulation of a psyche defines a person, and the
hierarchy of projects a life.

The decentring of mind from consciousness entails quite generally
that performance and overt activity becomes inadequate designators for
the cognitive sciences; and it breaks the link, in this domain, between
belief and/or ability and consciousness of that belief/knowledge of that
ability. In particular, the agent may be unaware of the springs and
internal conditions, as well as the external conditions and consequences,
of his/her intentional activity. For though it is analytic to the concept of
an intended act that the agent believes his/her act to possess a certain
quality (for the sake of which it is performed), it is not analytic that s/he
can say, is conscious of, or 'knows' what this quality is. Beliefs may be
unconscious, implicit or tacit; and the disjuncture between belief (or
ability) and consciousness of that belief may be due either to ignorance
or opacity, of which repression (resistance) is a special case, in which
mis- or non-recognition of the object (for example, motive) concerned is
causally generated by the effects of a structural formation of which the
object concerned is an essential part.

Now it follows from this second decentring that though psychic unity may be a goal, and is certainly an accomplishment, it is not (and cannot be) a presupposition of any science of psychology. Of course this reconstruction of the concept of a person (as a decentred disunity) in no way undermines the actuality of people as real objects (complex, structural ones) with emergent powers necessary *inter alia* for the reproduction of society. Moreover persons are already presupposed as one term in any scientific investigation. It is an error to believe in the possibility of any scientific, let alone social scientific, discourse which eliminates self-reference or indexicality. The date is an indispensable component of any scientific report. Because active *subjects* are a necessary presupposition of science, that they exist is transcendentally necessary. But such subjects are transcendentally real, not ideal; and, as such, they are also possible objects of scientific investigation. Moreover this second decentring does not imply any lessening in the force of the concept of *agency*. Dogs continue to bark when one understands how they do so, agents continue to act when one understands the phenomenon of agency as the effect of deeper structures. Of course the difference here is that such knowledge may be incorporated reflexively into the course of action itself, as in the human sphere beliefs are themselves causes.

It has been well said that if Copernicus showed that the earth was not the centre of the universe and Darwin demonstrated that humanity is not its *telos* or goal, Marx removed man (the individual tacitly gendered human subject) from the centre of the stage of history and Freud displaced consciousness from its nodal position as the unifying source of the individual's activity.[74] The significance of this fourfold decentring is profound. Henceforth human beings appear, like any other empirically given object, as phenomena, complex productions of structures they have not produced and of which they have no automatically privileged knowledge. Yet a human is still an agent, possessing powers, whose acquisition, development and exercise is a necessary condition for any scientific enterprise. The correct response to Bishop Bramhall's attempted *reductio* of Hobbes' actualism ('such a liberty as a river hath to descend down a channel')[75] is to welcome the comparison, as allowing a contrast between the *distinct* powers of people and things, in virtue of which, for example, the predicate 'free' is sometimes applicable to a person's situation. From the standpoint of transcendental realism, rivers, hydrochloric acid and humans are equally (1) agents, (2) products, (3) possible objects of scientific investigation. Any metaphysically significant differences between them must be located at the level of their different *kinds* of properties/powers, not in their possession, generation or susceptibility to scientific explanation *per se*. There are two further aspects to the Copernican decentring of man: (a) the establishment of a philosophical ontology or intransitive dimension; and (b) the establishment of a materialist (non-idealist) epistemology or transitive dimension. Propositions in (a) articulate the conditions of things independent of, but necessary for, science. Propositions in (b) articulate the mechanisms of the production of scientific knowledge (in various fields). A consequence of the elaboration of (b) is that knowledge, irrespective of object, must be viewed as a social process irreducible to a purely individual acquisition.

It is analytic to the concept of action that the agent could have acted otherwise. But an agent is only *free* to the extent that s/he is capable of realizing his or her real interests (which means knowing, acting on and bringing about a state of affairs satisfying them). Clearly not all actions are free in this sense. Now it is a necessary condition for the concept of action that the world is open, in the sense that the agent's activity makes a difference to the state of affairs that would (normally) otherwise have prevailed. As the world is open, and agency is real, and as society is only materially present in intentional human action, it follows that social phenomena only ever manifest themselves in open systems. And from this it follows that any possible social (or psychological) laws must be analysed as tendencies. Because society is in transformation, and to the extent that human beings are social products, these tendencies will be historical. And from this, as we shall now see, critiques of the leading philosophies of the human sciences quickly follow.

NOTES

1. See A. Kenny, *Freedom, Will and Power* (Oxford 1975), pp. 2ff.
2. See P. Strawson, *Individuals* (London 1959), p. 104.
3. See R. Harré and P. Secord, *op. cit.*, esp. ch. 5.
4. L. Wittgenstein, *Philosophical Investigations* (Oxford 1963), p. 161.
5. See A. Danto, 'Basic Acts', *American Philosophical Quarterly* 2 (1965), reprinted in *The Philosophy of Action*, A. White (ed.) (Oxford 1968).
6. See C. Whiteley, *Mind in Action* (Oxford 1973), p. 58.
7. J. Austin, *How to do Things with Words* (Oxford 1962), esp. p. 108.
8. W. Benjamin, *Illuminations* (London 1976), p. 259.
9. See D. Davidson, 'Actions, Reasons and Causes', *Journal of Philosophy* 60 (1963), reprinted in A. White (ed.), *op. cit.*, p. 80.
10. M. Scriven, 'Causes, Connections and Conditions in History', *Philosophical Analysis and History*, W. Dray (ed.) (New York 1966), p. 245.
11. See N. Chomsky's classic 'Review of B. F. Skinner's *Verbal Behaviour*', *Language* 35 (1959), reprinted in J. Fodor and J. Katz, *The Structure of Language* (New Jersey 1965).
12. Thus one could say, from the meta-standpoint of philosophy, that in the former case one has *two* sets of descriptions (one constitutive of social reality itself and one of a scientific understanding of it), in the latter case only one. So that if the understanding of the way reality is grasped is a

hermeneutic task, the sociologist or historian of social science is engaged in a *double hermeneutic*, in contrast with the single one of the sociologist or historian of natural science.

13. To coin a slogan: *intentions are personal, meanings are social* – in the sense that intentions are of (that is, belong to) persons, whereas meanings are always effectively given for them. Now it is only because language is always and everywhere already given, that one can use it as a vehicle with which to describe actions (and, in the special case of speech, to perform them), and thus, in the case of one's own actions, use it both to form intentions and to comment reflexively upon what is intended in or by an action (whether the action is communicative or not). Thus it is a mistake to identify the social meaning of an action with the agent's intention in performing it on some particular occasion. Cf. Weber's distinction between 'direct' and 'explanatory' understanding.

14. Of course reasons also explain the unintended results and consequences of intentional acts, but mediately, that is, through some act performed intentionally.

15. See J. Aronson, 'Explanation without Laws', *Journal of Philosophy* 66 (1969).

16. See D. Locke, 'Reasons, Wants and Causes', *American Philosophical Quarterly* 11 (1974).

17. The alleged asymmetry between the logics of practical and so-called 'theoretical' reasoning (see, for example, A. Kenny, *op. cit.*, pp. 81ff) ignores the fact that in open systems the same natural tendency may be manifested, and even realized, in a number of different ways.

18. See D. Davidson, 'Psychology as Philosophy', *Philosophy of Psychology*, S. Brown (ed.) (London 1974), reprinted in J. Glover (ed.), *The Philosophy of Mind* (Oxford 1976).

19. See A. MacIntyre, 'The Antecedents of Action', *British Analytical Philosophy*, B. Williams and A. Montefiore (eds.) (London 1966), pp. 211ff.

20. See, for example, S. Toulmin, 'Reasons and Causes', *Explanation in the Behavioural Sciences*, R. Borger and F. Cioffi (eds.) (Cambridge 1970), p. 21.

21. See S. Hampshire, *Thought and Action* (London 1959), ch. 2, and M. Ayers, *The Refutation of Determinism* (London 1968), pp. 28–32.

22. See *A Realist Theory of Science*, p. 107.

23. T. Huxley, *Methods and Results* (London 1894).

24. G. Santayana quoted in D. Armstrong, *A Materialist Theory of Mind* (London 1968), p. 9.

25. G. Santayana quoted in J. Shaffer, *The Philosophy of Mind* (New Jersey 1968), p. 70.

26. Thus not for the first time does transcendental idealism reveal only a paper improvement on empiricism. Note that just as the natural world (as distinct from our understanding of it) can only be changed by altering the initial conditions of supposedly deterministic universal laws (*qua* empirical regularities), so here human behaviour can only be changed by operating on stimulus conditions of a crudely physical kind – as in the most reductionist forms of the operant conditioning of Skinnerian behaviourism!

27. Inasmuch as the (α/β) distinction is invoked with respect to mental (and other typically unobserved and unobservable) acts, this criterion may be extended to cover them also.

28. See *A Realist Theory of Science*, ch. 2, sec. 5.
29. See D. Davidson, 'Actions, Reasons and Causes', p. 85.
30. P. Winch, *The Idea of a Social Science*, p. 29.
31. See, for example, A. MacIntyre, 'The Idea of a Social Science', PAS Supp. 41 (1967), reprinted in A. Ryan (ed.), *op. cit.*, pp. 19–20.
32. One can thus concur with Ricoeur when he says: 'The philosopher trained in the school of Descartes knows that things are doubtful, that they are not as they appear; but he does not doubt that consciousness is as it appears to itself; in consciousness meaning and consciousness of meaning coincide. Since Marx, Nietzsche and Freud this too has become doubtful' (*Freud and Philosophy* (New Haven 1970), p. 30). But add that the distinction between consciousness and its meaning (or adequate description) is not only a condition for a science *of* consciousness, but for any science which *uses* consciousness, and hence for *any* science at all.
33. As already remarked, the agent's special authority is never absolute. It derives in the last instance from the fact that what is to be explained consists in or depends upon episodes in his/her life (and therefore depends upon his/her unity and continuity as a biological individual), whether or not the episodes occurred prior to the acquisition of a language and the onset of reflexivity. Now because the episodes are episodes in *his/her* life, the agent is *ontologically* in a uniquely privileged position, but we know, since Freud, that the very privilege of his/her position may sometimes be so unbearable as to necessitate a compensating (equilibrating) repression, so that ontological privilege does not automatically carry over into *epistemological* authority. Of course the status of the agent's account may be reinforced by relativizing the *aims* of inquiry.
34. Aristotle, *De Motu Animalium*, 701 a 7ff.
35. The category of wants may be extended analytically to include needs, and more generally to signify the conative component in action (however it is on some occasion most felicitously described). Note that it is the fact that wants are grounded in beliefs that makes our wants rationally assessable. Now if an agent may be said to have an interest in X if X facilitates the achievement of his/her wants, then it follows not only that an agent may be unaware of his/her real interests, but that his/her real interests may be false, grounded in illusions.
36. See C. Whiteley, *op. cit.*, p. 57.
37. L. Wittgenstein, *Remarks on the Foundations of Mathematics* (Oxford 1956), pt. 2, sec. 77.
38. For as Freud stressed, 'we must learn to emancipate ourselves from the importance of the symptom of "being conscious"', *The Standard Edition of the Complete Psychological Works*, 14 (London 1953–64), p. 193.
39. See esp. D. Armstrong, *op. cit.* CSM is sometimes also referred to as the 'contingent-identity' thesis, because it is held to be a contingent fact that the mind is just the brain – shown not just by the logical possibility of disembodied existence, but by the empirical discovery that the brain is the physical 'seat' of mental functions.
40. Such alternatives are always open in principle on the frontiers of any branch of science (see *A Realist Theory of Science*, p. 180). And *here* one reaches the frontiers of the human sciences.
41. See, for example, A. Luria, *The Working Brain* (Harmondsworth 1970), and S. Rose, *The Conscious Brain* (Harmondsworth 1976).
42. See, for example, J. Beloff, 'Mind-Body Interactionism in the Light of the Parapsychological Evidence', *Theoria to Theory* 10 (1976).

43. In this respect I agree with Smart and Armstrong in holding that statements such as 'I am thinking now' are 'topic-neutral', in that, in Armstrong's words, 'they say that something is going on within us, something apt for the causing of certain sorts of behaviour, but they say nothing of the nature of this process' (D. Armstrong, *op. cit.*, p. 121).

44. CSM involves two steps: (1) the definition of a mental state, both in opposition to the classical view as an inner arena and to behaviourism as an outward act, as a (real) state of the person apt for the production of certain sorts of physical behaviour, so that the mind is seen as an inner arena identified by its causal relations to the outward act (see *ibid.*, pp. 82ff); and (2) the speculative identification of these inner processes with the physico-chemical workings of the brain (*ibid.*, pp. 89ff). SEPM accepts (1) in essentials but, seeing the inner arena as characterized by the possession of emergent powers, rejects (2).

45. See *A Realist Theory of Science*, p. 115.

46. CSM is logically coherent, MI is not. Society can never be reduced to individuals, because it is (despite social contract theory) a necessary condition for any intentional act, and not just for our understanding of it; whereas minds are certainly not a necessary condition for physico-chemical laws, as distinct from our understanding of them. Moreover, whereas no one would deny that there could be N-states without P-states (and the reverse is not self-evidently false), it is absurd to deny that there could be P-states without S-states or vice versa. On the other hand there is a problem about the consistent *statement* of CSM, which MI (unless forced into solipsism) avoids.

47. See, for example, H. Putnam, 'The Mental Life of Some Machines', J. Glover, *op. cit.*, p. 93; and J. Deutsch, 'The Structural Basis of Behaviour', *ibid.*, p. 69.

48. For instance, several studies, most notably those of Schacter, show that the same physiological state may be experienced in different ways and the same experience may be associated with different physiological states (so that, for example, stomach contractions and hunger may be out of phase).

49. See, for example, D. Davidson, 'Psychology as Philosophy', p. 102.

50. It is thus quite incorrect to argue that 'knowledge of the goals of a teleological machine is of value to the person who does not know the causal explanation of its behaviour, but to anyone who does know them, it is in principle dispensable' (C. Whiteley, *op. cit.*, p. 25). For the position at which I set a thermostat determines the resultant state of the room; and unless my actions (and hence my decisions, beliefs and desires) and the mechanical operations of the heating system can be incorporated into a single deterministic system, knowledge of the particular goals is indispensable. And indeed, in the normal case, it is knowledge of the principles of the machine that is superfluous.

51. See R. Taylor, *Metaphysics* (New Jersey 1966), pp. 8–10.

52. See, for example, D. Armstrong, *op. cit.*, pp. 365–6.

53. Notice that a materialistic (in the sociological sense) explanation of religion, which may issue in a real definition such as 'religion is the opium of the people', does not deny the existence of religious beliefs and practices. And inasmuch as the explanation situates these as, or as involving, illusions, they are explained in terms of other social realities (economic, political, cultural) distinct from those beliefs and practices. In any event, in preserving the sociological reality of their object, the sociologist's practice is directly analogous to that of the biochemist who identifies the chemical structure of

genes with DNA molecules, or that of the physicist who explains secondary qualities in terms of primary ones.

54. See B. Spinoza: 'If two things have nothing in common with one another, one cannot be the cause of the other' (*Ethics* (London 1959), pt. 1, prop. 3).
55. See, for example, D. Armstrong, *op. cit.*, pp. 49–53.
56. It is important to refrain from prematurely (that is, in advance of scientific theory) reifying *P*-states or powers as of entities either of a material or immaterial kind. It is likely, though by no means definite and certainly not necessary, that for every *P*-state there is some or other *N*-state, so that mind is only manifest in matter (though paranormal psychology contra-indicates this). But this does not affect the question of causality. Again, one need not speculate as to whether there is a direct *P*-trigger for *N*-mechanisms (as for example Eccles seems to believe) or whether, as seems more plausible, *P*-states transcategorially determine *N*-states triggering *N*-mechanisms. This again is in principle an open topic for scientific investigation.
57. For even if *N*-states determine the action of *N*-mechanisms, unless it is possible to predict the *N*-state which initiates a set of physiological and physical processes from antecedent *N*-states without recourse to *P*-states (or powers), mind is explanatorily irreducible (and hence, given the argument of sections 2 and 3, autonomously real).
58. Hypothetically, the paradigm may then be extended to cover the cases of the paranormal analogues of agency and perception (viz. psycho-kinesis and extrasensory perception respectively), where the suggestion is that a person's *P*-states may affect matter or another person's *P*-states without the mediation of his or her brain states. See, for example, J. Beloff, *op. cit.*
59. See, for example, L. Bloomfield, *Linguistic Aspects of Science* (Chicago 1939).
60. See, for example, W. Dray, 'Historical Understanding as Rethinking', reprinted in *Readings in the Philosophy of Science*, B. Brody (ed.) (New Jersey 1970).
61. See, for example, C. G. Hempel, 'Explanation in Science and History', reprinted in *Philosophical Analysis and History*, W. Dray (ed.) (New York 1966), p. 118 or *Aspects of Scientific Explanation* (New York 1963), p. 471; or K. Popper, *Objective Knowledge* (Oxford 1972), p. 179.
62. See, for example, C. G. Hempel, *loc. cit.* or A. Donagan, 'The Popper–Hempel Theory Reconsidered', W. Dray (ed.), *op. cit.*, p. 155.
63. See, for example, S. Lukes, 'Some Problems about Rationality', reprinted in B. Wilson (ed.), *Rationality* (Oxford 1970).
64. See C. Taylor, 'Interpretation and the Sciences of Man', *Review of Metaphysics* 25 (1971), reprinted in P. Connerton (ed.), *Critical Sociology* (Harmondsworth 1976), p. 164.
65. See, for example, B. Fay, 'Practical Reasoning, Rationality and the Explanation of Intentional Action', *Journal for the Theory of Social Behaviour* 8 (1) (1975), esp. pp. 90–1.
66. See, for example, D. Bloor, *Knowledge and Social Imagery* (London 1976), ch. 1 and *passim*.
67. S. Freud, *op. cit.*, 10. See also B. Fay, *op. cit.*, pp. 93–5.
68. See M. Godelier's distinction between contradictions *within* and contradictions *between* structures (*op. cit.*). Positivism, of course, with its tacit presupposition of closed systems, cannot think either of these species of real contradiction. Such contradictions may or may not be historically (or biographically) significant, that is, productive of transformations, such as

scientific discoveries, personality changes, social revolutions. But they contravene the requirement of empirical generality explicit in the deductive–nomological model and implicit in the Humean theory of causal laws. Consequently, change can only be explained consistently by invoking exogenous factors (for example, great men, the weather, luck, etc.).

69. See, for example, M. Hollis, 'Reason and Ritual', reprinted in A. Ryan (ed.), *op. cit.*
70. See, for example, D. Davidson, 'Psychology as Philosophy', p. 109.
71. See R. Harré and P. Secord, *op. cit.*, ch. 7.
72. See M. Hollis, *Models of Man* (Cambridge 1977), ch. 5.
73. See Q. Skinner, '"Social Meaning" and the Explanation of Social Action', reprinted in *The Philosophy of History*, P. Gardiner (ed.) (Oxford 1974).
74. See D. Adlam *et al.*, 'Psychology, Ideology and the Human Subject', *Ideology and Consciousness* 1 (1977), p. 38 and L. Althusser, 'Freud and Lacan', *Lenin and Philosophy* (London 1971), p. 201.
75. Hobbes and Bramhall, *Questions Concerning Liberty, Necessity and Chance*, 4 (London 1841).

Chapter 4

Philosophies

Metaphilosophical Preliminaries

An account of science can be criticized, or shown to be inadequate, in a number of ways. A *transcendental refutation* is obtained if it can be shown to be inconsistent with the possibility of science, or of certain generally recognized scientific activities. Clearly such a refutation itself presupposes a *transcendental analysis* – for one must know what the conditions of science's possibility are that the refuted account cannot sustain. Such an analysis will in general be able to show under what conditions, if any, the refuted account obtains: that is, what the conditions of possibility of the erroneous account itself are. I shall call such a transcendental demonstration a *transcendental situation*: it is an argument in the philosophy of the philosophy of science, rather than the philosophy of science, and it stands to Kant's 'Dialectic' rather as a transcendental analysis stands to his 'Analytic'. Both together comprise one sense of the term 'critique': what I shall call a *transcendental critique* (though I shall occasionally also use this concept just to denote a transcendental refutation).

In addition to such transcendental problems, an inadequate account of science may generate *theoretical, empirical* and *methodological* problems; and it may be subjected to criticism on these and at least one other kind of ground, viz. that of its *social* effects (which may be internal or external to science), for example as some or other *ideology*. Theoretical, empirical and methodological problems are problems of *theory-articulation, theory-confirmation* and *theory-application* respectively. Social problems pertain to the effects of the application, or the attempted application, of the account of science. Clearly it is not only inadequate accounts which encounter these sorts of problems: adequate ones may do so too, but they do not generate them in virtue of their falsity, and so cannot, for example, function as ideology.

Criticism of an account of science on theoretical grounds seeks either to show that the account is internally inconsistent or, if it is consistent, that it produces problems insuperable in its own terms. Such an *immanent critique* may suggest that there is a transcendental one, but it does not in itself enable us to identify it. Both transcendental and immanent critiques may be reinforced with *reductiones ad absurdum*. Reductios derive their force from a confrontation with, or affront to, our intuitions. They can never be absolutely decisive in philosophy. For it is always possible that it is our intuitions (or even the substantive scientific knowledge) that is at fault.

But transcendental and immanent critiques must be distinguished from what I shall characterize as an *explanatory critique*. Such a critique of an account of science presupposes not just a transcendental critique (which, *qua* refutation, corresponds in philosophy to the satisfaction of criteria for theory-preference in substantive science). It involves in addition an *explanation* of the reproduction of the account as an accepted and 'lived' body of beliefs, which necessitates a mode of substantive *sociological* explanation. Now such an explanatory critique, in so far as it allows one to show the account to be both *false* and *necessary ipso facto* enables the satisfaction of the minimal criteria for that account as 'ideological' (see Chapter 2). Such an explanatory critique entails of course an *evaluative* one. In general, in this study my criticism of philosophical systems is restricted to the level of immanent and transcendental critiques; in the sequel it is developed to the level of explanatory critiques, as I proceed from refutation and situation to substantive explanation.

Empirical criticism consists in confronting the account of science with a certain reading of history or set of sociological findings, indicating a variance between scientific practice and its explicit or implicit description in the account under attack. Thus criticism contrasting the complexity, diversity and apparent irrationality of actual practices with the simplicity, monism and stereotypifying idealism of leading philosophical accounts has assumed great importance in recent years – at least since the publication of *The Structure of Scientific Revolutions*. Indeed it is tantamount to the manifesto of 'the sociology of science'. It is, however, always vulnerable to normative counter-attack (as exemplified by Popperian responses to Kuhn), in which reality is judged more or less unfavourably in the light of the standards set by the idealized model of science. Such a stratagem can, however, only secure for the philosophical account a temporary or relative reprieve. For if the account is not to be dismissible as totally Utopian, it must, under certain conditions, be historically possible; and our evidence for unrealized historical possibilities can only be grounded in our *analysis* of what has been actualized, as revealed by historical and sociological research.

Methodological criticism is the counterpart in the applied or practical sphere to the other modalities of criticism in the realm, so to speak, of theory. Clearly, if an account of science is inconsistent with its possibility, it follows that it cannot be applied (though the converse is not the case). And as such it is subject to *direct* methodological criticism. But the *attempt* may still be made to apply an inapplicable theory. And such an attempt may generate in practice a range of highly significant effects. I shall characterize as *indirect*, criticism of a theory on the grounds of the effects of the attempts to apply it, whether or not it is in fact applicable. Such effects may be in principle manifest or latent; discursive or non-discursive; acknowledged or unacknowledged; and overt or covert. *Overt* effects are straightforward results or consequences of the theory. *Covert* effects presuppose, or depend upon, for their generation and efficacy aspects of reality which the account denies or cannot sustain. Their *identification* therefore generally presupposes a transcendental refutation. Covert effects may function tacitly or non-tacitly: in the former case they utilize (or depend upon) an implicit contradiction, in the latter case an explicit one (whether it is recognized as such or not).

The concept of a (tacit) covert effect allows us to pose an interesting question: if philosophy is indeed (as I argued in Chapter 1) an apodeictic discipline which can establish necessary truths about the world (that is, about what the world must be like for some social activity to be possible), then what happens if *what is necessary in practice is in theory or practice denied*? The result of such transcategorial inconsistency will be seen in the sequel to this study to be an 'algebra', having something of the nature of a logic of false consciousness, in which, for instance, the naturalization of science achieved in classical empiricism can be seen to be accomplished only at the necessary cost of the humanization of nature. Now the effects of such transformations, produced in the esoteric discourse of philosophy, are open questions for sociology. For philosophy, whether it likes it, admits it, or not, is a causal agent in society. And in Volume II I shall show how, if one wishes to understand the mode of production and reproduction of philosophical systems, they must be conceived as social objects. There I shall argue that it is in the generation of their (overt and covert) effects that the explanation of their efficacy as systems of thought very largely lies. Occasionally in this chapter I will indicate an ideological connection. But for the most part I will be content merely to criticize philosophically those efficacious ideologies that in the sequel I set out to explain sociologically. It is, however, worth emphasizing, in view of widespread misunderstanding on this point, that such philosophical criticism is both an indispensable prolegomenon to, and an essential ingredient of, sociological explanation. For the sociology of philosophy cannot be conducted in a philosophical vacuum. On the contrary, it presupposes a transcendental analysis of the activity that is the object of the reflection of the philosophical theory concerned; and, if the theory is false, a corresponding critique. For only in this way can the full array of the effects (including covert ones) of the theory be captured; and its mode of reproduction in any actual historical society be successfully delineated.

My investigation into the leading philosophies of social science may be conveniently introduced with a paradox. Positivism, grounded in the epistemological datum of the experience of the social scientific subject, produces some concept of the generality of its object, but at the price of rendering social activity quite *unlike* science; while hermeneutics, grounded in the ontological notion of the conceptuality of the object of social scientific understanding, manages partially to reconstitute the experience of subjects in society, but at the price of rendering social activity *insusceptible* to science. For the positivist, science is outside society; for the hermeneuticist, society is outside science.[1] And this paradox is reflected in the character of the debate, or rather the structure of the confrontation, between the two. The weaknesses of the one position find their antitheses in the strengths of the other. Positivism sustains embryonically adequate concepts of law (generality), ideology and society; hermeneutics embryonically adequate concepts of subject-ivity, meaning and culture. The self-authenticating experience of a subject (of the experience of *objects*) finds its reflection, or mirror image, in the constitutive conceptualizing activity of a (subject-) object (of the experience of *subjects*) or, in a significant refraction due to Gadamer, of a *subject* (of the experience of objects).

Now I have already suggested (in Chapter 1) that it is in the ontology of empirical realism and the conception of (tacitly gendered) man it presupposes that the analytical origins of this antinomic problem-field lie. Kantian syntheses – from Weber to Habermas – do not break from this underlying problem-field, and as a result merely (at best) artificially *conjoin* the partial insights of the principal disputants. Transcendental realism, in subjecting the underlying problem-field itself to critique, situates the possibility of a genuine *Aufhebung* (or sublation) of the quarrel between the champions of meaning and of law. Thus, on the new critical naturalism that emerges, justice is done both to the *conceptuality* (or concept-dependence) and to the *transfactuality* (or generality) of the subject-matter of social science. The production of meaning is seen as law-governed but not determined; and the conceptual activity of social agents as at once both necessary for, and necessitated by, social structures and subject to critique both for what it presents and for what it obscures. Now such an explanatory critique is itself a moment in the process it describes. So that social science, on this conception, is critical, self-reflexive and totalizing. And its objects are existentially, but not causally, intransitive; concept-dependent, but not conceptual; and transfactually efficacious, but irreducibly historical (that is, bound in space and restricted in time).

The Critique of the Positivist Tradition:
Explanation, Prediction and Confirmation

Positivism pivots on the Humean theory of causal laws, viz. that laws are or depend upon constant conjunctions of atomistic events or states of affairs, interpreted as the objects of actual or possible experiences. This theory itself follows ineluctably from the requirements that knowledge be certain and given-in-experience: the empiricist solution to the problem of knowledge, ascribing a predicate 'knowledge' to a subject 'man'. Such a solution presupposes, of course, both a conception of man as passive and autonomized in experience and a conception of the world as constituted by given and atomistic facts, so as to produce its duplex result: viz. that whatever is known is certain and given-in-experience and whatever is given-in-experience and certain is known. And it depends critically upon the ideologically supersaturated and philosophically underanalysed notions of 'experience' and 'facts'. Experience discharges a double (ontological/epistemological, explanatory/normative) ambiguity; while the facts supervise an impossible (transitive/intransitive or human/non-human) correspondence.

Most of the debate initiated by positivist philosophy of social science has not, however, been about the Humean theory as such, or about its structurally generative assumptions. Rather it has revolved around the associated (Popper–Hempel) model of explanation or its implications, such as a parity between explanation and prediction; or around Popper's polemical use of Nicod's criterion, which presupposes and implies that theory of laws, to generate a critique of what he calls 'historicism'.

The positivist account of science is based on two principles:

P_1: *the principle of empirical-invariance*, viz. that laws are or depend upon empirical regularities; and

P_2: *the principle of instance-confirmation* (or falsification), viz. that laws are confirmed (or falsified) by their instances (Nicod's criterion).

Flowing from P_1 are characteristic theories of causality, explanation, prediction (and its symmetry with explanation) and the development of science; and P_2 secretes various theories of demarcation and scientific rationality.[2] Underpinning both is the empiricist solution to the problem of knowledge mentioned above (P_0). The characteristic theory of explanation is implicit in Hume, was made explicit by Mill and Jevons, and has been enthusiastically promulgated in recent times by Popper and, above all, Hempel. On it, events are held to be explained by deducing them from one or more universal laws (in the sense of P_1, that is *qua* empirical invariances), together with a statement of their initial conditions. It should be noted that P_1 in its stronger or weaker (Kantian) forms continues to be accepted by almost all the factions of orthodox (non-transcendental realist) philosophy of science, including those which reject P_0.

In general, positivists have assumed the adequacy of their account of the natural sciences and have sought to show, with increasing difficulty, that it can be stretched to fit the social sciences too. Now it might be thought sufficient for my purposes here merely to demonstrate its inadequacy to the natural sciences and then pass on immediately to consider the positive case for hermeneutics. However, the recurrence of positivist themes within that tradition has already been noted. Moreover an examination of positivist philosophy of social science possesses independent value. First, in facilitating the recapitulation of significant differences between the social and natural sciences, now approached from the 'formal' rather than (as in Chapter 2) the 'material' side. Second, in order to allow the distillation of the proto-scientific achievements of that tradition, when tempered in practice by realism (that is, in its non-vulgar form).

I have shown elsewhere[3] that the common presupposition of P_1 and P_2, and hence of the theories based on them, is closed systems, that is, systems where constant conjunctions of events obtain. By considering the examples actually proffered by positivists of Humean causal laws, a strong prima-facie case can be made out for supposing that there are no (at least hitherto known) Humean causal laws, that is, empirical invariances (of an epistemically non-vacuous kind), and that therefore social systems are (as far as we know) open.[4] For all the alleged laws cited in support of the deductive–nomological model, or some other positivist fable, are taken from the natural sciences[5] or are false[6] or analytically, that is, definitionally, true or trivial, or too detailed or specific to count as laws in the requisite sense (for example, in virtue of their mentioning the names of individuals or particular spatio-temporal regions or so-called 'concrete universals', such as capitalism) – or even contain no element of generality at all.[7]

Humanists, hermeneuticists and other anti-naturalists, jointly comprising the anti-scientific romantic reaction which has always coexisted in symbiosis with positivism, have of course eagerly seized on this absence to demonstrate the refractory nature of society to scientific explanation (thereby of course implicitly accepting the positivist account of science). Positivists, for their part, have been forced *either* to modify their philosophical criteria *and/or* to cite, in extenuation, some feature of the social world to account for this gap between philosophical theory and substantive practice.

Thus examining the first option, nothing is more revealing than to observe the traces, in the pantheon of models currently advertised by deductivists,[8] of the rapid backsliding in which they have found it expedient to engage as they have successively loosened their criteria for laws and explanations, in order to accommodate deductive–statistical, inductive–probabilistic, partial, incomplete and elliptical explanations and so-called explanation sketches, until in the end their position reduces to the bland reassertion of the (transcendentally refutable, and refuted)[9] doctrine of regularity determinism. Now these extensions and modifications, besides in many cases suffering from internal difficulties of their own, all vitiate the point of the original deductivist position, with its Laplacean rationale. Lacking any epistemological grounding, they also lack an ontological one, in that they fail to get any grip on the *differentia specifica* of the social sciences. On the other hand, those explanation forms which are conceded to be both legitimate and prima-facie distinctive of the human sciences, such as genetic, functional and so-called rational explanations, are all analysed as presupposing deductive–nomological ones,[10] and so fail when confronted with the phenomenon of open systems. In short, positivism is caught in an impasse here.

The other option for positivism is to take one of the lines already anticipated by Mill and Comte respectively, and argue either that the empirical invariances that govern social life are so *complex* as to elude detection, or that they operate at some more *basic* (for example, neurophysiological) level. In this way characteristic 'interactionist' and 'reductionist' regresses are generated in the search for a more complete and/or atomistic state-description.[11] These lines rest of course on a confusion of generalization with abstraction and of empirical invariances with laws. And here again the positivist response to the phenomenon of open systems is only intelligible on the assumption of an unthinking commitment to the legend of regularity determinism.

Moving in the direction of realism, Scriven and D. and J. Willer have recognized the *normic* and *abstract* character of generalizations, without providing satisfactory analyses of them. Thus Scriven points out that the generalizations presupposed in social explanations such as (S_1) 'Strict Jews fast on the Day of Atonement', (S_2) 'Diligent pupils attend lectures', (S_3) 'Trade-unionists tend to vote Labour', typically contain, or at least should be construed as subject to the operation of, modifiers such as 'tends to', 'normally', 'typically', etc.[12] And he styles them as possessing a 'selective immunity' to apparent counter-examples.[13] But he does not furnish an adequate rationale for the use of the modifier and (despite the qualification 'apparent') leaves the basis of the selective immunity obscure. The key question is this: in what way is one justified in using statements like S_1–S_3 for explanatory purposes in open systems

– that is, when even, though their antecedents are instantiated, their consequents are unrealized? Similarly, D. and J. Willer, in identifying the error involved in 'interactionism', see that the empiricist mistakes generalization for abstraction,[14] but leave the status of abstraction unclear. Indeed in asserting that 'laws are not to be found in nature'[15] and glossing them as 'mental inventions',[16] they are in danger of lapsing into a rationalistic Kantianism in which it is the synthesizing procedures of scientific theory (presumably as embodied in the scientific community) that impose a determinate order on the world. Confining their criticism of empiricism entirely to what I called (in Chapter 1) the transitive dimension, they are unable to identify the ontology of (relatively) enduring and transfactually active mechanisms that grounds abstraction in science. And so they must inevitably resort to the notion of abstraction as involving the establishment of an isomorphism between theoretical non-observables and empirical observables:[17] that is, between 'rational thought' and the so-called 'empirical world'. But this will not unduly worry empiricists who are quite willing to concede a sham battle over knowledge as long as they retain the world!

Now it will be remembered that I argued (in the third section of Chapter 1) that laws cannot be constant conjunctions of events, because such conjunctions (1) are extremely rare, and (2) must in general be artificially produced. On the first count one has the problem of what governs phenomena in open systems. The empiricist must either say that nothing does (weak actualism) or that, as yet, science has discovered no laws (strong actualism). On the second count the identification of laws and constant conjunctions leads to the absurdity that human beings, in their experimental activity, cause or even change (rather than merely empirically identify) the laws of nature.[18] It leaves the experimental establishment, just as the first problem leaves the practical application, of knowledge without a rationale. Conversely, an ontology of transfactually active mechanisms irreducible to, productive of and occasionally (normally under artificial conditions) actually manifest in sequences of events, renders both processes immediately intelligible. Thus the correct corollary to draw from the absence of closed systems is not that there are no social laws (or that they are not strictly universal, that is, transfactually applicable, within their range). This would only follow if P_1 were true. It is rather that, as argued in Chapter 2, criteria for the rational assessment (replacement, acceptance, rejection, modification, diversification and development) of theories cannot be predictive. And so must be *exclusively explanatory*. Moreover once one allows that natural laws are normic, and transfactually applicable, the inadequacy of positivist and quasi-realist responses to open systems is shown up. And the problem, around which discussion has hitherto turned, of a difference in *form* between natural and social laws (explanations, etc.)

disappears – to be replaced by an altogether different problem (carrying with it a different, and less radical, contrast) relating to a difference in the conditions for their *identification*.

If the analysis of experimental and applied activity establishes a transcendental refutation of positivism, we are now in a position to transcendentally situate it. It is clear that closed systems are a condition – what I shall call a first-order condition – of the possibility of positivism. But what is the condition of possibility of closed systems? In general, experimental activity – which positivism cannot think (as it is inconsistent with its account of laws). So the second-order conditions of the possibility of positivism are spontaneously occurring closed systems and a particular (behaviouristic) model of man. Positivism can now be seen to involve the illicit generalization of a special case. For the identification of laws and empirical regularities, always illicit (and a category mistake), is impossible outside closed systems. So a second-order critique (see p. 52 above) of positivism consists in situating the spatio-temporally restricted (or, if one likes, historically transient) nature of closed systems (the special case). But a first-order critique consists in demonstrating the categorial differentiation, and the consequent illicit identification in positivism, of causal laws and empirical regularities. Note that this allows us to explain why positivism has a degree of *plausibility* in the natural, as opposed to the social, sciences – viz. because its first-order condition of possibility (closed systems) is sometimes satisfied there. Now the model of man which constitutes a second-order condition of positivism is in resonance with a substantive (pseudo-) scientific theory – behaviourism – in which it finds its echo and perhaps its source. This theory is accurate, and perhaps only, as a surface description of the behaviourist's own practice. Hence one has the paradox that in the very domain where positivism is most inapplicable and its philosophy most absurd, it is most fervently acted upon. The scenario is completed and begins to be explained when it is realized that this theory (behaviourism) is itself a putative object of social scientific explanation, that is, constitutes an aspect of social reality itself.

Positivist philosophy of social science can of course be criticized not only in virtue of its account of *science*, but in virtue of its implicit account of *society*. So stemming from the transcendental deduction of Chapter 2 there arises the possibility of a second transcendental situation of positivism. Now the transformational model implies that social laws are not only normic in form, but spatio-temporally restricted in scope. Positivism of course (despite its origins) cannot allow this. Note that if on the first score the *deducibility* requirement in the deductive–nomological model is violated, on the second score the *covering-law* one is. In short, transcendental analyses of science and society suggest that the subject-matter of social science is both law-like and irreducibly historical in character. *Law-like*, in opposition both to the 'findings' of the interactionist and reductionist wings of (behaviouristic) empiricism and to the humanistic defenders of a truistic (or the advocates of an exclusively *verstehende*) social science. *Historical*, in opposition both to the (rationalistic) individualism of praxology and to the ahistorical schools of structuralism, which (at best) can only account for the most species-general aspects of social life.

The transcendental refutation of positivism implies a radical critique of the Humean theory of causal laws and of the Popper-Hempel theory of explanation. And it implies, through the entailed critique of historicism,[19] a radical asymmetry between explanation and prediction.[20] In both the natural and social sciences laws are normic in form. In both cases theoretical explanation is analogical and retroductive, and historical explanation is conjunctural and retrodictive. In both cases law-like statements must be independently empirically tested and theoretically explained; and in both cases they are transfactually applicable. But, because of the absence of closed systems, decisive test situations are in principle impossible in social science, and so criteria for confirmation must be exclusively explanatory; and, because of the transformational character of social systems, social laws may be (although still universal within their range) historically restricted in scope.

Now explanation in open systems is in general accomplished by a four-phase process:

1. *Resolution* of a complex event into its components (causal analysis).
2. *Redescription* of component causes.
3. *Retrodiction* to possible (antecedent) causes of components via independently validated normic statements.
4. *Elimination* of alternative possible causes of components.

This model, which I shall dub the RRRE model of explanation in open systems,[21] testifies to the multiplicity and plurality of causes in steps (1) and (4) respectively. These features are also caught in Mackie's influential account of a cause as an INUS condition (that is, an Insufficient but Non-redundant part of an Unnecessary but Sufficient condition).[22] However his account is vitiated by an empiricist ontological commitment, and generative analyses of causality are preferable.[23] Note that the RRRE model highlights at phases (2) and (3) the key roles played by the activities of scientific redescription and the transfactual application of knowledge (both strictly incompatible with a Humean account).[24]

On the positivist model, explanation merely generalizes the problem, whereas in scientific and everyday life it resolves it, via the introduction of new (problem-solving, explanatory) concepts. It involves, that is to say, non-logical work. Transcendental realism and idealism agree about the necessity for, but disagree about the nature of, such work. Realism sees it as practical, as well as symbolic, with the explanations constructed in the scientific imagination subject not just to the cognitive constraints of coherence and plausibility, but to the material constraints of empirical test. And it distinguishes, accordingly, between the moment of theory and that of its open-systemic applications. Idealism correctly notes that explanations are situated in space and time: that they are forms of social exchange (and even production), not descriptions of (or inference tickets for predicting) a given world. But realism insists that this social process conveys ontological import, and regards it as subject to objective as well as intersubjective controls.

In addition to transcendental problems, positivism is embroiled in problems of theory-articulation and application (in the domains of, as it were, pure and applied philosophy). Among the problems of theory-articulation that it faces quite generally must be included the galaxy that revolves around the problem of induction. Among those specific to its account of social science must be included those stemming from the attempt to fit the deductive–nomological model to a necessarily open and intrinsically historical subject-matter, and those flowing from the inconsistencies of Popper's attack on historicism.[25]

In considering positivism's problems of theory-application, there are a number of points to note. Firstly, pure positivism is necessarily *inapplicable*. (This follows of course from its transcendental refutation.) Now inasmuch as positivism cannot think the phenomenon of open systems, and conceptualizes laws as correlations between discrete and atomistic events, it cannot do justice to the feature of social science that its laws cannot be plausibly construed as anything other than tendencies, and that its subject-matter requires the totalization of phenomena bearing internal relations to one another. Moreover, the fact that positivism leans on empiricist criteria for ascribing reality means that it cannot do justice to the feature of social science that its objects cannot be made empirically manifest. And this accounts for a constant slippage by positivist social theorists back to some form of behaviouristic individualism and a constant (verificationist) tendency to identify (or reduce) the object of study with (or to) its empirical grounds.[26]

Secondly, proto-science in the positivist mode is forced into more or less conscious realist stratagems, so that there are *inconsistencies* between different levels or aspects of the proto-scientist's practice. Thus Durkheim, having allowed that 'we can know causes scientifically only by the effects they produce'[27] and even that legal and moral rules 'can exist without being actually applied',[28] spoils this by insisting upon purely nominal and operational definitions of such causes and rules, and working with a Humean notion of laws.[29] Similarly, Comte, both in his definition of society and in his eschatology of the sciences, employs a pattern of explanation which is, in his own terms, 'metaphysical'. Inasmuch as the tacit acceptance of an empiricist ontology also vitiates the neo-Kantian tradition, it is instructive to contrast the Marxian and Weberian 'ideal types'. The former is not a one-sided accentuation in thought of an equivalent aspect of an undifferentiated empirical reality, but an attempt to grasp what is really accentuated (or, as it were, lop-sided) in reality; and its focus is causal, not taxonomic.

The third point to note is that the *attempt* may still be made to apply an inapplicable theory, such as positivism, rigorously and systematic-ally. And here I want to distinguish the kind of positivism to be found in social thinkers such as Durkheim, who combined their methodological commitment to positivism with elements of a realist scientific practice, from the vulgar or apologetic positivism characteristic of much of the contemporary 'behavioural sciences'. Now the far greater implausibility of positivism in social science is reflected in the even more detrimental effects of its attempted application. These effects stem partly from its liability to initiate reductionist and interactionist regresses; and partly because the very absence of decisive test situations, coupled with continuing formal allegiance to a *predictive* criterion, serves at once to mystify methodology, protect entrenched (or otherwise privileged) theory, stunt alternatives and/or encourage (a belief in) the unresolv-ability of theoretical conflicts – which, in practice, means their resolution in favour of the status quo. For the same inability of positivism to think this difference – that the human sciences must start their trek to scientificity without that priceless asset, available to the experimental sciences of nature, of sometimes being able to observe or detect in undisturbed fashion the operation of the latent structures of the world – enables it to afford to a system all the privileges (e.g., resist-ance to pseudo-falsification) properly accorded to scientific theories, when such theories may have no claim to that title at all, that is, rank as substantive ideology (in the sense elaborated on pp. 67–8). Positivism here plays a crucial defensive role for established social theories. Let us see how this happens.

Positivism's incapacity to sustain the notions of the stratification and differentiation of reality, and, accordingly, the distinctions between structures and events and open and closed systems, produces (or rather exacerbates) a situation in which, as noted in Chapter 2, undifferen-tiated events become the objects of only conventionally differentiated sciences. Now we know that the attempt to apply an inapplicable theory must in practice generate a range of covert as well as overt effects. Thus positivism's inability to sustain these distinctions, and *a fortiori* the problem of knowledge-production in the social sciences, enables it to give to a system, once it has got off the ground (or if it is otherwise privileged), the covert protection of a *CP* clause inconsistent with its ontology.[30] For, all theories, if interpreted actualistically, are falsified in open systems. Positivists (Popper, Friedman, etc.) typically exploit this theorem against, for example, Marxian economics, yet at the same time invoke a *CP* clause in defence of neo-classical theory. This uneven-handed approach is surely no accident. And in the sequel I shall show how it is that positivism, with its behaviourist implications (and presuppositions), comes to defend an a priori theory of rational action, praxiology, moulded in the lineage of utilitarian theory. In the meantime, it should be noted that any putative science can be regarded as constituted by the intersection of an epistemology and an ontology. Accordingly, it can always be reconstructed as the application of a theory of knowledge (in the transitive dimension) to a more or less specific object (in the intransitive one) such as man. Now the problem-field of the contemporary human sciences is defined in its social ontology by the couple behaviourism/praxiology, and in its general epistemology by the couple interactionism/reductionism: together they fix the vectors that determine a matrix of pseudo-sciences (under the dominance of an interactionist form of behaviourism). One effect of this problem-field is that praxiological content-injunctions are underpinned by empiricist ontological commitments: together they prohibit the juxtaposition of, and sustain the opposition between the terms, 'history' and 'theory' (and more generally, 'science'). But a moment's reflection shows that such a prohibition is already implicit in the structure of the D–N model. For in its nomological requirement it turns its back on history, and in its deducibility requirement it effectively shuts the door on science (any science that must study phenomena which only ever manifest themselves in open systems). Positivism thus functions in the philosophy of social science simultaneously as an *anti-historical histori-cism* and an *anti-scientific scientism*.

The Critique of the Hermeneutical Tradition I: Concepts, Reasons and Rules

I have already suggested that the hermeneutical tradition is determined *in the last instance* by its acceptance of an essentially Humean account of natural science, and more generally of an empiricist ontology. And that significant aspects of the thought of different hermeneutical writers can be reconstructed as dependent upon essentially positivist theories (or their generative presuppositions, such as the core structure P_0 noted on p. 124), either in pure or modified form. The principal modalities of such modification are inversion (or negation), displacement (of a theory on to a subject), transformation (of a theory about a subject) and condensation (viz. the fusion of such modified elements into a single more or less consistent theory or text). In this section and the next I want to focus on Winch's work (here reconstructing his model of explanation, in the fourth section subjecting it to detailed investigation); in the fifth section I will consider the hermeneutical and neo-Kantian traditions more generally.

Formally, Winch's work may be regarded as constituted by the conjunction of a linguistically transposed transcendental idealism and elements of a less rigorous epistemological and social romanticism or expressivism. Both conjuncts are residues of Wittgenstein's later philosophy, and to a lesser extent that of Collingwood. And it is the uneasy coexistence, and incomplete synthesis, of these two strands that accounts for the ambiguities and tensions in Winch's texts.

For Winch the social sciences (or 'studies') and philosophy are at one, in that their method is *conceptual* and their central category that of *meaning*, whereas the method of the natural sciences is *empirical* and their central category *causality*. Winch's idea of the natural sciences is Kantian, rather than simply Humean.[31] But, for him, they are still concerned with *causally regular* behaviour, and are founded on the observation of externally related elements, such as events and states of affairs. The social sciences, on the other hand, are concerned with meaningful, that is (for Winch) *rule-following*, behaviour, and are founded on the understanding of the rules constitutive of the forms of life under study. Their method is that of *Verstehen*, and their aim is the elucidation of conceptual connections between internally related elements, such as actions and the meanings they express.

What is Winch's concept of philosophy? And how does it enable him to assert an identity between it and social science? Winch's general approach to philosophy (as to natural science) is Kantian,[32] but his specific mentor is of course Wittgenstein. Now whereas for Kant the problems of philosophy (at least *qua* metaphysics) were to be resolved by seeing them as problems about the conditions, limits and forms of *knowledge*, for Wittgenstein they were to be resolved by seeing them as problems about the conditions, limits and forms of *language*. The rationalization of the denial of ontology, and the collapse of an intransitive dimension, in what I have called the *epistemic fallacy*,[33] thus takes on a linguistic form, in what could be called the *linguistic fallacy*.[34] (Of course the denial of a philosophical ontology merely results in the tacit presupposition of an implicit one – in this case of an actualist or expressivist one.) But now, in contrast to Kant, nothing outside mind (or culture) remains – as *Verstehen* displaces faith as the means of access to an effectively noumenalized social sphere.[35]

Given, then, that the problems of philosophy are to be reparsed as problems of language, Wittgenstein's particular contribution to their solution is to show that the elements of a language do not get their meaning by standing for some object, but by being used in a form of social life: so that roughly to know the meaning of a word (sentence, etc.) is to know the social rules that govern its use. And Winch's concern is to show how Wittgenstein's analysis of linguistic behaviour as rule-following 'may shed light on other forms of human interaction besides speech. The[se] forms are naturally those to which analogous categories are applicable: those, that is . . . [that] have a *meaning*, a *symbolic* character'.[36] Thus whereas the central theoretical problem of both philosophy (epistemology) and social science (sociology) is the eluci-dation of the concept of a social phenomenon in general, the specific branches of both are concerned with the elucidation of the concepts informing the various kinds of activity and forms of social life (science, art, religion, politics, etc.).[37]

As already noted on (p. 2), Winch has two main arguments for his contrast: an epistemological one, and an ontological one, in which the epistemological one is grounded. Occasionally, Winch seems committed only to the concept-dependence, or conceptuality, of society.[38] But in general his position seems to be that society is entirely conceptual in character.

> When the 'things' in question are purely physical the criteria [for 'sameness' and 'difference'] will be those of an observer. But when one is dealing with intellectual (or, indeed, any kind of social) 'things' that is not so. For their *being* intellectual or social, as opposed to physical, in character depends *entirely* [my italics] on their belonging in a certain way to a system of ideas or mode of living.[39]

Winch's point is, then, that essentially human behaviour exists only in concepts and concepts exist only in such behaviour. This does not mean that they are either fictional or purely individual constructs.[40] But the equation of the conceptual and the essentially human holds good even in the case of basic biological activities.[41]

We can now see why it is that, according to Winch, understanding social institutions cannot be a matter of grasping empirical generaliz-ations, as in the natural sciences. Winch's *claim* is 'that the concepts according to which we normally think of social events are logically incompatible with the concepts belonging to scientific explanation [in that] the former enter into social life itself and not merely into the observer's description of it'.[42] His great *insight* is that social life does not exist independently of the concepts in terms of which agents think their own existence. His *fork* is that the subject-matter of social science must consist just in those *concepts* or else be reducible to the purely *physical* aspects of behaviour (which are susceptible to an external and causal treatment).[43] The subject-matter of the social sciences has the unique property that it entertains beliefs about itself, and (for Winch) unless this were so, its subject-matter would disappear. Hence, as social scientists, our subject-matter must be defined by *its* criteria of significance and not by our own. For instance, to describe an action as praying (or voting) is to employ religious (or political) criteria, but what counts as praying can only be settled from *within* a form of life.

Winch's epistemological conclusions quickly follow from his onto-logical premises. For, given that the subject-matter of social science is constituted by the way in which agents conceptualize their conditions of existence, explanation is to be achieved by understanding (or, as it were, reconceptualizing) their conceptualizations; that is, by grasping the way in which they grasp (or understand) their existence. The social scientist may indeed introduce technical concepts, but they must be defined in terms of those of the societies under study, as the concept of liquidity preference is rooted in business practice;[44] so that our understanding of the aetiology of neuroses will be different in the case of societies (such as that of the Trobriand Islanders) where they have a different concept of fatherhood.[45] Thus the putative social scientist must, inasmuch as she employs a special vocabulary or set of techniques, undergo in principle *three* sets of socialization processes: into the general community into which s/he is born (or of which s/he is now a member); into the special community of social scientists; and into the community s/he is studying. But it is the third community that has epistemological priority; so that the mode of understanding achieved by the social scientist will ideally or actually be that employed by the people s/he is studying. *Verstehen*, or interpretative understanding, thus becomes logically necessary and sufficient for social scientific expla-nation. Regularities constitute at best evidence for the existence of rules. And 'sociological laws', in a neat inversion of the standard positivist line (as enunciated by Popper, Ginsberg, Abel, *et al.*), are now allowed only as possible heuristic devices for the achievement of *Verstehen* – inasmuch as they may be 'helpful in calling one's attention to features of historical situations which one might otherwise have overlooked and in suggesting useful analogies'![46]

I now want to show that Winch's argument for the conceptual nature of social reality is unsound, and that his anti-naturalist stance is based on an untenable theory of science. Any adequate account of social science must be able to do justice to Winch's intuition that the subject-matter of social science is concept-dependent, that is, to sustain the notion of its conceptuality, without committing itself to the position that it is *exhausted* by such conceptualizations or that such conceptualizations are *incorri-gible* (either intrinsically or merely for scientific purposes). Similarly, any adequate account of social science must accept that social causation depends upon the identification by the agents concerned of conceptual connections (that is, that social causation is conceptually and linguistically mediated), so that our knowledge of social causation depends upon our identification of these connections; that is, that social science depends upon *Verstehen*, without committing itself to the position that *Verstehen exhausts* social science, or that the ontology necessitated by its recognition requires a fundamentally different analysis from the normic one appropriate to the sciences of nature.

Social *explananda* indeed depend upon (or consist in) intentional human agency, so that reference to beliefs and other conceptual matter will in general be necessary for an adequate social explanation, but it will not – even where the *explanandum* is itself conceptual – in general be sufficient for it. For such action always, or almost always, has a *material* (or outer) aspect, so that it cannot be reduced to its *conceptual* component (or inner cause). Winch, correctly perceiving ideas to be distinctive of social reality, incorrectly infers them to be exhaustive of it. His own examples show this. Being in prison[47] or fighting in a war[48] is not just (or even perhaps necessarily) possessing a certain idea of what one is doing: it is being physically separated from the rest of society or being party to an armed conflict; and without the separation and the conflict, the concepts would lack the material substrate, as it were, essential for their correct application. Winch himself provides an excellent example of the material (physical) aspect of social behaviour in his discussion of a passage from the film *Shane*, when he explains the meaning of an interchange of glances in terms of 'the loneliness, the threat of danger, the sharing of a common life in difficult circumstances, the satisfaction in physical effort and so on'.[49] Winch cannot evade this objection by giving a (physical) behaviourist analysis of concepts without undermining the basis of his (physical/conceptual, empirical generalization/rule) contrast. Moreover it applies in principle even where the social *explanandum* is itself a belief. For beliefs cannot be dislocated from their intentional objects, and in particular the material practices (always involving, to a greater or lesser extent, the transformation of nature) in which they are inscribed.[50] Now just as social behaviour typically consists in something more than being in possession of the concept under which one's action falls (and some social behaviour – for example, infantile sexuality – may occur in the absence of *any* concept, or at least any concept amenable to a Winch–Wittgensteinian analysis), so some social behaviour, though not existing independently of *some* concept, exists independently of its *adequate* concept. Moreover in the case of some social behaviour the concept possessed by the agent may actually function so as to *mask*, repress, mystify, obscure or otherwise occlude the nature of the activity concerned.[51] Again this point is perfectly general and applies to concepts of beliefs (and other conceptual material), as much as to concepts of behaviour. In short, social life has a material aspect and agent's conceptualizations are corrigible.

Just as Winch's ontological claim depends upon the tacit acceptance of an empiricist theory of existence, so his epistemological contrast depends upon the tacit acceptance of P_1. That is, Winch takes it for granted that the application of the categories of causality and law presuppose empirical regularities. Now it is certainly the case, as Winch asserts, that one could know the probabilities for the occurrence of certain words in Chinese without being able to understand what was being said[52] (and, conversely, that understanding a language – in the sense of knowing (being able to use) the generative structures at work in the production of grammatical, contextually appropriate and meaningful sentences – does not enable one to make any predictions about verbal behaviour).[53] But transcendental realism also distinguishes statistical regularities from causal laws: regularities constitute at best grounds for laws, and laws exist and act independently of particular outcomes. Hence there is a complete epistemic symmetry here between the natural and the social sciences.

In his attempted reconciliation of the claims of *Erklären* and *Verstehen*, Weber had defined a sociological law as 'a statistical regularity which corresponds to an intelligible intended meaning'. Weber regarded statistical grounds as necessary, if not only (because of his general neo-Kantian commitments), then at least partly because of the problem posed by the possibility of a plurality of interpretations for any given piece of social behaviour. For Winch, at least in principle, this problem cannot arise. For it is always the interpretation of the culture concerned (more or less embellished by sociological concepts rooted in it) that is correct. (Any problem of verification must be reposed as one of communication or translation.) There is always in principle a *definitive interpretation* for any given form of social behaviour, because there is always in principle a determinate set of rules that the agents are following in it. For unless there were such a set of rules, on Winch's analysis, the behaviour could not properly be said to be 'social' at all.

Tables 4.1 and 4.2 summarize differences between positivism as represented by Durkheim, neo-Kantianism as represented by Weber, hermeneutics as represented by Winch, and transcendental realism with respect to the status of empirical regularities and agents' conceptualizations in a social scientific explanation. For Durkheim empirical regularities are necessary and sufficient; for Weber necessary but not sufficient; for both Winch and the transcendental realist critical naturalism developed here they are neither necessary nor sufficient. However, transcendental realism differentiates itself from Winch in holding that this is also the case in natural science; which is why its

Table 4.1 Status of Constant Conjunction of Events in Explanation

	Necessary	*Sufficient*
For explanation in social science		
Durkheim	✓	✓
Weber	✓	✗
Winch	✗	✗
Transcendental Realism (TR)	✗	✗
For explanation in natural science		
Winch	✓	✗
TR	✗	✗

position in the philosophy of social science is *naturalistic*. Turning to the status of agent's conceptualizations in a social scientific explanation, transcendental realism here agrees with Weber that reference to them is necessary but not sufficient, disagreeing thus with both Durkheim, on the one hand, and Winch, on the other. It disagrees with Winch, moreover, in holding such conceptualizations to be corrigible, and from Weber in holding that their correction may itself form an intrinsic part of a full social scientific explanation (see Chapter 2). However, in opposition to Durkheim, transcendental realism holds the corrigibility of such conceptualizations to be contingent; which is why its position is characterizable as a *contingently critical naturalism*. For transcendental realism, then, laws remain transfactual in form, but are now concept-dependent in their mode of operation. And concepts do not exhaust social reality, but rather themselves stand in need (in principle) of social explanation.

Given, then, that for Winch social life is to be explained by *rendering it intelligible* in the terms used by the agents under study (which is precisely what constitutes it as a form of *social* life), the reconstruction of a model for social scientific explanation depends largely upon the reconstruction of the way in which social phenomena are rendered intelligible in substantive social life. Winch's text is structured by four key concepts: the concepts of *concepts, meanings, reasons* and *rules*. On

Table 4.2 Status of Agent's Conceptions in Social Scientific Explanation

	Reference necessary for	*Reference sufficient for*	*Necessary correction in*	*Contingent correction in*
Durkheim	✗	✗	✓	
Weber	✓	✗		✗
Winch	✓	✓		✗
Transcendental Realism	✓	✗		✓

the whole they are not clearly differentiated. But, as a rough approximation, one could say that for Winch, social behaviour is necessarily (definitionally) symbolic or meaningful, and typically (though not necessarily) done for a reason; concepts are identified with meanings, and the category of meaning explicated in terms of that of rules. For Winch that people can act for reasons (or motives) depends upon the possibility of their behaviour being meaningful, that is, the existence of a framework of rules; but the converse is not the case.

Given the non-identity of meanings and reasons, and the lack of correspondence Winch posits between meaningful and intentional action (where the latter is conceived as action performed for a reason),[54] it seems wrong to reconstruct Winch's model explanation, as MacIntyre does,[55] in the following way:

A (i) N does A for reasons $R_1 \ldots R_n$.
   (ii) R_i is rendered intelligible by being set in the context of social rules and conventions $S_1 \ldots S_k$.

Rather, as the concept of rule is designed to explicate that of meaning rather than reason *per se*,[56] I think one should construe Winch's model of explanation as follows:

B 1 (i) N does A.
     (ii) A is meaningful, hence governed by rules $S_{a1} \ldots S_{ak}$.
B 2   Why does N do A?
         Either (a) because $S_{a1} \ldots S_{ak}$ prescribe it
             or (b) for reasons $R_1 \ldots R_n$.
         In case (a) no further explanation is required;
         in case (b) one can ask further:
B 3   Why does N possess (act for) reason R_i?
         Either (α) because $S_{i1} \ldots S_{ik}$ prescribe it or render it appropriate
         or (β) for higher-order reasons $R_{i1} \ldots R_{in}$
         or (γ) for no (further) reason at all (that is R_i is spontaneously or mechanistically caused).
         In case (α) no further explanation is required;
         in case (γ) no further social one is possible;
         in case (β) clearly one can ask again:

B 4   Why does N possess reason R_{ij}?
         Once more (α)-, (β)- and (γ)-type options open until eventually the explanation terminates in either rules or causes.[57]

Winch leaves it unclear whether rules *determine*, as is suggested by his actualism, or merely *constrain* (and enable), as is suggested by his expressivism.[58] However, Winch's ontological argument supports a transcendental idealist, rather than a romantic or 'open-texture' reading. For, because rules are constitutive of social reality, they cannot merely constrain or permit the performance of acts (of differentiable types). Otherwise there will be, as it were, bits or aspects of inexplicable social matter. Or rather, because what is social is so only in virtue of its being rule-governed (and so explicable), anything that is not completely explicable (that is, rule-governed) cannot in the respect in which it is not rule-governed be said to be properly 'social' at all. For were the same set of rules to be consistent with the performance of distinct acts, there would be no socially relevant ways of differentiating them. And so they could not be said to be *distinct* (types of) *acts* at all.

The Critique of the Hermeneutical Tradition II: Explanation and Understanding

I now want to undertake a detailed investigation of Winch's model of explanation. It will transpire, upon analysis, that it involves a transposition of familiar positivist themes, encapsulating *inter alia* an inadequate sociology.

1. Winch misconstrues the *explananda* of social science. Social science is not only concerned with actions, it is concerned with their conditions and consequences (including the states and relations of structures and agents). And it is concerned with what societies and persons are[59] (and may become), as well as with what they do. Moreover it is concerned with actions which are practical, not just symbolic: with *making* (poiesis), not just *doing* (praxis), or rather with doing which is not, or not only, *saying* (signifying or expressing).[60] Such making always possesses a material cause. So it is important to note the limits of all Vichian arguments for hermeneutics: *what we do not make, we have no privileged understanding of.*[61] And we make neither society nor ourselves. It follows from this that the social structure, motivation and the tacit knowledge (skills and competences) we employ in social interaction and the transformation of nature may all be more or less opaque to our understanding. Of course conceptual inquiries are important in social science – not only for their own sake, but as an essential prelude to causal ones. Now such causal inquiries require independent empirical checks. Hence the social sciences need accuracy in measurement (wherever possible), as well as precision in meaning: their interest

extends to the numbers of crimes and suicides committed, and to the conditions under which they occur, not just to the role these concepts play in social life and death. It is evident here that Winch effects a linguistic–idealist transposition of a fundamentally empiricist *explanandum*, in which signifying actions take the place of events and our authority as agents that of facts apprehended in the certainty of sense-perception.

2. It is not the case, as Winch supposes, that behaviour can be rule-governed without being intentional under the description for the class of acts that the rule prescribes. For Winch, in contradistinction from Weber, is prepared to bring under the category of social, that is, rule-governed, behaviour, cases where even though the agent *N* does not act for a reason, his act (such as voting Labour) still has a definite sense, viz. as long 'as he is aware of the symbolic relationship [sic] between what he is doing now and the government which comes into power after the election'.[62] Now I do not think this washes. For in the event that *N* voted (say because it was compulsory), but did not care how (suppose he flipped a coin or tossed a die), his vote causally contributed to the result. But though *N* voted intentionally, his action cannot be said to be intentional under the description 'voting Labour'. Moreover he is not following any rule in voting Labour. Thus although *N*'s vote *counts* as a vote for Labour, he cannot be said to have *cast* his vote for Labour (in the count the casting was imputed). So here Weber is right and Winch is wrong. A person can only be said to be acting meaningfully, or following a rule, when his action under the relevant description is intentional, that is, done for a reason.

3. On the other hand, it is not the case that all intentional behaviour is rule-governed. Here again Winch's position is roughly the inverse of Weber's, and shares an affinity with Durkheim's. In both Durkheim and Winch individual behaviour appears (ideally or constitutively) as the internalized effect or expression of social phenomena; there is no distinction between different kinds of commitment to norms/rules, and the sources of compliance are ignored. The result in both cases is an 'oversocialized conception of man' (see Model II of the third section of Chapter 2). In Winch this is a legacy of Wittgenstein's radical break from his earlier solipsistic individualism – which, however, merely displaces the solipsism from the 'I' of the isolated individual to the 'we' of the community, or rather the 'it' of a form of life.[63]

Now, as MacIntyre points out, for Winch 'the test of whether a man's actions are the application of a rule is . . . whether it makes sense to distinguish between a right and a wrong way in connection with what he does'.[64] What, then, is the wrong way of going for a walk or catching a bus? And if there is no wrong way of doing them, does this mean that they cannot be done intentionally?

Winch's linguistically transposed transcendental idealism lies at the source of the trouble here. For it is not the case that because there are more or less strict rules governing the use of predicates, there are more or less strict rules governing that to which predicates apply. Thus, although it is certainly the case that there are some activities, such as reading a book, which would be incorrectly *described* as 'going for a walk', it does not follow that there is a correct way of so doing. Similarly, although there are criteria for the correct application of the concept 'anarchist', there is no correct way of *being* one. In short, social reality is not identical to the conditions of its intelligibility; and the meaning of an action is not equivalent to its occurrence. The conditions of the possibility of knowledge (or description) of objects are not the same as (and do not determine) the conditions of the possibility of those objects (or vice versa) – in social life, just as in the natural sphere. The rules of digging are not rules for the correct application of the predicate 'digging': digging and applying the predicate 'digging' constitute different kinds of skill.

Thus it is not the case that all actions are, or can be modelled on, or can be explained in the same kind of way as, or are in any kind of correspondence with speech actions or their analogues (signifying and/or communicative actions). There is neither identity nor homology between what is real and what is knowable, or sayable: the limits of language are not the limits of the world. Concept and object, even where the object is itself a concept, remain distinct and, in general, dissimilar. Moreover, where rules are explanatorily relevant to both, the rules concerned may possess radically different properties and depend for their identification upon very different procedures. Thus even *if* language-use is rule-governed in the way Winch assumes, it does not follow that intentional actions generally are; or that the myriad of possible objects of scientific study dependent upon intentional agency can all be understood by reference to the rule-following paradigm.

4. The suspicion must arise that Winch is making over-extensive use of an undifferentiated category of rules: that he fails to identify the different kinds of rules at work in social life;[65] and, in particular, to distinguish those cases of social behaviour which are strictly rule-governed (such as traffic light behaviour) from those which are not (such as going for a walk). Most social life occurs within a framework of rules, but what happens within (and outside) the framework, though still social, is, rather like the moves in a game of chess (and the off-stage play), not determined by, and hence cannot be

completely explained by reference to, the framework. It follows from this that (at best) the rule-following paradigm requires supplementation by other models of explanation.[66]

Consider two contrasts Winch himself draws, between the life of an anarchist and that of a monk, and between the rules of style (with fuzzy boundaries) and the rules of grammar (with sharp ones).[67] In both instances the former, as it were, leave 'space' for individual decision and caprice that the latter fill. Now would it not be absurd to suppose that for every act there is in principle a finite number of concepts applicable to the anarchist's behaviour such that, as it were, at the intersection of them all it is completely fixed, so that no other way of acting is possible for the anarchist? (Remember that in a checkmate it is not that there is only *one* thing to do, but rather *nothing* to do.) This would be a rule-displacement of regularity determinism, based on the transposition of P_1: a linguistically mediated Laplaceanism at variance, moreover, with the non-actualist, 'expressivist' elements in Winch's thought.[68]

However, if Winch, on his model, allows undetermined aspects of social behaviour, a terrible trilemma confronts him. For he must either say (a) that nothing explains such aspects or (b) that they are unsocial or (c) that they are, after all, completely explicable in terms of some set of – perhaps as yet unknown – rules. (b) is surely out – for to say 'I do' with a nudge or a wink, though not prescribed by the liturgy, may be both meaningful and intentional. (c) incites a regress of rules, in both horizontal and vertical directions (along familiar interactionist and reductionist lines). Moreover, if the rules are unknown, then the behaviour cannot be intelligible to the agents concerned, and so, on Winch's ontological argument, cannot be either social or meaningful. And similarly in the case of (a). The only option for Winch is to concede that what happens within a framework of rules, though putatively intentional and social, cannot be completely explained by reference to the framework itself.

However, even to talk, as I have done, of a 'framework of rules' is to employ a potentially misleading (because spatial) metaphor. Rules are enabling conditions for the performance of acts and constraints upon action, but they do not exist apart from what they enable/constrain. Now Winch never distinguishes between constitutive and regulative rules. Winch's ontological argument suggests that the rules he is concerned with are constitutive – in which event he is left with the debris of an actualist definition of the social. Yet it is only in the case of regulative rules, for which sanctions and rewards are deemed appropriate, that it makes sense to talk, as does Winch, of mistakes (there is no wrong way of promising, though one may intend and fail to do so) – in which case he must take seriously the (prima-facie causal) question of the mechanisms of enforcement of (and resistance to) such rules. (Note, the rules governing linguistic behaviour are typically constitutive of speech acts, but regulative for the language-learner.) Now a rule normally tells us only what forms of action are possible (if it is *constitutive*) or permissible (if it is *regulative*): it does not normally tell us how to 'carry on'. It is only in the *para-anankastic* contexts of mathematics, language-learning, puzzles and problems – the true denizens of the late Wittgensteinian ontology – where the concept 'correct answer' is appropriate or where, as in liturgy, the focus of interest is restricted to the correct or successful performance of an act of a clearly defined, and more or less rigidly circumscribed, type, that the 'carrying-on' model is appropriate. (Ironically, in view of Winch's exemption of 'lunatics',[69] some forms of neurotic and psychotic behaviour also conform to this model.)[70] Is it significant that while linguistic behaviour is taken to be the paradigm of social action, the examples cited of rule-governed behaviour all tend to be signifying activities capable of a para-mechanistic interpretation, and indeed simulation? And that it is never asked how people behave when they are not acting 'socially', that is, in rule-governed fashion, as in a Brechtian or Wittgensteinian *Verfremdungseffekt*? In short, on this model, creativity (subjectivity), like intentionality, gets squeezed out. The play sphere is demarcated, the spectators arrive, only to find puppets, not players; a routine, rather than a game.

Related to this is the failure to distinguish rules which are *consciously* acquired and consciously (as in liturgy) or unconsciously (as in routine) applied, from rules which are *unconsciously* acquired and consciously (for example, in compulsive behaviour) or unconsciously (for example, in grammatical productions) applied. Again, there are both rules to which the agent does, and rules (contrary to Winch)[71] to which s/he does *not*, see an alternative. Compulsive, or traditional, behaviour is not, therefore, non-social.

Now, however the rules are conceived, Winch never considers the following questions: (a) what explains the rules themselves?; (b) what explains the agent's rule-observance on any particular occasion?; and (c) what explains the acquisition of the rules by the social individual in the first place? (a) must lead Winch in the direction of either an infinite regress or an asocial explanation of rules, so he must refuse it by positing rules as explanatorily ultimate givens. (b) is more difficult for Winch to evade. For it seems fair to ask what distinguishes the case where a rule is *followed*, in appropriate circumstances, from the case where it is *not*? (Could it be anything other than the fact that in the former case, but not the latter, the rule is causally efficacious?) For note that just as a rule does not in general single out a course of action as the one and only thing to do, reference to the rule cannot explain why it is accepted, interpreted (or applied) in the way that it is, and acted upon by the agent concerned. Rule and conduct are distinct. Moreover there can, in general, be no presumption that agents, when they are following rules, are *aware* of the rules they are following; and some agents must be unaware of some rules, or the concept 'learning a rule' would lack application. Hence rule and knowledge of the rule – whether implicit or explicit – are in principle distinct: *rule-following is not its own explanation*. (c) raises the spectre of another regress – in time. For clearly one cannot explain the acquisition of rules S_j by N by reference to S_j, so one needs to posit higher-order rules for acquiring rules, S_{ij}, etc. Now here there is a limit to a regress of some significance for the hermeneutical tradition generally. For individuals are not born social subjects: they are socialized (made social) and constituted as subjects in a process which is necessarily unavailable to their conscious reflection. The limits of *Verstehen* are thus set, at the highest estimate, by the onset of self-conscious monitoring and the acquisition of a language. It is important to note that the construction of individuals as subjects, their production as social beings, (creative) language-users and (skilled) social interactors is a continual process and cannot be dated, as an achievement, at some point in chronological time; so that this limit is, as it were, a *permanent* one.

Finally, note that Winch does not consider the question: 'What distinguishes the case where a rule is *broken* from the case where it is *changed*'? It requires a transcendental realist ontology to distinguish the case where a mechanism endures but is inactive or counteracted, from the case where it is transformed, since *empirically* there may be nothing to differentiate them. Now just as in nature an accident is not tantamount to a breakdown in the uniformity of nature, so, in the social realm, deviance is not equivalent to change (a fact that actualism obscures).

5. I have suggested that what happens within and outside the 'framework' has to be explained in causal terms. I now want to show that the rule-following paradigm itself *presupposes* the category of causality. If this is so, this not only undermines the basis of Winch's contrast, but opens the floodgates to a host of causal questions – including ones about the genesis, maintenance and efficacy of systems of rules, the limits of their compatibility and the conditions of their transformation.

Winch half-sees the problem here: 'What is the difference between someone who is really applying a rule and someone who is not?'[72] But asking the right question, he answers the wrong one. For instead of elucidating the *difference* between the cases, he merely – in behaviourist fashion – lists criteria for *deciding* between them (as if to describe a litmus test was to explicate the nature of the difference between an acid and an alkali). I suggest that the difference can only be explicated as follows: in the former case the rule provides the agent in the context in which his/her action occurs with a sufficient reason (or motive) for acting as s/he does. Now clearly this merely shifts the question to: 'What is the difference between someone who is really acting for a reason and someone who is not?': that is, to the nature of the distinction between real and professed (or avowed) reasons, at the necessity for which Winch again seems to hint,[73] but an analysis of which he once more fails to provide. Now I argued in Chapter 3 that a distinction between real and possible reasons (R_r/R_p) is a necessary presupposition of any theoretical or practical reasoning, and that there was no way of explicating the notion of a real reason save as a reason causally efficacious in bringing about the action concerned. Winch is faced with an acute embarrassment here. For *either* he must accept the R_r/R_p distinction, presupposing the category of causality, in which case it is at least logically possible that explanations may have to be given in terms unavailable to the agent (and perhaps inconsistent, and even incommensurable, with his/her conceptions); *or* else he cannot sustain the really applying S_j/not applying S_j distinction, central to any non-voluntaristic account of rules. ('For it is only in a situation in which it makes sense to suppose that somebody else could in principle discover the rule I am following that I can intelligibly be said to follow a rule at all.')[74]

Unless, then, one is prepared to eschew altogether a role for reasons (and rules) in the explanation of social phenomena or to terminate one's inquiry with the reasons (or rules) actually professed by the agent concerned, one needs a notion of real reasons as reasons causally efficacious in the production of the behaviour concerned, whether or not these are the reasons actually advanced by the agent *or* conjectured by the investigator. But this is itself only a corollary of the theorem that one needs, in philosophy, the concept of an object, even where the object is itself (or depends upon) a concept (meaning, reason or rule), existing independently of any particular characterization of it, whether by an agent, participant or observer (interlocutor/investigator); that, in fine, one needs, in philosophy, an intransitive dimension, irrespective of domain or object. Now this has the profoundly anti-Cartesian implication that no moment ever contains its own truth, or act its own criteria of intelligibility. In particular, society is not constituted by the way it makes itself intelligible to itself: it is not, as it were, an 'intelligible', but a possible object of *scientific* investigation – that is, of a non-identical but internal relation to itself.

6. Once it is accepted that the Winchian paradigm itself presupposes for its applicability the category of causality, the central claims of Winch's argument can be re-examined. Winch's acceptance of an essentially positivist account of natural science leads him to overstate the anti-naturalist implications of his model. For redescription and considerations of intelligibility play vital roles in natural science too. Moreover his two-tiered model of explanation (see p. 139), from meaningful actions to the rules that make them possible, exactly parallels the characteristic movement in natural science from manifest phenomena to the structures that (co-)produce them. Indeed, conceived merely as a regulative framework or general conceptual schema for the understanding of social phenomena (akin, say, to atomism in physics), enjoining the student of social affairs to investigate social phenomena as if they were rule-governed, Winch's model is not only formally consistent with a fundamentally realist research strategy in social science (if suitably qualified and inter-preted), it has already several notable achievements to its credit – in anthropology, social psychology and (arguably) psychiatry. Indeed, were he merely recommending a heuristic, Winch's programme would be unobjectionable (if limited). But of course Winch is doing something more than that: he is making a priori claims about the nature of social reality, and of philosophy.

   Now critical naturalism can certainly accommodate Winch's insight that social reality is pre-interpreted (or effectively shrouded by a veil of interpretative material). Moreover it can accept weaker versions of both his epistemological and ontological arguments (pinpointing the hermeneutic tasks of the social sciences and the conceptuality of its subject-matter, respectively), and an overlap, but not an identity, between philosophy and social science (see, the fifth section of Chapter 2). Furthermore it can sustain conceptual change, agency and a breakdown in the symmetry between explanation and prediction *without* abandoning the rule-following paradigm, so that in this respect it can strengthen the Winchian heuristic. However, in rejecting the implicit identities of social *being* and *thought* and *individual* praxis and *social* rule, it can situate the possibility of differential material interests in the transformation of nature (the material face of social life) and so deal with a nexus of problems centring around institutional (including conceptual) transformation and change, turning on the phenomena of class and power. And in rejecting the explicit identity of philosophy and social science, it can restore to both an autonomous (if connected) cognitive function and an emancipatory potential alike.

7. I now want to show that Winch's paradigm is incapable of dealing with a group of problems that gravitate around the phenomena of

conceptual conflict, interaction (including communication!) and
change, quite apart from non-conceptual forms (that is, institutional
ones generally). It is clear that if an act is only an act or a state of
mind, a state of mind in virtue of its being intelligible to the agent (or
rather the society of which the agent is a member) in a certain way,
Winch is in difficulties as soon as the possibilities arise of: (a) the
same agent (or society) interpreting the same ϕ (act or state of
mind) in different ways (over time); or (b) different agents
interpreting the same ϕ in different ways at the same time; or (c) the
same ϕ being interpreted in different ways for different purposes.
(a) makes all conceptual changes, and transformations generally,
impossible. But (b) and (c) rule out all conceptual diversity, and
hence *all* forms of communication, including education and argument
(learning/teaching and discussing). A moment's reflection shows why
this is so. For the possibility of *diversity* – in the sense of a non-
identity (or uniformity) in beliefs (and cognitive states generally)
and/or a discrepancy in wants (and volitional states generally) – *is a
condition of every genuine* – necessary (non-redundant) and/or
intelligible (significant) – *communicative act or episode*. For communication to be possible there must be *mutuality* (overlap); for it to
be necessary there must be *difference* (non-identity), in beliefs and
wants (and, underlying them, in descriptive presuppositions and
practical interests). Quite simply, there is nothing to be said *within* a
form of life, only *between* them (however precisely such forms are
individuated).

Now if conceptual (and volitional) variety is a condition of the
possibility of communication, then it must potentially be the case
that the parties to a communicative episode characterize the same ϕ
in different, and putatively inconsistent, ways; and so no ϕ can ever
be identified with its characterization within one of the interlocutor's
forms of life (say A). Conversely if, as in the Winchian paradigm, a
ϕ is so identified, communication and hence the acquisition of the
life-form A by agents in the first place become impossible. (Clearly
such a life-form cannot be reproduced, and cannot have been
produced, and so must exist – Platonically – outside time.) It follows
as a direct corollary of this that the acquisition of hermeneutic
knowledge, and *Verstehen* generally, is, on the Winchian paradigm,
either *unnecessary* – if the social scientist is *inside* the object life-form
– or *impossible* – if s/he is *outside* it. A transcendental refutation of
the hermeneutical tradition in its Winchian guise is thus obtained by
seeing that it is inconsistent with the possibility of communicative
activity (and hence of the acquisition of hermeneutic knowledge).
For communication is always potentially *between* (conceptually
differing) agents and *about* (recharacterizable) objects.

A special, and sociologically significant, example of (b) is provided by the case where the members of some tradition (for example, Christianity, anarchism, psychoanalysis) or the parties to some social relationship agree about the existence of the tradition or relationship, but interpret the tradition or describe the relationship in inconsistent or incommensurable ways (for example, what is work or redundancy to the capitalist may be exploitation or unemployment to the worker; therapy to the psychiatrist, rip-off to the patient, etc.).

It is clear that in order to sustain (a)–(c), and other affiliated modalities of conceptual work, one needs to sustain the concept of the intransitive reality of intentional agency; and to sustain this one needs to recognize that to possess the concept of a state of mind is neither a necessary nor a sufficient condition of it.[75] Conversely, it is clear that the result of the collapse of an intransitive dimension in Winch is a relativism, of such Heraclitean proportions (once it is confronted with the phenomenon, itself transcendentally necessary for hermeneutic work, of diversity and change) that ultimately rational discourse becomes impossible to sustain, until one is left with a solipsism of forms of life, outside time, of which individual agents are so many *Träger*.

8. I now want to examine the way in which characteristically positivist themes are reproduced in displaced or transformed form in Winch's model. For positivism, it will be recalled (see the second section), facts are given in sense-experience and are *certain*, and the scientist (in sense-experience) is *passive* and autonomized. In Winch these features reappear on a hermeneutical terrain. The interpretation of the object-culture is *definitive* (certain) and the ideal social scientist investigates his or her subject-matter with a *conceptual tabula rasa* (passively). (Of course the social scientist is a member of a community: the acquisition of hermeneutic knowledge is not individualistic.)

Now if S_1 is the community under study, S_2 the community of social scientists, and S_3 the community into which the social scientist is born, Winch's model may be represented as in the diagram below.

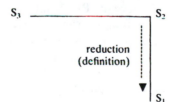

Knowledge consists, as it were, in the mimetic reproduction in S_2 of the thought-content of S_1. Socialization (immersion) into a form of life is assumed to be unproblematic. The definition or explication of the concepts of S_2 in terms of S_1 is as easy as (and is exactly isomorphic with) the reduction of theoretical concepts in natural science to observable ones. And the converse relationship of knowledge-acquisition (or justification), viz. $S_1 \rightarrow S_2$, is, like that between fact and theory in natural science, entirely unilinear. The object S_1 can thus be passively apprehended – hermeneutically intuited, if not empirically sensed. Its concept does not have to be reconstructed in S_2 in work: as in positivism, there is no transitive dimension in science here. Moreover, just as the objects of empirical knowledge (facts) only exist as sensibilia, so the objects of hermeneutic knowledge (societies) only exist as intelligibilia. S_1 is as incorrigible to the participants in *its* social life, as the facts are to the scientist in sense-experience. For were it to be corrigible, as it exists only in its self-characterization, it must literally cease to be. Of course there are differences. For whereas in natural science the sensibilia are for (of) the scientist, the intelligibilia are for (of) the object under study. This creates a problem of access. On the other hand, to counterbalance this, correspondence becomes easier. For while in natural science there is only one *subject* (or society), there are two kinds of *substance*; whereas in social science there are two subjects, but only one kind of substance – viz. ideational matter (that is, just the kind of matter in terms of which understanding is achieved and with which judgements of truth, adequacy, etc., are made).

In positivism the objects of experience are atomistic. For Winch, forms of life (constituted by internally related elements) themselves become *externally related*, discrete, 'loose and separate', at best conjoined but never connected. This leads *inter alia* to a neglect of their interpenetration, and to the absence of a category of totality capable of sustaining endogenous change.

In 'Understanding a Primitive Society' Winch begins to see some of the difficulties involved in the S_1/S_2 relationship: 'We must somehow bring S's conception of intelligibility (b) into (intelligible!) relation with our conception of intelligibility (a)'.[76] So the sociologist cannot be completely passive. But Winch never works through the implications of a rejection of the contemplative model of man together with the spurious objectivism it secretes. Doing so would entail abandoning the assumption of the ideal identity (or correspondence) of S_2 and S_1, that is, of scientific and lay accounts, rooted in the notion of the (ontologically grounded) incorrigibility of the latter, together with that of its corollary, viz. the neutrality (or indifference) of social scientific (and hence philosophical) discourse to social practice. In the same way Winch tries to escape from the more extreme relativistic implications of his model by positing certain 'limiting notions' – birth, death and sexuality – which are 'inescapably involved in the life of all known human societies in a way which gives us a clue where to look, if we are puzzled about the point of an alien system of institutions'.[77] But how do such limiting notions differ from Paretian 'residues'?[78] Further, is there not a certain arbitrariness (and ethnocentricity) in this trinity – after all, are not 'food, habitation and clothing' or 'language, power and production' equally 'inescapably' involved? Moreover it is unclear how, if the way these notions function in S_1 is to be exhausted by their manifest conceptualized (or conceptualizable) content, one is any better off; and how, if they are not, this is consistent with the kind of contrast that Winch still wishes to draw between the conceptual and the natural sciences. For in the latter case the 'point' of an alien system of institutions can only be grasped causally.

What of Winch the philosopher? Winch never stops for a moment to ask what (or whose) language-game *he* is playing. Unreflectively, and positivistically, he assumes that philosophy can be dislocated from the rest of the social totality and treated, *because this is how it is experienced*, as 'uncommitted inquiry'.[79] Of course it turns out that matters are not quite so simple: that he must be both 'master-scientist' and 'under-labourer' in one. Master-scientist – in virtue of the role accorded to conceptual inquiries (and *a fortiori* philosophy) in social science. Under-labourer – for how else is one to construe his activity, save as an attempt to remove 'some of the rubbish that lies in the way to (social) knowledge'?[80] But then, in a cruel dilemma, *here* is one practice about which Winch manifestly cannot be neutral.

Of course Winch is not the only hermeneutical philosopher in whom one finds transposed positivist themes (see, for example, Dilthey's psychologistic empiricism and individualism, Schutz's theory-free natural attitude, Gadamer's renunciation of knowledge at a (temporal) distance, Habermas's transcendental empiricism of interests, etc.). But, probably because of his philosophical ancestry, they are perhaps most evident in his work. Before turning to the hermeneutical tradition more generally, it is worth emphasizing the main points to have emerged from this critique. Firstly, the condition of all genuine communicative acts is the hermeneutical circle as such. And the condition of this is the intransitivity (and hence susceptibility to causal inquiries) of the conceptual equipment and other elements brought to bear in communicative episodes. Secondly, the identification of social being and thought must be rejected on two grounds. Ontologically, on the ground that social life has an irreducible material aspect. And epistemologically, on the ground that all conceptualizations are corrigible and potentially subject to critique (in the sense of the fifth section of Chapter 2). Thirdly, any adequate ontology of social science must be formally *non-actualist* and materially *relational*. That is to say, it must be able to sustain the notions of the stratification and differentiation of reality (including conceptual reality). And it must have broken from the problem-field structured around the relationship between the isolated individual and an abstract (ahistorical) society. For the flat undifferentiated ontology of empirical realism, whether in pure or transposed form, always functions to the same effect: science becomes easy and history impossible. (The more 'self-evident' reality becomes, the more effectively ideology is obscured.) And the sociology of individualism, whether in pure (that is, voluntaristic) or inverted form, squeezes out the mediating concepts (of class, power, interest, etc.) necessary to make sense of the arena in which both the action and the determination actually occur. For social life always occurs in a context which is prestructured and differentiated, in which socially differentiated individuals *act* (that is, articulate and apply) their various (and potentially or actually antagonistic) 'forms of life' *in* the processes of social interaction and material mutation that reproduce (and transform) the totalities of internally related fields of force that comprise societies. Such acting is work, and such work is history.

A transcendental refutation of positivism has been obtained by showing that it is inconsistent with the possibility of experimental (and applied) activity. A transcendental refutation of hermeneutics, in its Winchian manifestation, has been obtained by showing that it is inconsistent with the possibility of communicative activity. Thus if positivism produces an anti-historical historicism and anti-scientific scientism, one could say that one has here a *non-verstehende hermeneutics*. Let us see if other horizons fare any better.

The Hermeneutical Circle and the Logic of Emancipation

The three closely interrelated achievements of the hermeneutical tradition are the isolation of (1) the *pre-interpreted* character of social reality, (2) the *non-presuppositionless* character of social inquiry and (3) the *indexical* character of the expressions used both in social life and social science. However, it does not follow from (1)–(3) that social reality is exhausted by interpretative material, or that such material is not rationally corrigible or that a generalizing social science is impossible. Now (1)–(3) all cluster around the theme of 'the hermeneutical circle'. Failure to distinguish four different senses in which this notion has been employed – in effect, four different 'circles' – has been responsible for some confusion over the validity of the claims made on behalf of the universality of hermeneutics, on the one hand, and its distinctiveness to the social sciences, on the other. I want to argue that a hermeneutical circle (C_1) is a condition of any act of inquiry, whether in natural or social science, and that another (C_2) is a condition of any dialogue or intersubjective communication at all. In these senses hermeneutics is indeed, as for example Gadamer has claimed, *universal*. But two other circles are, as the more orthodox neo-Kantian tradition has maintained, *distinctive* of and necessary (but not sufficient) for the social sciences.

C_1 depends, quite generally, upon the non-presuppositionless character of any act of inquiry. It is this circle that Socrates was playing on in his reformulation of the Meno paradox: 'A man cannot inquire either about that which he knows, or about that which he does not know; for assuming he knows he has no need to inquire; nor can he inquire about that which he does not know, for he does not know about that which he has to inquire'.[81] Among the features that C_1 pinpoints is the necessity for antecedent (material) causes of knowledge in what I have called the transitive dimension of science. If C_1 could be called the *circle of inquiry*, C_2 is the *circle of communication*. I have already employed C_2 against Winch, and it can be expressed in the form of a dilemma: communication is either impossible or unnecessary. Communication is impossible unless some descriptive and practical presuppositions are shared in common; unnecessary unless there is the possibility of discrepancy (non-identity in objective content) between them. Both C_1 and C_2, turning on the transformational and communicative aspects of all cognitive activity, apply to the natural and social sciences alike.

In C_3 and C_4 one is trying to interpret what is said (or done) or has been made (or written) in some object-domain. Both apply, strictly speaking, only to social science. C_3 is a circle of inquiry into other existing societies, cultures, traditions, etc. It may be appropriately modelled on C_2, so that if C_1 is represented as 'C of 1' and C_2 as 'C of C', C_3 might be represented as 'C of $1(C)$'. C_4 is a circle of investigation into meaningful objects (or products), rather than subjects (or their actions or activities). In C_4 the original sense of the object has been, as it were, deposited in a text or text-analogue. The paradigm here is reading, not listening (the original subject being, as it were, a dead author rather than a living speaker). C_4 cannot be appropriately modelled on communicative acts or contexts. It could be represented as 'C of $1(T)$'. Among the features that C_3 and C_4 pick out, respectively, are the necessity for a *dialogical* model of social inquiry and the *non-logocentric* nature of reading[82] (that is, the impossibility of adequately conceptualizing reading as the recovery by the reader of the original intentions of the author), where 'reading' stands for the interpretation of meaningful products generally. A weak ('para-hermeneutic') analogue of C_4 may be applied to the case of the natural sciences on the condition that the highly metaphorical nature of talk of 'reading' the object-domain, *as if* it were meaningful, is appreciated.

Because all four circles concern meaning in some way and because of the holistic (or better, systemic) character of meanings – existing as they do only in virtue of (the use of) systems of difference – all four circles can be expressed in terms of part–whole relationships.[83] Of course there are family resemblances between the circles. Thus Heidegger gives a Socratic slant on C_4 when he tells us that 'any interpretation which is to contribute understanding must already have understood what is to be interpreted'.[84] And Habermas utilizes what I shall call the paradox of communication when he makes the point that 'interpretation would be impossible if the life-expressions were totally alien. It would be unnecessary if there was nothing alien about them. It must therefore lie between the two extremes'.[85]

There is a relative, but significant, difference in the cases of C_2 and C_3. In the normal communicative situation of C_2 the descriptive presuppositions that underpin the success of referential acts, etc., are tacitly presupposed. But occasionally they must be confirmed, negotiated, restored (*or* corrected) by the provision of use-substitutes for the expressions that fail. I shall take the presumption of success in the 'uptake' (transmission or exchange) of communicative intent (that is, what is intended in or by an utterance) as pragmatically defining a situation within a *common context of utterance* or 'mutual horizon'. Now if in C_2 our primary concern is with the isolation of 'speakers' meaning' within a common context of utterance, in C_3 it is with the *establishment* of a common context of utterance, and hence with the isolation of 'linguistic meaning' (with which any speaker's meaning must be expressed) in the object-culture concerned. Translation thus takes the place of redescription in the *process* of the establishment of a shared horizon.

The concept-dependent nature of social structures implies the necessity for *Verstehen* (the condition of which here is C_3). And inasmuch as *Verstehen* is always the operation of a subject one can appreciate the truth of Dilthey's remark that 'the first condition of the possibility of historical science lies in the fact that I am myself a historical being, that the historical researcher also makes history'.[86] Now once it is accepted that natural science is already a social activity, involving the hermeneutic tasks of utilizing (clarifying, exploiting) presuppositions and communicating (that is, C_1 and C_2), in pursuit of the para-hermeneutic objective of understanding (non-meaningful) nature, it is natural to say that social science, in virtue of its distinctive tasks of understanding the meanings expressed *by* other subjects (C_3) and *in* other objects (C_4), is engaged in a 'double hermeneutic'.[87] And, accordingly, to take the relationship between the two sets of descriptions – that is, between social scientific descriptions and lay descriptions (whether actual as in C_3 or imputed as in C_4) – as the central question of method in the social sciences. It is easy also to take the norm of adequacy as the achievement of an identity or correspondence between these descriptions (whether this achievement – *Verstehen* – is conceptualized logically, as in Winch, or psychologically (re-experientially), as in Dilthey). More often than not, this norm is rooted in the assumption of the incorrigible, because constitutive, character of lay accounts. And it has the inevitable corollary that scientific accounts are neutral with respect to lay practice (or more generally, that second-order discourses are indifferent to that which they seek to explain or explicate), a position rationalized by what in the third section I called the 'linguistic fallacy', whether this fallacy be expressed in metatheoretical or substantive form.

I have already examined these (transposed positivist) themes at work in Winch. But they are quite characteristic of the hermeneutical tradition generally, affecting even its dynamic and quasi-materialist variants. Thus for Schutz the postulate of adequacy demands that social scientific concepts 'must be constructed in such a way that the human act performed within the life-world by the individual actor would be understandable by the actor himself as well as for his fellow-men in terms of commonsense interpretations of everyday life';[88] for Garfinkel the proposal underlying ethnomethodology 'is that the activities whereby members produce and manage settings of organized everyday affairs are identical with members' procedures for making those activities "accountable"';[89] just as for Winch the subject-matter of social science is self-defining and its technical concepts must be 'logically tied' to those of the society under study.[90] The Wittgensteinian theme that philosophy 'leaves everything as it is',[91] and consists in 'uncommitted inquiry', in Winch is paralleled in the phenomenological tradition generally in the stamp of Husserl's original notion that philosophy 'does nothing but explicate the sense the world has for us all, prior to any philosophizing, and obviously gets solely from our experience – *a sense which philosophy can uncover but never alter*'.[92] This is echoed in the postulate of ethnomethodological indifference, and more subtly in the notion of the 'incorrigibility of the resources used to generate social interaction'.[93] Wittgenstein's insistence that 'to give the essence of propositions means to give the essence of all description, therefore the essence of the world',[94] is echoed in Gadamer's dictum that 'being is manifest in language', itself reflecting Heidegger's view that 'language is the house of being'.[95] And the linguistic fallacy even finds a quasi-materialist displacement in Habermas's reformulation of the goal of social emancipation as '*communication* free of domination' and 'a general and unforced consensus'.[96]

I have argued that the conditions of being are not the conditions of the linguistic expression of being, that lay accounts are corrigible and susceptible to critique, and that social science (and, at a remove, philosophy) always and necessarily consists in a semantic, moral and political intervention in the life of the society under study (in such a way that they continually condition, mediate and self-reflexively transform each other). I now want to approach the assumption of the ideal identity of scientific and lay accounts by considering Gadamer's objective-idealist critique of it.

My discussion in the last section showed how that assumption inevitably generates an analogue of basic statements, constituting certain foundations of knowledge, and necessitates a contemplative model of man; and how, accordingly, one must reject any monism of forms of life, and conceive them, instead, as in thoroughgoing interaction. Gadamer, in breaking from that standpoint, and the latent solipsism that informs it – be it at the level of the ego (Schutz), group (Garfinkel) or language-game (Winch) – substitutes the dialogical norm of *fusion* for the logocentric norm of *immersion*. *Verstehen* now consists in the melting of horizons, and truth no longer resides in being but in becoming. An active subject and a plurality of traditions are now recognized from the outset. However, as Betti, Hirsch and others have pointed out,[97] without some notion of the meaning of the meaningful object *for* the subject or *in* the culture that produced it (that is, of an intransitive target of hermeneutic investigation), it becomes difficult to sustain any notion of adequacy (or correctness) for interpretations at all. Lacking the concept of reference to speakers' intentions, Gadamer lapses into a (judgemental) relativism, in which the notion of the corrigibility of interpretations cannot be maintained (or can only be maintained by appeal to the practices of the tradition within which the interpretation is circumscribed, which merely displaces the problem of adequacy on to those practices). Thus there is change, but not development; melting, but not transformation; a circle, but not a spiral. Moreover, for similar reasons, Gadamer is also vulnerable to a dynamic variant of the Winchian dilemma. For although it is clear, at least in principle, how communication *within* a common context of utterance can be sustained, it is unclear how such a common context could ever come to be *established*. For this necessitates the attempt to establish speakers' intentions by providing use-substitutes for the expressions concerned. For Gadamer such activity must be pointless. Of course this dilemma does not apply with anything like the same force in

C_4 as in C_3. But even in C_4 permissiveness over interpretations is constrained: (a) by the requirements of communicating within and between traditions still concerned, rightly or wrongly, with speakers' (Marx's, Freud's, Plato's, Gadamer's) intentions – and note, any C_4 presupposes or depends upon *some* C_2; and (b) by social scientific analysis, which is concerned to explicate the role or function or mode of production of the meaningful object within the society in which it was originally formed.

To argue for the ineliminability of the concept of speakers' intentions is not to fall back into logocentrism. In fact two errors must be avoided. On the one hand, while it is true that one can only understand another culture or text in one's own terms, what one is trying to understand is an *other*. And to this extent it is salutary to remember the old hermeneutic dictum that meaning must be read out of, not into, a text. Moreover it is vital to retain an intransitive dimension if the possibility of an understanding, which is anything other than a self-understanding, and the susceptibility of meaningful objects to critique alike are to be retained. Speakers' intentions are *not* the object of such an analysis, but reference to them (in our language) is indispensable for it. On the other hand, while the metaphors of a fusion of horizons or a mediation of meaning-frames may be acceptable in the metalanguage of philosophy, they must not be hypostatized as a representation of historiographical or even anthropological practice. Because, of course, for us there is only one horizon; the melting is always in the here and now: there is no Archimedean position outside some language or point outside historical time. The mediation of L_2 and L_1 is always either in L_1 or L_2; it cannot be in both (or neither). We cannot escape from our language (or time), that system of differences we exploit to produce meaning and in virtue of which meaning is produced for us. The supposition of the possibility of a (logocentric) correspondence, if interpreted as a logical thesis, is meaningless or at the very best unverifiable (as there is no possible way in which it could be checked). But, if interpreted empirically, as a claim about what is known *about* actual languages *in* particular languages, it is false (the systems of difference never exactly fit). Moreover it is politically reactionary, in that it reinforces the authority of dominant interpretations (or 'ways of reading'),[98] as well as rendering the carriers of meaning – conceived as cross-culturally, trans-historically valid – immune from critique.

Gadamer's hermeneutical heresy thus does nothing in itself to counteract the effects of the assumption of the identity of social being and thought. This inevitably results either in an absolutism, based on the notion of the incorrigibility of lay accounts or the self-authenticity of traditions, or in a relativism, generated by the collapse of an intransitive dimension in the domain of thought itself. Conversely, when, as for example in Habermas's version of critical theory, a material aspect is granted to social life and it is conceded to possess a structure which requires something more than hermeneutic analysis, it still tends to be assumed that the apprehension or revelation of this structure in thought is sufficient for the changing of it; so that if thought is no longer the substrate of social being, it is still the efficient cause of social change. But of course awareness of false consciousness neither necessarily dissolves that consciousness, nor necessarily renders the mechanisms producing it inoperative. Similarly, the recovery of some object in consciousness does not automatically render it susceptible to rational conscious control.

The chronic failure of the hermeneutical tradition lies in its inability to sustain the conditions necessary for a *non-idealist critique of ideas*: viz. (1) the possibility of rational corrigibility; and (2) the possibility of non-ideational causality. Correction of the first error situates the possibility of a *critique*. Such a critique is both emancipatory and self-reflexive – *emancipatory* inasmuch as the necessity for false ideas can be explained; *self-reflexive* inasmuch as social science is a part of the totality it seeks to explain. Such a critique thus assumes the shape of an emancipatory spiral rather than a hermeneutic circle; and it constitutes an explanatory production, not simply a semantic exchange.

Correction of the second error sets the spiral in a *material* context; so that although it is worked out in the discourse of social science, and explicated in that of philosophy, this process of elaboration has practical (extra-theoretical) conditions and causes, whose *elaboration* is itself the work of the spiral. This restores to social science, and philosophy, real and autonomous, but *limited*, emancipatory roles. They no longer hold the key to history, but neither are they epiphenomena of it. Such a spiral thus has, as it were, a (potentially variable) centre of gravity in social practices *outside* itself.

Now it is the constant tendency of philosophy to suppose that the question of the limits and conditions of philosophy is itself a purely philosophical one. But of course this is not so. For philosophy is *in* and *of* history. Thus not only is the question of the limits of reason *in part* a social scientific one, but the limits social science describes may be *in part* quite non-discursive. And so what I called in the first section an explanatory critique of reason cannot be engaged outside the context of some theory of history. Moreover, as such a theory cannot be deterministic, and on the assumption that the transformational conception applies to philosophy also, there is no reason to suppose that the explanation of philosophies will differ in logical form or mode of production from that of any other social object.

Conclusion

It is the contention of this book that the human sciences can be sciences *in exactly the same sense*, though *not in exactly the same way*, as the natural ones. The move from manifest phenomena to generative structure that was seen in Chapter 1 to lie at the heart of rational theory-construction in science is possible here also – precisely in virtue of the distinct properties and powers of the objects of the social and psychological sciences elaborated in Chapters 2 and 3. Now the human sciences, like any other, take intransitive objects. But the processes of the production of their intransitive objects may be causally connected, and internally related, to the processes of the production of the knowledge (or mystification or repression) of which they are the objects (so that one could say that one is dealing with *object*, not *process*, intransitivity here). The human sciences and philosophy thus appear as distinct moments of the very same totalities they describe and explicate. Subject and object of knowledge are now neither – as in the materialism of the Enlightenment (on the whole still plausible for the experimental sciences of nature) – unconnected; nor are they, as in absolute idealism (or its materialist *alter ego*), identified. That there is a *causal* connection between them is a condition of the possibility of a critique. But that this causal connection is itself a *conditioned* one is a condition of the possibility of any non-idealist (or non-reductionist) critique. And the untenability of idealism and reductionism follow as straightforward consequences of the transformational and emergent powers naturalism developed here.

In this chapter we have seen how the notion of the self-evidence of the empirical world in positivism is reflected in that of the self-characterization of a society in hermeneutics. And I have argued that the source of these errors lies in the anti-scientific trinity of empirical realism, sociological individualism and the epistemic fallacy. Together they underpin a conceptual field, in which the key notions of a stratified and differentiated reality (including a conceptually articulated reality) cannot be sustained. The hermeneutical tradition is correct to stress that social reality is pre-interpreted, so that *Verstehen* is a condition of social science. But such interpretations are always and everywhere set in a field already crossed by different practical interests in the material transformation of nature. So that if every science must free itself from the 'tissue of tenacious errors'[99] secreted by the existing currency of mind, the obstacles at work in the human sciences will be the more powerful for being tied to definite interests in the position-practice system reproducing the existing social order. Hence if the real point of Vico's claim is that if we did not first understand one another, we could not understand the natural world at all, this must be counterbalanced by the recognition of Comte's insight. Social science is thus at once easier to initiate and more difficult to develop than natural science. And this is not paradoxical at all.

In Chapter 1 I argued that only a transcendental realist account of science and philosophy can sustain the intelligibility of experimental activity and scientific development, and an adequate account of the philosophy/science relation. In Chapter 2 a transformational model of social activity was developed; and it was shown how this model entails both a relational conception of the subject-matter of sociology and a number of ontological limits on (and conditions for) naturalism, viz. the activity-, concept-, and space–time-dependence of social structures. I argued that the epistemological fact that social structures only ever manifest themselves in open systems means that criteria for the rational assessment of theories must be *explanatory* and non-predictive; while the relational consideration that social science is internal to its subject-matter lays the ground for a kind of *critique* in which, without the addition of any extraneous value judgements, one can pass immediately from facts to values, or more precisely from explanatory theories to practical imperatives. In Chapter 3 a causal theory of mind was developed; and it was argued that reasons can and must be causes for any theoretical or practical activity to be possible, and that only a synchronic emergent powers materialism is consistent with the meta-physical and scientific data. In Chapter 4 both the positivist and hermeneutical traditions, in their philosophically dominant forms, have been subjected to transcendental refutation; so that both the 'positive' and 'negative' parts (see p. 6) of our transcendental argument are complete. In the sequel to this study the critical naturalism elaborated here will be set to work on philosophical materials. But this book stands on its own. And the positive theories of society and mind developed here must be creatively applied to, and tested against, that is, in the critical explanation of, the more general phenomena which are the effects of the structures experienced as social life and consciousness.

NOTES

1. See the 3rd Thesis on Feuerbach: 'The materialist doctrine . . . forgets that circumstances are changed by men and that the educator must himself be educated. This doctrine must, therefore, divide society into two parts, one of which ["science"] is superior to society'. Conversely, the incorrigi-bility attributed to science in positivism is displaced on to society, in the guise of the conceptual being and products of social actors, in the hermeneutical tradition, effectively rendering such conceptual life at once self-explanatory and immune from criticism.

2. See *A Realist Theory of Science*, app. to ch. 2, esp. pp. 127–32.
3. *Loc. cit.*
4. But for a critique of the possibility of such laws see the third section of Chapter 1 and for an a priori argument as to why social systems must be open see Chapter 2, fifth section.
5. As when Popper says: 'If we say that the cause of the death of Giordano Bruno was being burnt at the stake, we do not need to mention the universal law that all living things die when exposed to intense heat' (*The Poverty of Historicism* (London 1960), p. 147).
6. 'You cannot, without increasing productivity, raise the real income of the working population' ('Prediction and Prophecy in the Social Sciences', *Conjectures and Refutations* (London 1963), p. 343).
7. See, for example, A. Donagan, 'The Popper–Hempel Theory Reconsidered', *Philosophical Analysis and History*, W. Dray (ed.) (New York 1966).
8. See, for example, C. G. Hempel, *Aspects of Scientific Explanation* (New York 1963), esp. ch. 12.
9. See, *A Realist Theory of Science*, esp. ch. 2, sec. 5.
10. See, for example, C. G. Hempel, *op. cit.*, pp. 449, 309 and 471 respectively.
11. See *A Realist Theory of Science*, p. 77.
12. M. Scriven, 'Truisms as the Grounds for Historical Explanation', *Theories of History*, P. Gardiner (ed.) (New York 1959), p. 465.
13. *Ibid.*, p. 464.
14. D. and J. Willer, *Systematic Empiricism* (New Jersey 1973), p. 23.
15. *Ibid.*, p. 45.
16. *Ibid.*, p. 118.
17. *Ibid.*, p. 26.
18. These alternative absurdities correspond to the horns taken by strong and weak actualism respectively. They constitute a displaced material paradox of idealism. For just as idealism sees the *necessity* of the causal connection as explicitly imposed by women, so here its *universality* must be viewed as similarly produced. However this is not just counter-intuitive; it involves a manifest contradiction. Hence the hush on ontology.
19. It should be noted that historicism – in the sense of deductively justified predictability – is straightaway untenable in open systems and so is in general just as invalid in nature as in society. Popper's 'logical' refutation of historicism (see *The Poverty of Historicism*, pp. 6–7) turns on the internality of social science with respect to its subject-matter. And it is upon this feature that both the well-known Merton effects (of self-fulfilling and self-defeating predictions) and the emancipatory potential of social science also depend. Note that the internality of social science presupposes the openness of the *natural* systems within which the relevant social phenomena occur, and hence presupposes the general untenability of historicism in the sphere of nature too. It should be added that although the Merton effects appear as unintended consequences of human actions, the phenomena of which they treat (such as prices) are equally *conditions* of such actions; so that one should not say, as Popper does, that the subject-matter of social science consists in such consequences, but rather that it is reproduced through (or in virtue of) them.
20. See *A Realist Theory of Science*, pp. 136–7. Note in particular that the familiar distinction between causes and symptoms may be broadened into a contrast between theories which are explanatory but non-predictive (such as Darwin's, Marx's or Freud's) and generalizations (for example, about

capital–output ratios or suicide rates) which may be accurate predictors but are totally non-explanatory. The irreducibly historical nature of social systems (and the conjunctural determination of social events, including historical transformations) provides of course another reason for the absence of the requisite parity in social life.

21. *Ibid.*, p. 125.
22. See J. L. Mackie, *The Cement of the Universe* (Oxford 1974), p. 62.
23. Of course the INUS model is only one of causality, whereas the RRRE model is a general schema for the explanation of events in open systems. However, even in this limited respect the INUS account is defective. First, by omitting the crucial notions of necessity, generation and power it is susceptible to well-known paradoxes. Second, inasmuch as the concept of an INUS condition presupposes the possibility of Humean causal laws, as talk of sufficient conditions and causal regularities indicates, it must be rejected. If, on the other hand, it gestures merely to the possibility of explanations for significant differences in a world characterized by multiple-('*I*'), over-('*N*') and plural-('*U*') determination, then it is unobjectionable, but by the same token unilluminating. By contrast, non-anthropomorphic generative analyses can immediately explain *why* it is that we pick out the particular factor that, in the *pragmatic* context of our concerns, we do: namely, because it is the factor which, in the *real* context of the genesis of the event, made the difference, tipped the balance, produced the outcome. Paradigmatically, such a factor is an agent or structure, but it may also be a condition (present or absent), state or event. In any case, one needs to be able to sustain the notion of a real difference between the cause and all the other conjuncturally necessary conditions which, as Mill noted, on the Humean view have equal warrant to that title.
24. In the explanation of concrete events, laws typically merely function as grounds for the explanation. Moreover their application is never automatic and always requires trained judgement. Thus if it is the case that social causation depends upon the identification of meanings, it is equally the case that the application of knowledge of social causation (and laws) depends upon the correct identification of the social situations to which the law-like statements apply. This is, or at least depends upon, a hermeneutic task *par excellence* and corresponds exactly to the necessity for appropriate descriptions of events in both the theoretical and applied work of the natural sciences.
25. Popper's own criterion of falsifiability, and his theories of causality, explanation and scientific rationality all depend for their application upon precisely the historicist transformation (viz. of conditional into uncondi-tional predictions) that he so roundly condemns. Such a transformation is of course quite improper in open systems. But it is doubtful if his targets were in fact guilty of it (see A. Ryan, *op. cit.*, pp. 215–9).
26. See T. Parsons' definition of a theory as 'confined to the formulation and logical relation of propositions containing empirical facts in direct relation to the observation of the facts and the empirical verification of the propositions' (*The Structure of Social Action*, p. 48).
27. E. Durkheim, *The Division of Labour in Society*, p. 48.
28. E. Durkheim, *Rules of Sociological Method*, p. 7.
29. Contrast S. Lukes' argument in a recent study (*Power: A Radical View* (London 1974), pp. 24–5) that one must move not only from the 'one-dimensional' identification of power and conflict, but from the 'two-dimensional' view which allows the *possession* of power in the absence of

overt conflict (see Durkheim above and Weber's definition of power), to the 'three-dimensional' view where power is conceived as *exercised* in the absence of any actual observable conflict: that is, as a *tendency* in the sense of Chapter 1, section three.

30. See *A Realist Theory of Science*, ch. 2, sec. 4.
31. See *The Idea of a Social Science* (henceforth *ISS*), esp. pp. 17, 124 and 134.
32. Thus for Winch the central question of philosophy is the question of what it is to say that reality is intelligible (see *ISS*, pp. 8–15). Cf. 'Reality is not what gives language sense. What is real and what is unreal shows itself in the sense that language has' ('Understanding a Primitive Society' (henceforth 'UPS'), *APQ* 1 (1964), reprinted in B. Wilson (ed.), *Rationality* (Oxford 1970), p. 82).
33. See *A Realist Theory of Science*, esp. p. 36.
34. This consists in the view that statements about the world can always be transposed into linguistic terms, that is into statements about the language one uses to describe the world. It finds its *locus classicus* in Wittgenstein's *Tractatus*: 'To give the essence of propositions means to give the essence of all description, therefore the essence of the world' (London 1961, s. 4.711); and 'That the world is my world shows itself in the fact that the limits of my language (of the only language I can understand) mean the limits of *my* world' (*ibid.*, p. 62). But it recurs as a continuing motif in modern analytical philosophy. Thus P. Strawson in *Individuals* (London 1959), p. 17, explicates the notion of the ontological priority of one type of particular over another in terms of the dependence of our ability to *talk* about the latter on our ability to talk about the former, but not vice versa. And more generally it is reflected in substantive social science in the kind of view of which the following is a gem: '"Suicides" cannot correctly be said to exist (i.e. to be "things") until a categorization has been made. Moreover, since there exist great differences between the interested parties in the categorization of real-world cases, "suicides" can generally be said to exist and not exist at the same time' (J. Douglas, *The Social Meanings of Suicides* (New Jersey 1967), p. 196).
35. Kant, like Winch, wished to deny the applicability of the category of causality to a sphere (let us call it 'S'), but he held, unlike Winch, that one could have empirical–causal knowledge of minds. The neo-Kantians effectively transformed Kant's noumenon/phenomenon distinction into a nature/culture one, thereby identifying mind with S (extending it to include the social world generally), adding the faculty of hermeneutic knowledge to that of empirical knowledge. Winch, in company with most other modern hermeneuticists, drops the empirical–causal half of the neo-Kantian synthesis (but fails to restore a noumenal realm), so managing to achieve what Kant held to be impossible – viz. the definition of an authentic procedure of *knowledge* for a sphere (S) to which the category of causality is inapplicable.
36. *ISS*, p. 45.
37. *Ibid.*, pp. 40–2.
38. For example *ibid.*, p.125.
39. *Ibid.*, p. 108.
40. *Ibid.*, p. 127.
41. *Ibid.*, p. 131.
42. *Ibid.*, p. 95 (see also p. 47).
43. *Ibid.*, pp. 88, 100.
44. *Ibid.*, p. 89.

45. *Ibid.*, p. 90.
46. *Ibid.*, p. 135. See also p. 113.
47. *Ibid.*, p. 122.
48. *Ibid.*, p. 127.
49. *Ibid.*, p. 130.
50. Once one situates beliefs in the context of human activities and remembers that these are typically regularized in the form of structured practices, with both material and ideational components (or aspects), then one can readily allow both ideational causes of material changes and non-ideational causes of ideational ones.
51. See E. Gellner, 'Concepts and Society', B. Wilson (ed.), *op. cit.*, esp. p. 18, n. 1.
52. *ISS*, p. 115.
53. See H. Hart, *The Concept of Law* (Oxford 1961), pp. 87ff; and L. Wittgenstein, *Remarks on the Foundations of Mathematics* (Oxford 1956), esp. pp. 142–51.
54. See *ibid.*, pp. 49–51.
55. A. MacIntyre, 'The Idea of a Social Science', A. Ryan (ed.), *op. cit.*, p. 18.
56. But contrast 'motive is a rule which depicts the social character of the act itself' (P. McHugh *et al.*, *On the Beginnings of Social Inquiry* (London 1974), p. 27), and of course intentionalist (Gricean) analyses of meaning.
57. See 'what has to be accepted, the given, is – so one could say – forms of life' (L. Wittgenstein, *Philosophical Investigations* (Oxford 1963), p. 226).
58. One might try to reconcile these themes either by locating the source of novelty, diversity, change, etc., at the level of reasons, interpreting reasons expressively and meanings actualistically, and/or by interpreting the former as individual and the latter as social phenomena. However, the first line does not seem very plausible in view of Winch's actual remarks about rules (being context-dependent) – see *ISS*, p. 81 – and reasons (being intelligible) – *ibid.*, p. 92. And the second line also seems ruled out by Winch's strong use of the private language argument (see *ibid.*, pp. 32–3 and *passim*). This ambivalence is of course already present as an unresolved tension in Wittgenstein's analysis of rules. This is in difficulty as soon as one asks how it is that a language-game gets started, or what happens when there is more than one way of carrying on.
59. See A. MacIntyre, *op. cit.*, p. 25.
60. The hermeneutical tradition, in its non-dynamic form, typically only pays attention to doing, which it models on saying (or hearing). But although all saying is doing, not all doing is saying; and although all making involves doing, doing encompasses making of radically different sorts. In its more dynamic form, the hermeneutical tradition still treats doing as saying/hearing, but these are now conceived, agentively, on the model of making. But although change is now emphasized, lacking a concept of an intransitive dimension, what is past (or different) cannot be subjected to critique. Interpretations differ, horizons fuse and melt away, but remain incorrigible (save at best in terms of criteria – of authenticity, etc. – intrinisic to the self-defining traditions concerned).
61. That this specifies a real limit is not only because our products may take on 'a life of their own' (see J. Habermas, *Knowledge and Human Interests* (London 1972), p. 146) but, more radically, because on the transformational model, our activity presupposes that they have such a life prior to, and independent of, ours. In formulating his prospectus for his New Science (see ch. 1, n. 3 above), Vico overlooked the old Lucretian dictum: '*nullam*

rem e nihilo gigni divinitus unquam' – not even God can make something out of nothing.

62. *ISS*, p. 51.
63. One consequence of this is that, as private rules (in principle) require public criteria, in the event of any discrepancy between an actor's and the social definition of a situation, 'society is right'. Cf. 'the point of the concept of a rule is that it should enable us to evaluate what is done' (*ISS*, p.32).
64. A. MacIntyre, *op. cit.*, p. 21; *ISS*, p. 31.
65. The error involved in the *epistemic fallacy* – of confusing or failing to distinguish being (including conceptual being) from thought, and a concept from knowledge of a concept – becomes both more plausible and more insidious when the reality one is concerned with is itself thought. For idealism has always seemed more reasonable (and even 'obvious') when the real (intransitive) object can be construed as being governed by the same kind of rules as the transitive process of knowledge-production. But of course thought remains distinct from any particular thought (or description) of it. Once existentially distinguished, not only do both become (potentially) corrigible, but their relationship becomes an open topic for inquiry. Thus one can allow that here, as in the social sphere generally, object and concept are causally connected and even internally related, without positing either an identity or a correspondence. Truth no longer inheres in being. Both the series (nexus) in which being occurs and the series (nexus) in which truth judgements are made now possess (non-identical) material causes of their own; so that neither can be collapsed into the other. (Incidentally it is worth noting that a correspondence theory of truth is far more plausible in the conceptual than in the natural sciences. For what concept or ideational object could correspond to, say, a laser or (*pace* Merleau-Ponty) a nebula? Hence the appeal for empiricists of Tarski's theory, which displaces the requisite correspondence from the problematic relationship between unlike elements (viz. language and nature) on to one between like elements (viz. two languages). But of course physics is not *about* a language. And so metaphysically we are back to square one.)
66. See D. Shwayder, *The Stratification of Behaviour* (London 1965), pt. 3.
67. *ISS*, pp. 52–3.
68. See Winch's remarks about novelty and the envisaging of alternatives (*ibid.*, pp. 93 and 63–5 respectively).
69. *Ibid.*, p. 53.
70. See A. Lorenzer, 'Symbols and Stereotypes', *Critical Sociology*, P. Connerton (ed.) (Harmondsworth 1976).
71. *ISS*, p. 65.
72. *Ibid.*, p. 29.
73. *Ibid.*, p. 47.
74. *Ibid.*, p. 40.
75. It is important to avoid supposing that it is because action typically has an outer aspect (so that it cannot be reduced to its inner cause) that there is a relatively fixed referent for conflicting (changing, differing, etc.), and an exchange of, characterizations of social phenomena. For although the material aspect of action may often be pragmatically sufficient for this purpose, it is neither necessary (in the case of beliefs) nor sufficient (on pain of a behaviourist analysis of mental phenomena). Note that once we allow the intransitivity of beliefs, we can situate both direct reference to, and varying descriptions of, them.
76. 'UPS', p. 99.

77. *Ibid.*, p. 107.
78. See *ISS*, pp. 103–9 for Winch's strictures on Pareto's residues/derivations distinction.
79. *Ibid.*, p. 102.
80. See J. Locke, 'Epistle to the Reader', *Essay Concerning Human Under-standing* (New York 1959), p. 14.
81. Plato, *Meno, Dialogues* (Oxford 1953), 80d.
82. See J. Derrida, *Of Grammatology* (Baltimore 1974); and J. Culler, *Saussure* (Glasgow 1976), esp. pp. 106–14.
83. See, for example, C. Taylor, *op. cit.*, p. 156.
84. M. Heidegger, *Being and Time* (Oxford 1967).
85. J. Habermas, *op. cit.*, p. 164.
86. W. Dilthey, *Gesammelte Schriften*, 7 (Munich 1937), p. 278, quoted in W. Outhwaite, *op. cit.*, p. 25.
87. See, for example, A. Giddens, *New Rules of Sociological Method* (London 1976), p. 162.
88. A. Schutz, *The Phenomenology of the Social World* (London 1972), p. 220.
89. H. Garfinkel, *Studies in Ethnomethodology* (New Haven 1967), p. 1.
90. P. Winch, *ISS*, p. 89.
91. L. Wittgenstein, *Philosophical Investigations*, p. 124.
92. E. Husserl, *Cartesian Meditations* (The Hague 1960), p. 177.
93. A. Giddens, *op. cit.*, p. 16.
94. L. Wittgenstein, *Tractatus*, 5.4711.
95. M. Heidegger, 'Letter on Humanism', *Philosophy in the Twentieth Century*, W. Barret and H. Aitken (eds.) (New York 1961). See also note 34 above.
96. J. Habermas, *Towards a Rational Society* (London 1971).
97. See, for example, J. Llewelyn, *Beyond Metaphysics?* (London 1985), ch. 6.
98. See P. Feyerabend, *Science in a Free Society* (London 1978), pt. 1.
99. See G. Bachelard, *La Formation de l'esprit scientifique* (Paris 1938), *passim*.

Postscript

In this postscript I want to comment in some detail on two important critiques of the book or its project, by Ted Benton and Alan Chalmers respectively;[1] to respond rather more briefly and mainly *en passant* to some other lines of criticism and development of the work; and to conclude with a provisional assessment of the progress made by the research programme it attempted to initiate.

My intention in writing *The Possibility of Naturalism* (henceforth *PON*) was to utilize the transcendental realist account of science, which I had elaborated in *A Realist Theory of Science*[2] (henceforth *RTS*), to 'underlabour' for the human sciences in their perplexed and perilous state. It seemed to me that if, as I had shown, laws were not constant conjunctions of events but transfactual tendencies of structures, if the deductive–nomological model of explanation was false and if the aim of science was not prediction and control but explanation and (potentially) emancipation, there was at least a chance of a chance (the possibility of a possibility) that the human sciences might be or become sciences in the same sense, though not of course in the same ways (cf. p. 159), as the experimental sciences of nature. This chance I set out to realize in Chapters 2 and 3 via a transcendental deduction of the properties that societies and people must possess if they are to be (or demarcate the sites of) possible objects of knowledge for us, rounding off the book in Chapter 4 with transcendental refutations of the currently dominant – positivist and hermeneutical – traditions in the philosophy of the human sciences. I had attempted to vindicate the possibility of a new critical naturalism. But *that* possibility could only be actualized in the substantive practices of the various human sciences. My task had been the Lockean one of removing a priori objections and clearing conceptual bottlenecks and methodological roadblocks in their way[3] – and to attempt to illustrate how the available space could be used by choreographing a few sequences for their play.

Alan Chalmers calls into question the whole project of *PON*, whereas Ted Benton objects only to the manner of its execution. For both of them transcendental realism represents an advance on existing rival, orthodox accounts of science. But both think that the description of science given in *RTS* – or more specifically omissions from it – mars my programme for the human sciences. For Chalmers it is 'theoreticist', in

167

that I concentrate on fundamental as distinct from phenomenological laws;[4] on theoretical, i.e. universally (transfactually) applicable, knowledge as distinct from technical knowledge, i.e. 'knowledge applicable only to artificial situations of a specified kind';[5] and on the explanatorily significant rather than the more craft-orientated, 'practically efficacious' modes of intervention highlighted by, for example, Cartwright and Hacking.[6] For Benton, it is 'experimentalist', in that I concentrate on classical experimental physics and chemistry at the expense of biology and the life sciences, ignoring in the process 'a range of natural sciences in which experimental closure is not an available means of empirical control on theory'[7] and where 'historicity and qualitative transformation pose epistemological and methodological problems . . . comparable with those encountered in the [human] sciences'.[8]

I accept that in *RTS* I focused on theoretical, explanatorily significant or 'fundamental' experimental physics and chemistry and that in *PON* I took over this paradigm in reassessing the problem of naturalism. The reason for this bias in *RTS*, as I perhaps did not make sufficiently clear at the time,[9] was that my strategy was one of *immanent critique*. These were precisely those aspects of science on to which the schools and traditions I was arguing against had fastened. Clearly, philosophical contestation and debate would become altogether impossible if one was going to shift one's opponent's premises at the outset. This would be akin to supposing one might score a goal by realigning the goal posts. Similarly in *PON* it was these 'classical' aspects of science which formed the backdrop to the debate about the possibility of naturalism and in relation to which the human sciences were invariably negatively evaluated, caricatured or contrasted. The argument of *PON* was conducted on the existing discussants' chosen terrain; and it sought to show how (even) on the existing terms of discussion, *adequately analysed*, new (and potentially critical) types of the human sciences were possible.

However, *RTS* was not supposed to be an exhaustive account of all of physics and chemistry, let alone all the (natural) sciences. It was a start, not a conclusion – founding, or so I hoped, a research programme into the sciences, based on a more adequate – transcendental realist – conception of those aspects on which philosophers had typically dwelt. In the same way the project of *PON* logically requires complementary comparative studies into the potential and prospects of the human sciences in relation to a whole range of other features, periods and kinds of sciences and other non-scientific (e.g. literary, dramatic) practices too.[10]

This raises two other issues, both to do with the logic of philosophical argument:

1. Ted Benton objects to the fashion in which I introduce the

expression 'intransitive dimension' in one way and then proceed to define or redefine or use it in other and apparently incompatible ways.[11] But the sort of consistency we should seek in a philosophical work which is genuinely innovative = transformative (cf. p. 37) is not of the static, formal–logical sort. It is rather *developmental consistency*: the sort of consistency shown in nature when a tadpole turns into a frog or an acorn into an oak; or the sort shown within science by different but connected theories in an ongoing research programme. This involves the sort of historical, developmental logic at work in the progressive and deepening reunderstanding of a problem, position, person or concept – just the *transformational* sort that one would expect if it is the case, as I argued on p. 8, that philosophy can be a conceptual science, able to surprise (and change) us.[12] Of course at the (temporary) end of the day the reader will have to be satisfied that a self-consistent and coherent account is available.

Can psychological and sociological mechanisms be consistently characterized, at the end of the day, as intransitive? Yes – in the sense that they exist and act, at any moment of time (punctually), independently of the knowledge of them, though of course there may (and will normally) be causal interdependency between the processes of the production and reproduction/transformation of the mechanisms and those of their knowledges (cf. p. 47).[13] But what of the knowledge-mechanisms themselves? They too can become the intransitive objects of a meta-epistemic investigation[14] and so on indefinitely, defining an in principle open-ended and recursive ontogeny.

2. Several critics have objected to the profusion of terms which I have used to specify the newly identified realm of the non-empirical (and non-actual) real or its cognates – powers, tendencies, structures, generative mechanisms, transfactuality, normic statements, etc. This is not due to any fondness of mine for neologism or jargon. What one is dealing with here is a network, 'family' or constellation of concepts, which are interdefined, but which will latch on in differential ways to different readers' experiences or vantage points. Here again, in any authentically innovative or transformative philosophical work the writer is trying to introduce the reader to a new way of thinking, and aspects of the logical penumbra or open texture of different terms will 'take' with different readers. So one gives, as it were, a multiplicity of routes into the new network, in the hope that the reader will get a feel for it. Here again, though, when the shades of night fall, one ought to be able to see how the different terms 'hang together'.

There is one term in particular that is used in the text of *PON* in a doubly ambiguous way: 'structure'. In the first place I use it to refer to both the abstract form or type and the particular concrete instantiation or token of it. Following Andrew Collier,[15] I think it often useful to distinguish between the abstract *structure* and the concrete *structuratum* – structures exist only as *structurata* and all *structurata* are structured.[16]

Secondly, I often use the term 'structure' and 'generative mechanism' as if they were synonyms. It now seems to me to be better to use the term 'generative mechanism' to refer only to the causal powers of ways of acting of structured things. Such things either (a) just *are* or (b) more normally *possess* their causal powers.[17] Only in the former case will structures and generative mechanisms be the same.[18] One consequence of this is that just as in general events are multiply (conjunctively) determined, so the possibilities arise (i) that the same mechanism (for example, the market) may sustain (or undermine) a multiplicity of distinct structures which, as it were, converge on it; and (ii) that the same structure (say, that of the nation-state or the family) may be reproduced (or transformed) by the joint activity of a number of different mechanisms. Another consequence is that just as the same type of event may be determined by a (disjunctive) plurality of mechanisms (see p. 129), so (i) the same kind of mechanism may sustain alternative structures and (ii) the same structure may be reproduced by a variety of different types of mechanism.[19]

I move on now to consider the detailed criticisms which Alan Chalmers and Ted Benton make. Although there are points of overlap and common threads in their critiques, it will be most convenient to take them separately, dealing with the points they raise seriatim.

Besides the case which I have already conceded to Chalmers that there are phenomenological – purely descriptive – as well as fundamental – or explanatory – laws, and technological or craft-orientated as well as theoretical knowledge, I would also happily grant that there are good arguments for realism other than those which I have advanced.[20] Moreover I would not only accept, but insist, that transcendental realism is fallible, as corrigible as the outcome of any other piece of human argument.[21] I, like Chalmers, regard it as merely 'the best account [at present] available'.[22] I would, however, add the rider that it is (at present) uniquely consistent with the historical emergence, practical presuppositions and substantive content of the sciences; and that it possesses the further virtue of reflexive self-consistency in that it can situate its own emergence, fallibility and transformability. I would further admit that transcendental realism, insofar as its premises are forms of historical praxis (such as the experimental interrogation of nature), which may come to be superseded, may be adequate to only one historically specific mode of science. It may even be that science itself comes to be replaced by some other kind of cognition. These are not entirely idle speculations. For in the first place they underline the historicity, relativity and potential (essential) transformability of all our cognitive achievements (including philosophical knowledge). And in the second place they permit the clarification of what is involved in assent to the premises and so, if, as Chalmers accepts (subject to a proviso to be discussed below), the reasoning is correct, to the conclusions of transcendental realism. It involves assent to the general 'belief-worthiness' or credibility of science. If, and insofar as, one believes that the knowledge produced by the systematic and wherever possible experimental investigation of nature is the best available, then one must be committed, if transcendental realism is the best reconstruction of scientific practice, to, for instance, the idea that the world is structured, differentiated and changing. A transcendental inquiry into the conditions of the possibility of astrology[23] is not going to be enlightening unless one believes in astrology as a source of practically efficacious or reliable knowledge. Ted Benton's remark about the need to assume the rational justifiability of the epistemic practices of science before strong ontological conclusions are drawn[24] is correct. Science presupposes, in practice, that the world has certain general characteristics, characteristics which transcendental realism – fallibly and incompletely – begins to specify. But one need only accept these presuppositions if one is willing – as most of us are most of the time – to declare one's hand with science.[25]

Chalmers takes specific objection to one of my arguments, which he dubs my 'ontological argument'. He alleges that I am wrong to argue that in an experiment, the experimenter is a causal agent of the sequence of events, but not of the law which the sequence enables her to identify. For the experimenter only causes the sequence 'in the sense that she assembles the appropriate experimental arrangement. But what happens when she has done so is dependent on the way the world is. The generative mechanism at work causes the sequence of events, not the experimenter. The ontological argument works only if the experimenter is taken to be the cause of the sequence of events, as opposed to the experimental set-up'.[26] But Chalmers' objection trades on a natural and non-malignant ambiguity in the term 'cause', which I note at *RTS* p. 252 when I say that I use the term 'to refer both to the antecedent event, condition or agent which triggers a mechanism and to the mechanism (and *a fortiori* the law it grounds) itself'. The experimental situation is as follows: The experimenter's activity, ϕ, is, in an experimental context, a necessary condition or cause of the experimental set-up, S. S includes whatever antecedent – stimulus and/or releasing – conditions are necessary for the operation of the mechanism, M. S is in turn a necessary condition or co-cause, together with the activity of M, for the sequence of events E_a, E_b, which allows us 'empirical access' to the *modus operandi* of M and the law it enables us to ground. The agent is a cause of the sequence of events E_a, E_b (but not of the law it empirically grounds) in the simple sense that without her activity, in the experimental context, S, and so the sequence E_a, E_b, would not have been forthcoming. This is not to deny that S might have occurred without her activity. This would correspond to the case of the naturally occurring locally closed systems which one finds in some astronomical contexts. But then *ex hypothesi* ϕ would not have been necessary for S. The cause of a co-cause of a phenomenon is, I think, rightly regarded as a cause of it. This does not give ontological parity to the agent, set-up and mechanism. For the set-up might have occurred without the agent, and the mechanism exists and acts (and the law holds) in general in nature independently of both. My so-called 'ontological argument' is sound.

There remains to discuss the general moral which Chalmers wishes to draw. Chalmers reckons my 'theoreticism' persists into my philosophy of social science – which takes place at a level 'too removed from that of practically efficacious intervention'.[27] This is asserted rather than proved. It could be maintained that philosophers of the human sciences have typically emphasized the cognitive over the conative and the conative over the affective side of human beings.[28] However, I do not think this is what Chalmers is getting at. He seems rather to be denying the need to work with generic concepts like society, social structure, human needs, ideology and emancipation (and presumably along with them concepts like gender and class). Yet a perusal of, say, the debates in Britain around Thatcherism and the Welfare State or the nature of socialism (or even, say, the state of higher education) reveal that they revolve around precisely such issues and take place at precisely this level of abstraction (which then feeds down into and informs the most mundane political actions and the most prosaic social practices).

Chalmers does however have one specific complaint concerning the premises of my transcendental arguments in the philosophy of the human sciences. But as this worries Ted Benton too, I will discuss their points together. Benton claims that my characterization of intentional action begs the question in favour of certain ('Durkheimian or Marxian, or rather some versions of these'[29]) as against other research traditions. I find this strange. For these traditions have typically had difficulty in sustaining the concept of *intentional agency*, which has been a relative strength of the neo-Kantian, Weberian and hermeneutical traditions (or rather some versions of these) (cf., e.g., pp. 37, 123, 138 above). Conversely, where the Durkheimian, non-historicist or non-humanist Marxian and structural–functionalist traditions have scored is in stressing the law-governed character of social forms. The synthesis attempted in *PON* seeks to preserve and reconcile both the subjective, intentional and conceptual, and the objective, conditioned and structural, aspects of social life. Why then does my argument in Chapter 2 take the form of an analysis of what must be the case for intentional agency to be possible? In the main because, pursuing my strategy of immanent critique, this is a good anti-naturalist premise – a premise which my opponent, the anti-naturalist, is almost bound to concede. However, could it not be that by starting there I may be, as Alan Chalmers suggests, entrapping myself in a tissue of tenacious truisms (pre-scientific reflections of the ideology of the day)?[30] Now I think that this, or something very like it, is what happens with the Winchian insight into the conceptuality of social life. I start, but do not stop, with intentional agency. I use it to establish the transformational model of social activity, the relational conception of society, the deduction of the possibility of social science and, with it, of explanatory (and putatively emancipatory) critiques, including critiques of commonsensical action descriptions. It is true that the concept of intentional agency remains intact at the end of Chapter 2. But it seems impossible to deny the phenomenon, in an article with a *point*, without being subject to a *tu quoque* argument. Of course intentionality must be interpreted broadly. In particular, as Freud put it, 'we must learn to emancipate ourselves from the importance of the symptom of "being conscious"' (see p. 116, n. 38 above). Moreover intentionality is not taken as an unexplicated datum in *PON* as a whole, as distinct from Chapter 2. There is an analysis of it in Chapter 3; and an argument to the effect that, without it, there would be no human science, as distinct from science of bodily movement (which would have difficulty in talking about itself), at all.

Intentionality is the *sine qua non* of the very problem – of naturalism – which I set out to resolve in *PON*. Perhaps Alan Chalmers' real objection is to any philosophical discussion about, as distinct from substantive discussion in, the human sciences. But then, as he notes, the advice to be specific is remarkably vague!

I have already granted to Ted Benton that we need to reappraise the possibility of naturalism from a multiplicity of scientific (and indeed extra-scientific) perspectives. He 'remain[s] convinced that the outcome of such investigations would be a confirmation of the broad outlines of Roy Bhaskar's realist model, if not of some of its more detailed articulation'.[31] The main thrust of his critique is that by failing to consider the biological and other life sciences, I am driven to unnecessarily anti-naturalist conclusions, thus tending to reproduce the traditional nature/culture divide, which can be traced back (at least) as far as Cartesian dualism. Now were I to rewrite *PON* today I would stress the way in which social order is embedded and conditioned by the natural order from which it is emergent and on which it in turns acts back.[32] An ecological orientation to social life is as important as is recognition of our biological being – both are insufficiently elaborated in the book.

Ted Benton is critical of my definition of a series of ontological, epistemological and relational limits of naturalism. Let me take these in order. The three ontological limits I featured in Chapter 2 were the activity-, concept- and space–time-dependency of social structures.[33]

It certainly is the case, as Benton correctly points out, that social structures can exist independently of the activities they govern (contrary to the claim made on p. 38) – at least insofar as:

(a) the activities they govern may not be those which sustain (or undermine) them[34] and/or
(b) they are internally related to other structures which are reproduced (or transformed) in human praxis.

Thus a structure of power may be reproduced without being exercised and exercised in the absence of any observable conflict (i.e. without being manifest) (cf. p. 162, n. 29) so long as it is sustained by human practices – the practices which reproduce or potentially transform it. In this sense the thesis of the activity-dependence of social structures must be affirmed. Social structures exist materially and are carried or transported from one space–time location to another only in or in virtue of human praxis. This does not, *contra* Benton, entail commitment to methodological individualism:[35] it is merely a condition for avoiding reification. Nor does recognition of the activity-dependence of social structures presuppose a residual 'problematic of the subject'.[36] On the contrary, the relational conception of society breaks completely from this. Not only is the focus switched from the subject to relations, but these relations, although they include intersubjective ones, are between positioned practices and between the human beings who fill them and nature and materially or institutionally realized social products (such as machines and firms) (see pp. 40–41).[37] What remains of individualism is a residual truth: that nothing happens in society save in or in virtue of something human beings do or have done (cf. pp. 30, 39–40).

My second ontological limit – that 'social structures, unlike natural structures, do not exist independently of the agents' conceptions of what they are doing in their activity' (pp. 38) – does seem to me to be exactly right. Of course these conceptions may not be correct or fully adequate. It is just this possibility which:

(a) grounds the fact that the double hermeneutic necessary for the understanding of social life is a contingently critical one (see p. 138);
(b) makes the concept of ideology possible; and
(c) establishes the feasibility of the project of an explanatory (and putatively emancipatory) critique.

I thus cannot agree that the concept-dependence of social structures has 'no special epistemological [consequences], *vis-à-vis* the natural sciences, where similar disparities between science and "common-sense" persist'.[38] For it presages the dissolution of fact/value and theory/practice dichotomies (see the last section of Chapter 2[39]) in a way which has only weak and partial analogues in the natural sphere.[40]

The third ontological limit – that social structures, unlike natural structures, may be only relatively enduring (so that the tendencies they ground may not be universal in the sense of space–time invariant) – only marks a necessary limit in relation to standard philosophical conceptions of physics and chemistry. I have already explained my immanent–critical reasons for taking these sciences (or rather standard conceptions of them) as my baseline for a re-examination of the possibility of naturalism in the human arena. There certainly is historicity and geographicity in nature (e.g. in biology and geology) and probably – through cosmology (and especially cosmogeny) – extending into the domain covered by chemistry and physics too. The relevant difference is that it is far faster and (e.g. in cities) denser than is normally the case in nature. It would be better perhaps to say that social structures and mechanisms are *more highly space–time specific* than natural (e.g. biological and geological) ones typically are; rather than to say that they are (more) space–time-dependent. For the argument is not that spatio-temporal locations are in themselves causally efficacious. It is rather that reference to space–time locations (e.g. classical Athens, mid-twentieth-century Liverpool, the Pacific Rim) may be irreducible in social scientific explanations – just insofar as they mark the site or space–time duration of certain geo-historically specific and internally related ensembles of structures, powers and tendencies. *Formally* such ensembles might have been found elsewhere. But *materially* this is not so. They are the unique and irreversible products of determinations which have converged on specific places at specific times. To conclude on space–time, what the transformational model of social activity brings to the fore are the following:

1. The recursivity of social structures as social products, subject to transformation like any other social product and hence (potentially) only relatively enduring with respect to the phenomena they explain.
2. The possibility of endogenous (e.g. in virtue of the possession of auto-subversive tendencies by a structure), as well as exogenous, sources of change.
3. The spatio–temporally moored, geo-historically reproduced, distantiated and transformed transformative character of the social process.

Ted Benton next turns to the epistemological limits to naturalism. The most important of these is that social phenomena only ever occur in open systems. It follows from this that criteria for theory-development cannot be predictive and so must be exclusively explanatory (cf. pp. 45–6).[41] There are two extreme reactions to the intrinsic openness of social systems. The first is to effectively deny the existence of *any* a posteriori controls on theory, or at least controls independent of their various practical (open-systemic) applications. This is Andrew Collier's response in characterizing the human sciences as 'epistemoids' rather than sciences properly so-called.[42] But why cannot a theory be subjected to non-predictive empirical test? The second is to regard the use of a battery of statistical techniques as providing a more or less fully adequate surrogate for experimental closure. This is Benton's response: 'The classic experimental closure is [merely] one technique (class of techniques) among many'.[43] But there are significant limits to measurement (see p. 46 above) and the use of statistical methods in the human sciences.[44] And of course there is no reason to suppose that the social world is not statistically open.[45]

None of this rules out *conditional* predictions in social science; and a powerful explanatory theory will be capable of situating *ex ante* unlikely possibilities long before they are realized.[46] William Outhwaite has nicely caught the spirit of my position when he characterizes it as 'ontologically bold and epistemologically cautious'.[47] We can be certain that society exists and has certain general features. Its existence (and some of these features) are after all transcendentally necessary conditions for any knowledge, including any knowledge in the natural sciences. But we must exercise some modesty and prudence in our cognitive claims about specific structures and mechanisms in social science – partly because of what Outhwaite calls 'their general messiness and fluidity'.[48] However, critical naturalism does at least situate the possibility of adjudicating – with respect to their comparative explanatory power – between rival theories within and between research programmes.[49] My motive in insisting, *contra* Benton, on an epistemological limit to naturalism in the human sciences is part of an attempt to shift the emphasis away from predictive accuracy to explanatory power. These are in any event asymmetrical in the natural sciences.[50] But historically the goal of predictive accuracy in the human sciences has been associated with historicist–fatalist or instrumentalist–manipulative or elitist–social-engineering approaches to their subject-matter. To these I want to counterpose the enlightenment and emancipation that depth explanation *may*, but will not necessarily, bring.

Finally, Benton takes issue with my relational limit. This pivots on the causal interdependency between social objects and social knowledge already noted. First Benton suggests that there is an analogous interdependency in the natural world – in experimental activity.[51] But the real structure, mechanism or law 'accessed', as distinct from the pattern of events produced, in an experiment is not a causal result of the experiment (cf. p. 171–2 above). Next Benton turns to my suggestion that social structures may become more 'visible' or 'accessible' in periods of crisis, strain or transition (see p. 48). I do believe that there is much to be said in favour of the thesis of the methodological primacy of the pathological.[52] But it is not logically necessary to my case. It could be that a period of calm and growing confidence among the oppressed, approximating perhaps to a Habermasian 'ideal speech situation', is most conducive to the discursive redemption of the relevant validity claims. Such states – be they of crisis or calm – in any case would only motivate, not justify, the proto-scientific transformation P→T (see p. 49). So if, as is likely, a crisis or any other kind of historical turning point ideologically divides social agents (as Benton suggests), the theory to be preferred will be the one embedded in a practical research programme yielding hypotheses, subject to empirical test, of greater explanatory power (and *ceteris paribus* emancipatory potential). Certainly the exploited, oppressed, etc., have a direct material interest in such a programme that their exploiters, oppressors, etc., do not. But a historical turning point *may* see the birth of a new ideology rationalizing the position or condition of the dominated, instead of the transformation P→T.

In any event my discussion of the relational status of social ideas is only a lead-in to the argument, which I advance on pp. 50–3, as to how the ontological specificities of the subject-matter of social science make possible a non-arbitrary procedure for arriving at real definitions of forms of social life. Such definitions will be capable of generating explanatory hypotheses, subject to non-predictive but empirical test. And such hypotheses will be embedded in practical research programmes yielding critiques of structures generating falsity among other ills. Such structures may come to be transformed through the theoretically and practically *transformed transformative praxis* of the agents who were reproducing them. This is the heart of my deduction of the possibility of an explanatory and *ceteris paribus* emancipatory social science. I could sum up my response to Ted Benton's critique by saying that whereas, if *PON* is perhaps not too red, it is certainly insufficiently green; he, for his part, tends to systematically underestimate the categorial differences, summed up in my ontological limits, which do not so much impede as enable the construction of explanatory social science – with critical import and, at least in so far as there is an emancipatory spiral at work in history, practical effect.

Some readers have found the argument of *PON* insufficiently 'dialectical' for their taste.[53] As I am currently writing a book on the topic of dialectic, I shall limit my remarks to two orders of comment here. The first, negative, order is this. Although Marx's criticism of Hegelian dialectic remained constant from 1843 to 1873, a definite positive re-evaluation of it occurs about the time of the *Grundrisse* (1857).[54] What accounts for Marx's (and Engels's subsequent) recourse to dialectics? My conjecture is that it took the place of critical realism as the missing methodological fulcrum of Marx's work. For Marx never theorized his critique of empiricism, which remained implicit, in the way he theorized his critique of idealism – and which indeed formed his *Ausgang* from philosophy into substantive social science and history. He thus never developed his continuing commitment to simple material object realism into that explicit commitment to scientific realism, which his work presupposed and for which his 'dialectics' acted as a surrogate. In the same way, Marx's theme of objectivity (cf. the 'intransitive dimension') remained underdeveloped in comparison with that of labour (cf. the 'transitive dimension'); just as the theme of normativity lagged behind that of historicity. Finally, Marx was, in his maturity, first and foremost a political economist and then a historian and a political activist, but not a philosopher. There was thus a fivefold lopsided development within the thought of Marx, which has passed over into Marxism and which helps to explain the enormous 'overloading' of the concept within it.

The second, positive, order of comment is this. Transcendental realism and critical naturalism accentuated the categories of structure, differentiation and change at both the ontological and epistemic levels, and in the natural and social spheres alike. But these are by no means the only previously underanalysed categories required for the understanding (and making) of (especially human) history. The categories of process, negation, contradiction and development, together with those of reflexivity and totality – stressed or highlighted by those within the dialectical tradition – demand adequate analysis and critique. The resulting system will, I think, deepen and enrich, but still be developmentally consistent with, transcendental realism and critical naturalism.

I want to conclude this postscript with a balance sheet of work done within the critical naturalist – or as it is often called, critical realist[55] – framework. Since the first edition of *PON* was published in 1979, there have been at least four major book-length expositions of the critical realist point of view.[56] More, or at least as, important is the work that has been done, within the critical realist perspective, over the whole field of the sciences – from psychoanalysis to biology, Marxism to linguistics, feminism to urban studies. In a collection of essays, based on papers delivered at the annual conference of the Standing Conference on Realism and the Human Sciences since 1985, which we hope to be in a position to publish shortly,[57] we aim to report systematically on the work that is being done and on some of the controversies and issues generated. That there would be such a ferment of activity within and around the critical realist research programme is just what I wanted in writing *PON*. Its job was to underlabour for the concrete research practices of the various human sciences and on occasion to act as midwife to them. But at the same time as we advance our concrete work, there is need also to deepen our understanding and critique of the philosophical tradition we have inherited and which is ever giving birth to new ideologies which threaten the critical human sciences. Sometimes these new ideologies are merely reincarnations of old and familiar ones, but even where this is the case, they still have to be understood and critiqued in their contemporary forms. Positivism and hermeneutics are the ancient and probably still the most potent foes of the critical human sciences. But they are not alone.[58] So long as humanity survives and pays any attention to the condition of itself and its environment, there will always be a need for new, ever-deepening and more practically efficacious critical philosophy of and for the human sciences.

NOTES

1. T. Benton, 'Realism and Social Science: Some Comments on Roy Bhaskar's "The Possibility of Naturalism"' (henceforth *RSS*, *Radical Philosophy* 27 (Spring 1981); and A. Chalmers, 'Is Bhaskar's Realism Realistic?' (henceforth *BRR*), *Radical Philosophy* 49 (Summer 1988).
2. First edition, Leeds 1975; second edition, Hassocks and New Jersey 1978.
3. For instance, I wanted to shift the emphasis in the human sciences away from the purely *formal* relations of similarity or dissimilarity, association or non-association, etc., to such *substantial* relations as generation, connection, interaction and change. (Cf. A. Sayer, *Method in Social Science: A Realist Approach* (London 1984), p. 82.) Thus change is a substantial, difference is a formal, relation – a point that has devastating implications for the entire philosophical tradition, which has accepted Plato's analysis of negation and change in terms of difference. (See my forthcoming *Philosophy and the Idea of Freedom* (Oxford 1989).) Again, causal connection is a substantial, constant conjunction a formal, relation – a point with equally devastating implications for Humean and Kantian analyses of causality and law as constant conjunction or that plus some subjective contribution of mind. (See *RTS*, esp. chs. 2 and 3).
4. *BRR*, p. 20.
5. See A. Chalmers, 'Bhaskar, Cartwright and Realism in Physics', *Methodology and Science* 20 (1987), p. 94.
6. *BRR*, pp. 20–2. See N. Cartwright, *How the Laws of Physics Lie* (Oxford 1983); and I. Hacking, *Representing and Intervening* (Cambridge 1983).
7. *RSS*, p. 19.
8. *RSS*, p. 20.
9. See *RTS*, p. 260 and cf. my *Scientific Realism and Human Emancipation* (henceforth *SR*) (London 1986), p. 14.

10. Cf. *SR*, p. 119.
11. *RSS*, pp. 14–5.
12. Such a dialectical, transitional logic – of the type characteristic of a process of immanent critique – would involve the loosening, stretching and (explicated) changing of meanings. Cf. my 'Rorty, Realism and the Idea of Freedom', *Reading Rorty*, A. Malachowski (ed.) (Oxford 1988), reprinted in my *Reclaiming Reality* (henceforth *RR*) (London 1989).
13. There is no question of subject–object identity here. 'Concept and object, even where the object is itself a concept, remain distinct and, in general, dissimilar' (p. 142). (Cf. also p. 92 and p. 116, n.32.) This does not make self-knowledge impossible. It is rather that what is known is distinct from its cognition.
15. This is what I have called the ontic$_2$ of a higher-order epistemic$_2$ (within ontology). See *SR*, p. 37.
15. *Scientific Realism and Socialist Thought* (Hemel Hempstead 1988), ch. 3.
16. Another terminological innovation of his is to distinguish, within the class of open systems, the category of *laminated systems*. These are '*structurata* whose elements are necessarily bonded by an irreducible plurality [or, in my terms, multiplicity] of structures (e.g. human individuals have mental and physical structures; human societies have economic, political and ideological structures)', *ibid.*, Glossary. Cf. also *SR*, pp. 109–10.
17. See *RTS*, p. 180.
18. This precision was suggested to me by Andrew Sayer, *op. cit.*, pp. 84, 96ff.
19. These possibilities are explored in a hitherto unpublished paper by John Lovering, 'Critical Realism: Lessons for Socialist Research'.
20. See *BRR*, p. 22.
21. Cf. *RTS*, p. 260 and *SR*, pp. 11–12.
22. *BRR*, p. 19 and *passim*.
23. Cf. *BRR*, p. 19.
24. *RSS*, p. 14.
25. Cf. *SR*, pp. 18–19.
26. *BRR*, p. 19.
27. *BRR*, p. 22.
28. See *SR*, p. 127.
29. *RSS*, p. 16.
30. *BRR*, p. 23.
31. *RSS*, p. 20.
32. Cf. *SR*, esp. ch. 2.1–2.3.
33. In *SR*, ch. 2, I added a fourth ontological limit, viz. social-relation-dependency (see SR, p. 137); and a fourth, critical, limit to the other three types (see *SR*, p. 133). But I think these are implicit in the argument of *PON*, ch. 2.
34. See W. Outhwaite, *New Philosophies of Social Science* (London 1987), p. 54.
35. *BRR*, p. 19.
36. *RSS*, p. 20.
37. Cf. *SR*, pp. 130, 155.
38. *RSS*, p. 17.
39. Cf. also my 'Scientific Explanation and Human Emancipation', *Radical Philosophy* 26 (Autumn 1980), reprinted in *RR*, and *SR*, ch. 2.5–2.7.
40. See *SR*, 178 and p. 189, n. 103.
41. Of course whether one has on any particular occasion actually achieved a

closure in the natural world, although in principle ontologically determinate, is or may be epistemically problematic – for reasons pointed out by
Duhem. See *SR*, p. 36.
42. See *Scientific Realism and Socialist Thought*, ch. 4.
43. *RSS*, p. 19.
44. See A. Sayer, *op. cit.*, ch. 6; and P. Manicas, *A History and Philosophy of
the Social Sciences* (Oxford 1987), ch. 13.
45. Cf. *RTS*, p. 142.
46. Cf. M. Burawoy, 'The Limits of Wright's Analytical Marxism and an
Alternative', *Berkeley Journal of Sociology* XXXII (1987), pp. 59–60, on
the 'prophetic power' of revolutionary social science.
47. *New Philosophies of Social Science*, p. 34.
48. *Op. cit.*, p. 53.
49. Cf. E. O. Wright, 'Reply to Burawoy's Comment on "Reflections on
Classes"', *Berkeley Journal of Sociology* XXXII (1987), p. 78.
50. Cf. *RTS*, pp. 134–9.
51. *RSS*, p. 19.
52. Cf. A. Collier, *op. cit.*, ch. 4.
53. See, e.g., G. Carchedi, 'A Critical Note on Bhaskar and Systems Theory',
Radical Philosophy 33 (Spring 1983).
54. See my 'Dialectics', *A Dictionary of Marxist Thought*, T. Bottomore *et al.*
(eds.) (Oxford 1983), reprinted in my *RR*.
55. See *RR*, ch. 1.
56. Viz. W. Outhwaite, *op. cit.* (see also his *Concept Formation and Social
Science* (London 1983)); P. Manicas, *op. cit.*; A. Sayer, *op. cit.*; and
A. Collier, *op. cit.* Also worth noting are T. Benton, *The Rise and Fall of
Structural Marxism* (London 1984); J. Isaac, *Power and Marxist Theory: A
Realist View* (Ithaca 1987); T. Lovell, *Pictures of Reality* (London 1980);
and G. McLennan, *Marxism and the Methodologies of History* (London
1981).
57. This collection is provisionally entitled *Realism and the Human Sciences*,
R. Bhaskar and S. Clegg (eds.).
58. A point made by Michèle Barrett in an unpublished talk, 'Explaining
Women's Oppression'. See also my *RR*, ch. 9 and *passim*.

Bibliography

(NB: This bibliography contains only works specifically cited in the text or notes.)

Adlam, D., *et al.*, 'Psychology, Ideology and the Human Subject', *Ideology and Consciousness*, 1 (1977).

Adorno, T., (ed.), *The Positivist Dispute in German Sociology*, Heinemann (London 1976).

Althusser, L., *For Marx*, Allen Lane (London 1969).

Althusser, L., *Lenin and Philosophy*, New Left Books (London 1971).

Althusser L. and Balibar, E., *Reading Capital*, New Left Books (London 1970).

Anderson, P., *Considerations on Western Marxism*, New Left Books (London 1976).

Aristotle, *De Motu Animalium*, OUP (Oxford 1952).

Armstrong, D., *A Materialist Theory of Mind*, Routledge & Kegan Paul (London 1968).

Aron, R., *Philosophie critique de l'historie*, Gallimard (Paris 1969).

Aronson, J., 'Explanation without Laws', *Journal of Philosophy*, 66 (1969).

Austin, J., *How to do Things with Words*, Clarendon Press (Oxford 1962).

Ayers, M., *The Refutation of Determinism*, Methuen (London 1968).

Bachelard, G., *La Formation de l'esprit scientifique*, Vrin (Paris 1938).

Barnes, S. B., *Interests and the Growth of Knowledge*, Routledge & Kegan Paul (London 1977).

Barrett, M., 'Explaining Women's Oppression' (unpublished talk 1987).

Beloff, J., 'Mind-Body Interaction in the Light of the Parapsychological Evidence', *Theoria to Theory*, 10 (1976).

Benjamin, W., *Illuminations*, Fontana (London 1976).

Benton, T., *Philosophical Foundations of the Three Sociologies*, Routledge & Kegan Paul (London 1977).

Benton, T., 'Realism and Social Science: Some Comments on Roy Bhaskar's "The Possibility of Naturalism"', *Radical Philosophy*, 27 (Spring 1981), reprinted in *Radical Philosophy Reader*, R. Edgeley and R. Osborne (eds.), Verso (London 1985).

Benton, T., *The Rise and Fall of Structural Marxism*, Macmillan (London 1984).

Berger, P. and Pullberg, S., 'Reification and the Sociological Critique of Consciousness', *New Left Review*, 35 (1966).

Berger, P. and Luckmann, T., *The Social Construction of Reality*, Allen Lane (London 1967).

Berlin, I., *Vico and Herder*, The Hogarth Press (London 1976).

Bhaskar, R., *A Realist Theory of Science*, 1st edn (Leeds 1975), 2nd edn, Harvester Press and Humanities Press (Hassocks and New Jersey 1978).

Bhaskar, R., 'Forms of Realism', *Philosophica*, 15 (1) (1975).

Bhaskar, R., 'Feyerabend and Bachelard: Two Philosophies of Science', *New Left Review*, 94 (1975), reprinted in my *Reclaiming Reality*.

Bhaskar, R., 'On the Possibility of Social Scientific Knowledge and the Limits of Naturalism', *Journal for the Theory of Social Behaviour*, 8 (1) (1978), reprinted in *Issues in Marxist Philosophy*, J. Mepham and D. Ruben (eds.), Harvester Press (Hassocks 1979), and my *Reclaiming Reality*.

Bhaskar, R., 'Scientific Explanation and Human Emancipation', *Radical Philosophy*, 26 (Autumn 1980), reprinted in my *Reclaiming Reality*, Verso (London 1989).

Bhaskar, R., 'Dialectics', *A Dictionary of Marxist Thought*, T. Bottomore *et al.*, (eds.), Blackwell (Oxford 1983), reprinted in my *Reclaiming Reality*, Verso (London 1989).

Bhaskar, R., *Scientific Realism and Human Emancipation*, Verso (London 1986).

Bhaskar, R., 'Rorty, Realism and the Idea of Freedom', *Reading Rorty*, A. Malachowski (ed.), Blackwell (Oxford 1988), reprinted in my *Reclaiming Reality*, Verso (London 1989).

Bhaskar, R., *Reclaiming Reality*, Verso (London 1989).

Bhaskar, R., *Philosophy and the Idea of Freedom*, Blackwell (Oxford 1989).

Bhaskar, R. and Clegg, S. (eds.), *Realism and the Human Sciences* (provisional title) (forthcoming).

Bloomfield, L., *Linguistic Aspects of Science* (Chicago 1939).

Bloor, D., *Knowledge and Social Imagery*, Routledge & Kegan Paul (London 1976).

Brennan, J., *The Open Texture of Moral Concepts*, Macmillan (London 1977).

Buchdahl, G., *Metaphysics and the Philosophy of Science*, Blackwell (Oxford 1969).

Burawoy, M., 'The Limits of Wright's Analytical Marxism and an Alternative', *Berkeley Journal of Sociology*, XXXII (1987).

Burtt, E., *The Metaphysical Foundations of Natural Science*, Routledge & Kegan Paul (London 1964).

Carchedi, G., 'A Critical Note on Bhaskar and Systems Theory', *Radical Philosophy*, 33 (Spring 1983).

Cartwright, N., *How the Laws of Physics Lie*, OUP (Oxford 1983).

Chalmers, A., 'Bhaskar, Cartwright and Realism in Physics', *Methodology and Science*, 20 (1987).

Chalmers, A., 'Is Bhaskar's Realism Realistic?', *Radical Philosophy*, 49 (Summer 1988).

Chomsky, N., 'Review of B. F. Skinner's *Verbal Behaviour*', *Language*, 35 (1959), reprinted in J. Fodor and J. Katz, *The Structure of Language*, Prentice-Hall (New Jersey 1965).

Chomsky, N., *American Power and the New Mandarins*, Penguin (Harmondsworth 1969).

Cicourel, A., *Method and Measurement in Sociology*, Free Press (New York 1964).

Colletti, L., *Marxism and Hegel*, New Left Books (London 1973).

Colletti, L., 'Marxism and the Dialectic', *New Left Review*, 93 (1975).

Collier, A., *R. D. Laing: The Philosophy and Politics of Psychotherapy*, Harvester Press (Hassocks 1977).

Collier, A., *Scientific Realism and Socialist Thought*, Harvester Press (Hemel Hempstead 1988).

Collingwood, R. G., *An Essay on Metaphysics*, OUP (Oxford 1940).

Colvin, P., 'Ontological and Epistemological Commitments and Social Relations in the Sciences', *Sociology of the Sciences Yearbook 1977: The Social*

Production of Knowledge, E. Mendelsohn, P. Weingart and R. Whitley (eds.)
D. Reidel (Dordrecht 1977).

Coward, R. and Ellis, J., *Language and Materialism*, Routledge & Kegan Paul
(London 1977).

Culler, J., *Saussure*, Fontana (London 1976).

Danto, A., *Analytical Philosophy of History*, CUP (Cambridge 1965).

Danto, A., 'Basic Acts', *APQ* 2 (1965), reprinted in *Philosophy of Action*,
A. White (ed.), OUP (Oxford 1968).

Davidson, D., 'Actions, Reasons and Causes', *Journal of Philosophy*, 60 (1963),
reprinted in A. White (ed.), *op cit*.

Davidson, D., 'Psychology as Philosophy', *Philosophy of Psychology*, S. Brown
(ed.) (London 1974), reprinted in *Philosophy of Mind*, J. Glover (ed.), OUP
(Oxford 1976).

Davie, G., *The Democratic Intellect*, Edinburgh University Press (Edinburgh
1961).

Derrida, J., *Of Grammatology*, Johns Hopkins (Baltimore 1974).

Deutsch, J., 'The Structural Basis of Behaviour', J. Glover (ed.), *op cit*.

Dilthey, W., *Gesammelte Schriften* (Munich 1937).

Donagan, A., 'The Popper–Hempel Theory Reconsidered', *Philosophical
Analysis and History*, W. Dray (ed.), Harper & Row (New York 1966).

Douglas, J., *The Social Meanings of Suicide*, Princeton University Press (New
Jersey 1967).

Dray, W., 'Historical Understanding as Re-thinking', B. Brody (ed.), *Readings
in the Philosophy of Science*, Prentice-Hall (New Jersey 1970).

Duhem, P., *The Aim and Structure of Physical Theory*, Atheneum (New York
1962).

Durkheim, E., *The Division of Labour in Society*, Free Press (New York 1964).

Durkheim, E., *The Rules of Sociological Method*, Free Press (New York 1964).

Durkheim, E., *The Elementary Forms of Religious Life*, Free Press (New York
1965).

Eagleton, T., *Criticism and Ideology*, New Left Books (London 1976).

Edgley, R., *Reason in Theory and Practice*, Hutchinson (London 1969).

Edgley, R., 'Reason as Dialectic', *Radical Philosophy*, 15 (1976).

Elias, N., 'The Sciences: Towards a Theory', *Social Processes of Scientific
Development*, R. Whitley (ed.), Macmillan (London 1974).

Fay, B., 'Practical Reasoning, Rationality and the Explanation of Intentional
Action', *Journal for the Theory of Social Behaviour*, 8 (1) (1978).

Feyerabend, P., *Science in a Free Society*, New Left Books (London 1978).

Freud, S., *The Standard Edition of the Complete Psychological Works*, The
Hogarth Press (London 1953–64).

Gadamer, H.-G., *Truth and Method*, Sheed and Ward (London 1975).

Gallie, W. B., 'Essentially Contested Concepts', *Proceedings of the Aristotelian
Society*, 56 (1955–6).

Garfinkel, H., *Studies in Ethnomethodology*, Prentice-Hall (New Jersey 1967).

Gellner E., 'Concepts and Society', B. Wilson (ed.), *Rationality*, Blackwell
(Oxford 1970).

Georgescu-Roegen, N., *The Entropy Law and the Economic Process*, Harvard
University Press (Cambridge, Mass. 1971).

Geras, N., 'Marx and the Critique of Political Economy', R. Blackburn (ed.),
Ideology in Social Science, Fontana (London 1972).

Geras, N., 'Althusser's Marxism: An Assessment', *Western Marxism: A Critical
Reader*, G. Stedman Jones *et al*. (eds.) New Left Books (London 1977).

Giddens, A., *New Rules of Sociological Method*, Hutchinson (London 1976).
Giddens, A., *Studies in Social and Political Theory*, Hutchinson (London 1977).
Godelier, M., 'System, Structure and Contradiction in *Capital*', R. Blackburn (ed.), *op. cit.*
Goldmann, L., *Marxisme et sciences humaines*, Gallimard (Paris 1970).
Habermas, J., *Towards a Rational Society*, Heinemann (London 1971).
Habermas, J., *Knowledge and Human Interests*, Heinemann (London 1972).
Hacking, I., *Representing and Intervening*, CUP (Cambridge 1983).
Hampshire, S., *Thought and Action*, Methuen (London 1959).
Hanson, N. R. *Patterns of Discovery*, CUP (Cambridge 1965).
Hare, R., *Freedom and Reason*, Clarendon Press (Oxford 1963).
Harré, R., *The Principles of Scientific Thinking*, Macmillan (London 1970).
Harré, R. and Madden, E., *Causal Powers*, Blackwell (Oxford 1975).
Harré, R. and Secord, P., *The Explanation of Social Behaviour*, Blackwell (Oxford 1972).
Harrison, R., *On What There Must Be*, Clarendon Press (Oxford 1974).
Hart, H., *The Concept of Law*, Clarendon Press (Oxford 1961).
Heidegger, M., *Being and Time*, Blackwell (Oxford 1967).
Heidegger, M., 'Letter on Humanism', *Philosophy in the Twentieth Century*, W. Barret and H. Aiken (eds.), Harper & Row (New York 1971).
Hempel, C. G., *Aspects of Scientific Explanation*, Free Press (New York 1963).
Hempel, C. G., 'Explanation in Science and History', W. Dray (ed.), *op. cit.*
Hesse, M., *The Structure of Scientific Inference*, Macmillan (London 1974).
Hobbes, T. and Bramhall, *Questions Concerning Liberty, Necessity and Chance* (London 1841).
Hollis, M., 'Reason and Ritual', A. Ryan (ed.), *The Philosophy of Social Explanation*, CUP (Cambridge 1973).
Hollis, M., *Models of Man*, CUP (Cambridge 1977).
Hollis, M. and Nell, E., *Rational Economic Man*, CUP (Cambridge 1975).
Horton, R., 'Lévy-Bruhl, Durkheim and the Scientific Revolution', *Modes of Thought*, R. Finnegan and R. Horton (eds.), Faber & Faber (London 1973).
Hume, D., *Essays Moral and Political*, 2 (London 1875).
Hume, D., *Enquiries Concerning Human Understanding and the Principles of Morals*, Clarendon Press (Oxford 1962).
Hume, D., *A Treatise on Human Nature*, Clarendon Press (Oxford 1967).
Husserl, E., *Cartesian Meditations*, Nijhoff (The Hague 1960).
Huxley, T., *Methods and Results* (London 1894).
Issac, J. *Power and Marxist Theory: A Realist View*, Cornell University Press (Ithaca 1987).
Jarvie, I., 'Reply to Taylor', *Universities and Left Review* (Spring 1959).
Kant, I., *Critique of Pure Reason*, N. Kemp Smith (trans.), Macmillan (London 1970).
Keat, R. and Urry, J., *Social Theory as Science*, Routledge & Kegan Paul (London 1975).
Kenny, A., *Freedom, Will and Power*, Blackwell (Oxford 1975).
Körner, S., *Categorial Frameworks*, Blackwell (Oxford 1970).
Kotarbinski, S., 'Praxiology', *Essays in Honour of O. Lange* (Warsaw 1965).
Koyré, A., *Metaphysics and Measurement*, Chapman & Hall (London 1968).
Kuhn, T. S., *The Structure of Scientific Revolutions*, 2nd edn, Chicago University Press (Chicago 1970).
Labriola, A., *Essays on the Materialistic Conception of History* (Chicago 1904).
Lacan, J., *Ecrits*, Tavistock Publications (London 1977).

Lakatos, I. 'Falsification and the Methodology of Scientific Research Programmes', *Criticism and the Growth of Knowledge*, I. Lakatos and A. Musgrave (eds.), CUP (Cambridge 1970).

Lecourt, D., *Proletarian Science?*, New Left Books (London 1977).

Lefebvre, H., 'What is the Historical Past?', *New Left Review*, 90 (1975).

Lévi-Strauss, C., *The Savage Mind*, Weidenfield & Nicolson (London 1976).

Llewelyn, J., *Beyond Metaphysics?*, Macmillan (London 1985).

Locke, D., 'Reasons, Wants and Causes', *American Philosophical Quarterly*, 11 (1974).

Locke, J., *Essay Concerning Human Understanding*, Dover (New York 1959).

Lorenzer, A., 'Symbols and Stereotypes', *Critical Sociology*, P. Connerton (ed.), Penguin (Harmondsworth 1976).

Lovell, T., *Pictures of Reality*, BFI (London 1980).

Lovering, J., 'Critical Realism: Lessons for Socialist Research' (unpublished paper 1988).

Lukács, G., *History and Class Consciousness*, Merlin Press (London 1971).

Lukes, S., 'Some Problems about Rationality', B. Wilson (ed.), *op. cit.*

Lukes, S., 'Methodological Individualism Reconsidered', A. Ryan (ed.), *op. cit.*

Lukes, S., *Durkheim*, Allen Lane (London 1973).

Lukes, S., *Power: A Radical View*, Macmillan (London 1974).

Luria, A., *The Working Brain*, Penguin (Harmondsworth 1970).

Lyons, J., *Chomsky*, Fontana (London 1970).

McHugh, P. *et al.*, *On the Beginnings of Social Inquiry*, Routledge & Kegan Paul (London 1974).

MacIntyre, A., 'The Antecedents of Action', *British Analytical Philosophy*, B. Williams and A. Montefiore (eds.), Routledge & Kegan Paul (London 1966).

MacIntyre, A., 'The Idea of a Social Science', A. Ryan (ed.) *op. cit.*

Mackie, J., *The Cement of the Universe*, Clarendon Press (Oxford 1974).

McLennan, G., *Marxism and the Methodologies of History*, Verso (London 1981).

Mandelbaum, M., 'Historical Explanation: The Problem of Covering Laws', *The Philosophy of History*, P. Gardiner (ed.), OUP (Oxford 1974).

Manicas, P., *A History and Philosophy of Social Sciences*, Blackwell (Oxford 1987).

Mannheim, K., *Ideology and Utopia*, Routledge & Kegan Paul (London 1960).

Marković, M., 'The Problem of Reification and the *Verstehen-Erklären* Controversy', *Acta Sociologica*, 15 (1972).

Marx, K., *The German Ideology*, Lawrence & Wishart (London 1965).

Marx, K., *The German Ideology* C. Arthur (ed.), Lawrence & Wishart (London 1974).

Marx, K., *Capital*, 1, Lawrence & Wishart (London 1965).

Marx, K., *Capital*, 3, Lawrence & Wishart (London 1966).

Marx, K., *Selected Works*, Lawrence & Wishart (London 1968).

Marx, K., *Early Writings*, Penguin (Harmondsworth 1975).

Marx, K., *Grundrisse*, Penguin (Harmondsworth 1975).

Mepham, J., 'The Theory of Ideology in *Capital*', *Radical Philosophy*, 2 (1972).

Mill, J. S., *A System of Logic*, 8th edn (London 1961).

Myrdal, G., *The Political Element in the Development of Economic Theory*, Routledge & Kegan Paul (London 1953).

Myrdal, G. *Value in Social Theory*, Routledge & Kegan Paul (London 1959).

Nagel, E., *The Structure of Science*, Routledge & Kegan Paul (London 1961).

Ollman, B., *Alienation*, CUP (Cambridge 1971).

Outhwaite, W., *Understanding Social Life*, Allen & Unwin (London 1975).
Outhwaite, W., *Concept Formation in Social Science*, Routledge & Kegan Paul (London 1983).
Outhwaite, W., *New Philosophies of Social Science*, Macmillan (London 1987).
Parsons, T. *The Structure of Social Action*, Free Press (New York 1959).
Plato, *Meno, Dialogues*, OUP (Oxford 1953).
Polanyi, M., *The Tacit Dimension*, Routledge & Kegan Paul (London 1967).
Pompa, L., *Vico*, CUP (Cambridge 1975).
Popper, K., *The Poverty of Historicism*, Routledge & Kegan Paul (London 1960).
Popper, K., *The Open Society and its Enemies*, Vol II, Routledge & Kegan Paul (London 1962).
Popper, K., *Conjectures and Refutations*, Routledge & Kegan Paul (London 1963).
Popper, K., *Objective Knowledge*, Clarendon Press (Oxford 1972).
Putnam, H., 'The Mental Life of Some Machines', J. Glover (ed.), *op. cit.*
Putnam, H., *Philosophical Papers Vol II, Mind, Language and Reality*, CUP (Cambridge 1975).
Quine, W. V. O., *Word and Object*, MIT Press (Cambridge, Mass. 1960).
Ravetz, J., *Scientific Knowledge and its Social Problems*, Clarendon Press (Oxford 1971).
Ricoeur, P., *Freud and Philosophy*, Yale University Press (New Haven 1970).
Rose, S., *The Conscious Brain*, Penguin (Harmondsworth 1976).
Ryan, A., *The Philosophy of the Social Sciences*, Macmillan (London 1970).
Sartre, J.-P., *Critique of Dialectical Reason*, New Left Books (London 1976).
Sayer, A., *Method in Social Science: A Realist Approach*, Hutchinson (London 1984).
Sayer, D., 'Science as Critique: Marx v. Althusser', J. Mepham and D. Ruben (eds.), *op. cit.*
Schutz, A., *Collected Papers* 1, (The Hague, 1967).
Schutz, A., *The Phenomenology of the Social World*, Heinemann (London 1972).
Schutz, A., 'Problems of Interpretative Sociology', A. Ryan (ed.), *op. cit.*
Scriven, M., 'Truisms as the Grounds for Historical Explanations', *Theories of History*, P. Gardiner (ed.), Free Press (New York 1959).
Scriven, M., 'Causes, Connections and Conditions in History', W. Dray (ed.), *op. cit.*
Searle, J., 'How to Derive "Ought" from "Is"', *Philosophical Review*, 73 (1964).
Searle, J., *Speech Acts*, CUP (Cambridge 1969).
Shaffer, J., *The Philosophy of Mind*, Prentice-Hall (New Jersey 1968).
Shwayder, D., *The Stratification of Behaviour*, Routledge & Kegan Paul (London 1965).
Skinner, Q., '"Social Meaning" and the Explanation of Social Action', *The Philosophy of History*, P. Gardiner (ed.), OUP (Oxford 1974).
Slack, J., 'Class Struggle Among the Molecules', *Counter Course*, T. Pateman (ed.), Penguin (Harmondsworth 1972).
Spinoza, B., *Ethics*, Dent (London 1959).
Stedman Jones, G., 'The Marxism of the Early Lukács', G. Stedman Jones *et al.*, *op. cit.*
Stockman, N., 'Habermas, Marcuse and *Aufhebung* of Science and Technology', *The Philosophy of the Social Sciences*, 8 (1) (1978).
Strawson, P., *Individuals*, Methuen (London 1959).

Swinburne, R., 'The Objectivity of Morality', *Philosophy*, 51 (1976).
Taylor, C., 'Neutrality in Political Science', A. Ryan (ed.), *op. cit.*
Taylor, C., 'Interpretation and the Sciences of Man', P. Connerton (ed.) *op. cit.*
Taylor, R., *Metaphysics*, Prentice-Hall (New Jersey 1966).
Therborn, G. *Science, Class and Society*, New Left Books (London 1976).
Timpanaro, S., *On Materialism*, New Left Books (London 1975).
Toulmin, S., 'Reasons and Causes', *Explanation in the Behavioural Sciences*, R. Borger and F. Cioffi (eds.), CUP (Cambridge 1970).
Vico, G., *Scienza Nuova*, trans. as *The New Science of Giambattista Vico*, Cornell University Press (Ithaca 1969).
Walsh, W. H., *Kant's Criticism of Metaphysics*, Edinburgh University Press (Edinburgh 1975).
Watkins, J., 'Ideal Types and Historical Explanation', *British Journal for the Philosophy of Science*, (3) (1952), reprinted in A. Ryan (ed.), *op. cit.*
Watkins, J., 'Historical Explanation in the Social Sciences, *BJPS*, 8 (1957), reprinted in M. Brodbeck (ed.), *Readings in the Philosophy of the Social Sciences*, Macmillan (New York 1969).
Weber, M., *The Methodology of the Social Sciences*, Free Press (Chicago 1949).
Weber, M., *Economy and Society*, Bedminster (New York 1968).
Whiteley, C., *Mind in Action*, Clarendon Press (Oxford 1973).
Willer, D. and J., *Systematic Empiricism*, Prentice-Hall (New Jersey 1973).
Winch, P., *The Idea of a Social Science*, Routledge & Kegan Paul (London 1959).
Winch, P., 'Understanding a Primitive Society', *American Philosophical Quarterly*, 1 (1964), reprinted in B. Wilson (ed.), *op. cit.*
Wittgenstein, L., *Remarks on the Foundations of Mathematics*, Blackwell (Oxford 1956).
Wittgenstein, L., *Tractatus Logico-Philosophicus*, Routledge & Kegan Paul (London 1961).
Wittgenstein, L., *Philosophical Investigations*, Blackwell (Oxford 1963).
Wright, E. O., 'Reply to Burawoy's Comment on "Reflections on Classes"' *Berkeley Journal of Sociology*, XXXII (1987).
Wright, G. H. von, *Norm and Action*, Routledge & Kegan Paul (London 1963).
Wright, G. H. von, *Explanation and Understanding*, Routledge & Kegan Paul (London 1971).

Index of Names

Index of Subjects